A NEW NO-MAN'S-LAND

**ILLUMINATIONS:
CULTURAL FORMATIONS OF THE AMERICAS SERIES
JORGE CORONADO, EDITOR**

A NEW NO-MAN'S-LAND

WRITING AND ART AT GUANTÁNAMO, CUBA

ESTHER WHITFIELD

UNIVERSITY OF PITTSBURGH PRESS

Published by the University of Pittsburgh Press, Pittsburgh, Pa., 15260
Copyright © 2024, University of Pittsburgh Press
All rights reserved

Printed on acid-free paper
10 9 8 7 6 5 4 3 2 1

Cataloging-in-Publication data is available from the Library of Congress

ISBN 13: 978-0-8229-6764-4
ISBN 10: 0-8229-6764-2

Cover art by Alexander Beatón
Cover design by Melissa Dias-Mandoly

CONTENTS

Acknowledgments

vii

INTRODUCTION. BORDERLANDS

3

CHAPTER 1. TRANSLATION

39

CHAPTER 2. GUARDS

69

CHAPTER 3. HOME

104

CHAPTER 4. THE FUTURE

139

Afterword

173

Notes

175

Works Cited

189

Index

215

ACKNOWLEDGMENTS

This book has been many years in the making. As time passed and it remained unfinished its subject matter would, in a more just world, have slipped into the realm of recent history. And yet Guantánamo—as a military prison on a US naval base, bordering but separated from a province and city in eastern Cuba—has endured for more than twenty years. For this reason I acknowledge, first, the people whose lives have been consumed, derailed, or destroyed by this extrajudicial construct.

I acknowledge and thank what I think of as a broad, eclectic and informal coalition of organizations and individuals—lawyers, journalists, scholars, former detainees, writers, and artists—who have labored unwaveringly to keep Guantánamo in the public eye. Among these, I am grateful for their generosity to me, personally, of Marc Falkoff, Carol Rosenberg, Debi Cornwall, Erin Thompson, Wells Dixon, Aliyah Hussein, Liz Ševčenko, Jonathan Hansen, and Edmund Clark. Mohamedou Ould Slahi, Ahmed Errachidi, and Moazzam Begg have graciously shared time that is particularly precious given their lost years. Don E. Walicek, Alexandra S. Moore, Jana K. Lipmann, A. Naomi Paik, and Peter Hulme are exemplary scholars who engage compassionately with the

ACKNOWLEDGMENTS

challenges of Guantánamo, and I am deeply appreciative to have been able to work with each of them across various contexts.

In Guantánamo, Cuba, Pedro Gutiérrez Torres, Alexander Beatón Galano, José Ramón Sánchez, Daniel Ross, and Jorge Núñez have shared knowledge, experience, and creative work with patience and humor, and welcomed me into their homes. In the United States and beyond, I am grateful to the community of Cuban Studies scholars to which I am fortunate to have belonged for much of my professional life. I thank in particular Jacqueline E. Loss, my friend and collaborator for more than twenty-five years, and, for their vitality and probing responses to this project over the years of its evolution, I am grateful to Guillermina De Ferrari, Katerina Gonzalez Seligmann, Rachel Price, Marilyn Miller, César Salgado, Odette Casamayor, Anke Birkemaier, Omar Granados, Guillermo Irizarry, Elzbieta Sklodowska, Antonio José Ponte, José Quiroga, Licia Fiol-Matta, Lena Burgos Lafuente, Arnaldo Cruz-Malavé, Vicky Unruh, Christina Civantos, Jessica Gordon-Burroughs, and Holly Ackerman. Dara E. Goldman was a warm and gracious interlocutor on Guantánamo and Cuba until her untimely passing in 2022; like many in our community of scholars, I continue to feel her loss. The death of José Quiroga, a magisterial Cubanist and beloved mentor to me and many others, in January 2024 is a further loss to this community.

This project has benefitted from institutional support at many levels. A grant from the National Endowment for the Humanities Dialogues on the Experience of War program, inherited from my former colleague Keith Brown, opened my perspective on the United States' twenty-first-century wars through the experience of their veterans in Rhode Island, and afforded the pleasure of collaborating with Debbie Weinstein, Jane Gerhard, and Meg McBride. Between 2014 and 2022, Brown University's Center for Public Humanities and Center for Latin American and Caribbean Studies sponsored three symposia on Guantánamo and its extensions across the world, and put in face-to-face conversation many of the actors and activists whose work I most admire. Grants from the Watson Institute for International Studies and the Pembroke Center for Teaching and Research on Women provided funding in the early stages of this project; its final stages were supported by a faculty fellowship from the Cogut Center for the Humanities, and a visiting scholar position at Harvard University's David Rockefeller Center for Latin American Studies. I have presented work in progress from

ACKNOWLEDGMENTS

this project far and wide, and I am especially grateful to my hosts at New York University, Tulane University, the University of Puerto Rico, Stony Brook University, the University of New Hampshire, SUNY Geneseo, the Cuban Heritage Collection, the University of Edinburgh, the University of Graz, and Harvard's Cuba Studies Seminar.

My home departments at Brown University, Comparative Literature and Hispanic Studies, have been continuous sources of intellectual stimulation, professional support, and kindness. I am grateful to my colleagues in both departments; to Tracy Miller, Carol Wilson-Allen, and Tiffany Lewis for their warmth and efficiency; and to the doctoral and undergraduate students who, over and over again, have found new ways to see texts and questions I thought I knew well. Michelle Clayton is an extraordinary scholar, reader, and friend; writing sessions with her, Leila Lehnen, and Ravit Reichman (who suggested the title of this book) brought me out of solitude at crucial moments.

I am lucky to be surrounded by friendship in many forms, and I thank the friends whose curiosity has helped me to think more clearly. My husband, Jeff Seul, and my children, Ellis and Carys, enrich my life in innumerable ways, and I am deeply thankful to each of them. My mother and sisters have followed the book's progress from afar, with the care and confidence in me that they have always shown. Much of this book was written during the COVID-19 pandemic, which claimed the life of my father, John Whitfield. His presence permeates its pages: he never let pass an opportunity to share his enthusiasm for my research, from accompanying me on my first visit to Cuba in 1992 to charming my friends (and babysitting my young daughter) in Guantánamo City in 2016. I dedicate this book to him.

Parts of this book have been previously published in articles and book chapters. I am grateful for permission to reprint from the following: "Natural Borders and Animal Life: Inhabiting Guantánamo," *The Routledge Companion to Twentieth and Twenty-First Century Latin American Literary and Cultural Forms*, edited by Guillermina De Ferrari and Mariano Siskind, Routledge, 2022, pp. 225–33; "Guantánamo, Cuba: Poetry and Prison on Divided Ground," *Comparative Literature*, vol. 72, no. 3, 2020, pp. 299–315; "Art, Ecology and Repair: Imagining the Future of the Guantánamo Naval Base," *Sargasso: A Journal of Caribbean Literature, Language and Culture*, nos. 1–2, 2017–2018, pp. 49–65;

ACKNOWLEDGMENTS

"Guantánamo and Community: Visual Approaches to the Naval Base," *Guantánamo and American Empire: The Humanities Respond*, edited by Don E. Walicek and Jessica Adams, Palgrave Macmillan, 2017, pp. 149–72; and "Cuban Borderlands: Local Stories of the Guantánamo Naval Base," *MLN*, vol. 130, no. 2, 2015, pp. 276–97.

A NEW NO-MAN'S-LAND

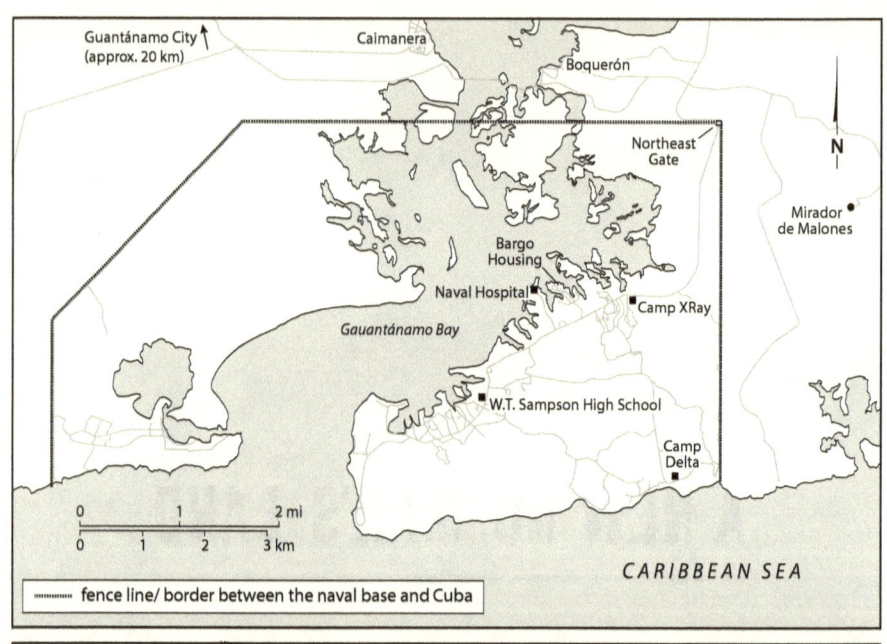
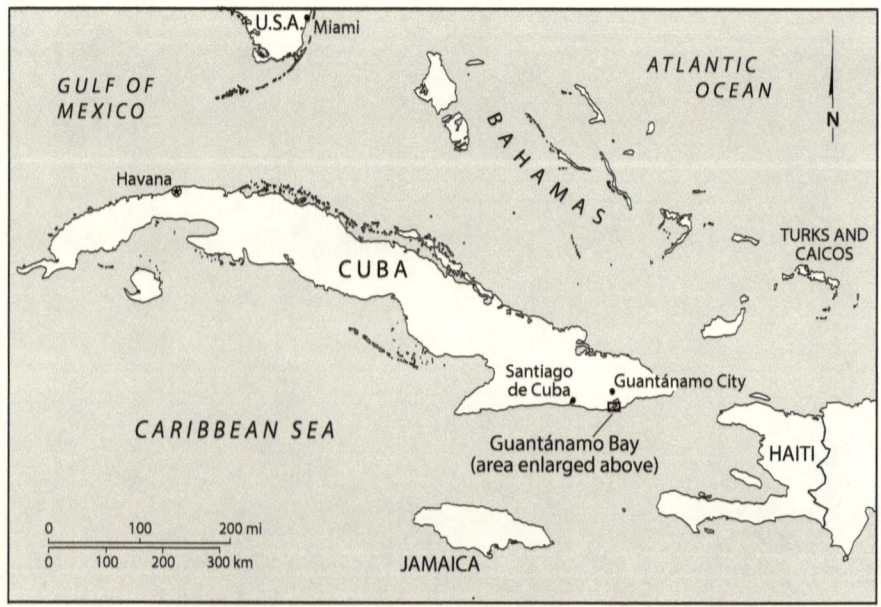

FIGURE I.1. GUANTÁNAMO BAY AND CUBA. CARTOGRAPHY BY BILL NELSON.

INTRODUCTION

BORDERLANDS

To the iguanas, especially to Princess, cats, banana rats, hummingbirds, our dear friend the sea, and even the pesky, noisy woodpeckers: I wish to thank you for your companionship and for bringing light into our lives in such a dark place as Guantánamo

Mansoor Adayfi, *Don't Forget Us Here:*
Lost and Found at Guantánamo

It's impossible to write about The Base
Without comparing yourself to its victims

José Ramón Sánchez, "Los quilos"

Iguanas, cats, banana rats, hummingbirds, the sea, and woodpeckers. That Yemeni writer Mansoor Adayfi, who was held without charge for fourteen years at the American military prison at Guantánamo Bay, should close his memoir by extending thanks to these companions comes as a surprise. Adayfi was, after all, held at one of the most notorious detention sites of the twenty-first century, a site whose legal contortions and human rights abuses have outraged advocates, activists and scholars since the US government's hurried and clandestine opening of detention camps at its naval base in eastern Cuba in January 2002. It is a site, moreover, where the Cuban government has vigorously protested what it considers to be the United States' illegal occupation of the territory, enabled by a lease in perpetuity granted through the unequal negotiations of the Cuban-American Treaty of Relations in 1903, and where a heavily guarded and land-mined fence line prohibits passage between Cuba and the base. And yet, in acknowledging the comfort he drew from the presence of creatures who know no borders, and from "our dear friend" (366) the Caribbean Sea that marks a limit to the base just as it surrounds the island of Cuba, Adayfi acknowledges an alternative Guantánamo, of sympathies, solidarities, and sharing of both space and experience. José Ramón Sánchez, a poet living near the base in the Cuban city of Guantánamo, weaves similar sympathies into his more than one hundred poems about the base, the long shadow it has cast over the region's history, and the impossibility of seeing it firsthand, as well as the solitudes that bind Cubans to men detained at the base even as their lives are vastly different. As Sánchez writes in "Impossible," the project of the poet moved by sympathy but restrained by politics becomes to "write second-hand poetry," to "take the words of others, images others saw for me" (*Black Arrow* 21).

For the past two decades, Guantánamo has been a battleground for two deeply consequential, if partially metaphorical, wars. One is Cuba's long-entrenched so-called war on imperialism that, since the early 1960s, has underpinned the David versus Goliath metaphor of the country's relations with the United States, and has justified decades of militarized social programs and defensive measures in the name of revolution. The other—more immediately recognizable for its relation to Guantánamo—is the President George W. Bush–era war on terror, whose divisions and detritus linger stubbornly into the present day. Nevertheless, despite the endurance of both wars and the centrality of Guantánamo Bay Naval Base to each of them, they are not Guantánamo's only story, nor are they the focus of this book. Instead, *A New No-Man's-Land* traces a Guantánamo that persists despite the enmities that have engulfed it: Guantánamo as a literary and artistic region, as a natural environment, and as a human experience, where the force of multiple hostilities on contested ground is met by articulations of survival, solidarity, and care.

The forty-five square miles of Naval Station Guantánamo Bay, as the leased territory known as GITMO is officially named, have since 2002 been inhabited by populations of vastly distinct experiences, housed in close proximity to one another: detainees originally from over thirty countries primarily in Europe and the Middle East, often captured in Afghanistan or Pakistan; military personnel and military families from the United States; contract workers from Caribbean countries, particularly Jamaica, as well as from the Philippines; and, in the shorter term, lawyers and journalists from across the globe. Cubans reside at the base, as workers who chose to stay after diplomatic relations with the United States ended in 1961, and as refugees who have crossed the mined and surveilled Guantánamo Bay to seek asylum. Many more Cubans live with the base as they inhabit a broader Guantánamo, particularly the border towns of Caimanera and Boquerón, once economically connected to the base, but now restricted zones secured by the Cuban military. Acknowledging these experiences and the differences among and within them, this book approaches Guantánamo as both the naval base and its geographic extensions into Cuban territory, and as a borderland region whose inhabitants often have in common limited access to power and self-representation, mobility restricted by geography if not captivity, and immersion in political languages that have ascribed rigid roles as "enemy combatant" or "patriot," "revolutionary" or "dissident." This is, moreover, a borderland region that, while physically isolated in its locale at the eastern edge of Cuba, extends a network of familial, linguistic, and cultural connections into the Caribbean and—given the multiple colonial and imperial histories that converge in the region—across much of the world.

The Guantánamo base is as notorious for its sui generis legal status as for its de facto territorial separation: initially presented by the Bush government's lawyers as beyond the reach of the US Constitution, and cut off from Cuba and otherwise reachable only by military-operated air and sea transport, it met former secretary of state Donald Rumsfeld's reported criterion of "the legal equivalent of outer space."[1] Cuba's Guantánamo province, while deeply tied to the base and its labor economy until the 1960s, has since then lived only the aftereffects of the former relationship, its border towns in particular designated as high-security zones with restricted access from elsewhere in Cuba. At the same time, even as its economic and institutional entities are part of tightly structured national networks, its six-hundred-mile distance from the economic and cultural metropolis of Havana has bequeathed it its own form of isolation. To read these two Guantánamos as one—which is the project of this book, and its referent when it names "Guantánamo" as a borderland region, rather than either the base, the province, or the provincial capital Guantánamo City—is to trace connections and affinities in the face of both complete physical separation and vast asymmetries.

Asymmetries are simultaneously the steepest challenge and the source of deepest texture to mapping Guantánamo as a borderland region, just as they often are to comparative work writ large.[2] I regard as asymmetrical those relationships that take shape in this region—across the fence line dividing the base from Cuba, and within the base and the detention camps themselves—which are marked far less by their minimal similarities than by their vast differences, differences marked as much by scale as by content alone. This understanding of asymmetry draws initially, ironically—and, indeed, with horror—on the term *asymmetric warfare*, common in the field of international relations. Steven D. Smith has summarized the term, with reference to scholarly and military sources, as "any warfare where the opposing combatants are at opposite ends of a political or tactical spectrum of unequal abilities or means to engage on equal footing"; specifically, where combatants are "unequal in military power, politics, population or technology" (2). While the tactics of *asymmetric warfare*, and related terms such as *guerilla warfare* and *irregular warfare*, have long histories, the recent use of this particular term coincides with the post–9/11 conflict and the centrality to it of nonstate actors, among them, ostensibly, Guantánamo's so-called unlawful enemy combatants. And yet the most localized use of this term in relation to Guantánamo is also its most chilling: in response to the suicides of three detainees in June 2006, Rear Admiral Harry B. Harris Jr., then commander of Joint Task Force Guantánamo, is reported to have said: "I believe this was not an act of desperation, but an act of asymmetrical warfare waged against us."[3]

International relations scholars, notably Christine Sylvester, have brought to the fore the human dimensions of "asymmetrical warfare," observing that the nonconventional subject positions from which it is waged bring with them a host of experiences unacknowledged in this and other kinds of warfare (1). The asymmetrical relationships that this book explores, however, align most closely with what Lisa Lowe has read as "intimacies" across four continents. Lowe's "intimacies" are relations forged in the aftermaths of colonial projects, rarely involving geographic closeness but aligning experiences that are necessarily particular in their local details; they must be traced across distinct archives to discern their "constellation of asymmetrical and unevenly legible intimacies" (18). Guantánamo's compassionate asymmetries approximate, too, the late nineteenth-century anticolonial friendships, "minor narratives of cross-cultural collaboration between oppressors and oppressed," which Leela Gandhi approaches as "innovative border crossing, visible in small, defiant flights from the fetters of belonging toward the unknown destinations of radical alterity" (6–7). At the same time, the peculiarities and constraints of the Guantánamo borderland region, in particular the spatial organization of its detention camps and the impassibility of the fence line, produce variations on "intimacy" and "friendship." Some, like relationships between guards and cellmates, are born of a stiflingly close physical proximity, while others, like those between Cubans and detainees, are rooted in the absolute impossibility of communication.

Asymmetries in the archive of texts and art that maps the Guantánamo borderland region are multiple. While not all have as their axis the fence line between Cuba and the base, some of the most prominent are inevitably governed by the stark differences between writing as a citizen of a deeply regulated and invigilated late socialist state, with an established if highly prescriptive and underresourced infrastructure of cultural institutions, on the one hand, and, on the other, as a temporary and often involuntary resident of a US-controlled territory, chosen precisely for its precarious relationship to the US Constitution but conscripted into a dubious program of patriotic defense.

A first asymmetry in the archive of what I am calling the Guantánamo region is one of scale. In short, and perhaps surprisingly, the corpus of Cuban creative work contributing to a borderland reading of Guantánamo is scant in comparison to such work produced on the base itself, notwithstanding the far smaller and more transient population of the latter. Despite its enduring presence in Guantánamo Province, Cubans have no access to the base, very little information about its operations, and few incentives to discuss it publicly or draw it into the sphere of national culture. In the post–9/11 period, Cuban state media published little on the plight of detainees at Guantánamo, even as major newspapers in the United States, Europe, and the Middle East reported consistently on the legal issues and human rights questions emerging from operations at the detention centers at the base. While the Cuban national film industry has on occasion, over the six decades since its institutionalization, referenced the base directly and indirectly—notably in José Massip's *Guantánamo* (1965) and Tomás Gutiérrez Alea's *Guantanamera* (1995)—as have some nationally prominent literary figures, the topic has largely been left to a small number of writers, artists, and filmmakers in Guantánamo Province. It is these who, in poetry, short fiction, art, and film, articulate peculiarly local engagements with the base's presence, and with the local histories of fraught neighborliness and clandestine migration that this presence has generated.

Related to the asymmetrical scale of the corpus of work from each side of the Guantánamo fence line is a similar asymmetry in the visibility and accessibility of each corpus. Despite the chaotic and extrajudicial nature of its founding, the purportedly clandestine imperative of its operations and the no doubt remaining "known unknowns" surrounding these, Joint Task Force Guantánamo has at various points in its existence been surprisingly, and perhaps paradoxically, solicitous in its claims to transparency. As Rebecca A. Adelman observes in a 2013 article, Joint Task Force Guantánamo has published photographs of its facilities, offered admittedly pre-scripted press tours, and maintained its own relatively robust internet presence through a website whose home page announces the commitment to "safe, humane and legal detention operations" (Adelman, "Safe, Humane"). These heavily curated gestures at rendering detention operations visible have been abundantly supplemented by the thousands of pages of military and legal documentation—some unclassified and some released as part of unauthorized WikiLeaks "document dumps"—as well as by testimonies, lists, and summaries collated by such vitally important advocacy efforts as those of Witness to Guantánamo; the Guantánamo Testimonials Project at the Center for Study of Human Rights in the Americas at the University of California, Davis; Healing and Recovery After Trauma; the *New York Times*' "Guantánamo Docket"; the Center for Constitutional Rights; and British journalist Andy Worthington's "Guantánamo Files," as well as by the growing corpus of published memoirs written by former detainees. Cuba's Guantánamo, on the other hand—particularly inasmuch as its forms of expression depart from, or simply fail to echo, the anti-imperialist narrative that the revolutionary government has championed since the early 1960s—is much less accessible. Cuban writers have long had limited access to the internet, and literary and artistic work produced on the island—particularly in its nonmetropolitan areas, among them Guantánamo Province—circulates sparsely in international contexts. Moreover, individuals' experiences of living near the base have largely been co-opted into the collective narrative of the Cuban Revolution, in its national dimension as well as its local version: that of a Guantánamo region whose proximity to the US base brought moral ruin to surrounding towns before the revolution's triumph, and subsequently delivered economic devastation and threats of potential violence. In a particularly sinister vein, the Cuban government's repression of its own citizens—those who have attempted to seek asylum at the base as well as the political dissidents incarcerated in the barely acknowledged provincial prisons situated only tens of miles from the base's notorious detention centers—is largely absent from the state-sanctioned record and instead emerges piecemeal from Cuba's highly imperiled independent journalists, exiled activists, and scattered references in fiction and poetry. Cuban Guantánamo's is, consequently, a scant archive, dwarfed by the copious documentation, reportage, and witness accounting pertaining to the detention centers on the base.

A not dissimilar asymmetry presents itself in the legibility, and related legitimacy, of the naval base and detention center's textual and visual record vis-à-vis that of Cuban Guantánamo. There is in the former a pendulum-like play between extremes of surplus and scarcity. On the one hand, what Joseph R. Slaughter, recalling Ranajit Guha, has termed the "bloodless prose of counterinsurgency" ("Life, Story, Violence" 469) and "the massive (and growing) public archive of documentary texts from the U.S. 'war on terror'" (469) has been so prolific in terms of sheer page count, with the WikiLeaks Guantánamo-related document dump of 2011 alone including over seven hundred documents, that its legibility is compromised, inasmuch as it demands practices of reading that renounce concision and coherence. On the other hand, much of this documentation—excluding that released by WikiLeaks, atypical and legally problematic for its lack of redactions—has been heavily censored in the form in which it is publicly available. The writing and art of detainees while held at Guantánamo have been subjected to myriad, externally imposed constraints on their legibility, ranging from the confiscation and classification of detainee poetry, especially that published in reduced and carefully screened form in Marc Falkoff's *Poems from Guantánamo* (2008), to Mohamedou Ould Slahi's *Guantánamo Diary*, a long set of letters published in 2015 after years of legal wrangling, with entire pages blacked out, and detainee artwork first exhibited in New York in late 2017, only to invite a military ruling that no more such work be permitted to leave the detention centers. While accessibility and the local scale of distribution, rather than legibility, is the primary obstacle to reading many of the texts in what I am calling Guantánamo's Cuban archive, the bars to legibility posed by censorship of writing and art by detainees at the naval base have sinister analogs on the other side of the border. Setting aside the practices of self-censorship that Antonio José Ponte, among others, has traced through the six decades of the revolutionary regime, expression of opposition to the Cuban government has been overtly suppressed, often through the incarceration of its authors and a public discrediting of their personal and political writing. This finely calibrated discrediting, bolstered by a watertight surveillance state and the readily wielded accusation of collaboration with the US government and intelligence services, forecloses avenues to verification of many dissidents' claims, such that they are deprived of legibility and legitimacy. Indeed, dissident writing, like most dissident activity in Cuba, is so expertly cast as illegitimate by Cuban institutions, both political and cultural, that to read it alongside less audacious, and thereby more institutionally commended, Cuban work, entails suspending documented verifiability as a criterion, and trusting the word of those whom state power has the means to vilify. It is in this spirit that I count among Cuban Guantánamo's textual production the newsletters of dissidents and political prisoners, printed and distributed in Guantánamo Province without government authorization, some later uploaded to the internet and others held in the personal collections of now-exiled contributors.

With regard to their disciplinary location, or more specifically, the area studies within the purview of which they have fallen, the base and Cuban Guantánamo are different and asymmetrical. The base has been addressed abundantly from within American studies, even as much scholarly work in this field—by Naomi Paik, Jonathan Hansen and Jana K. Lipman, for example—has extended to broader theoretical questions and geographies. Similarly, while the prolific legal scholarship on the detention centers brings to bear international law, most notably with regard to the Geneva Conventions, it must of necessity do so in tandem with the various aspects of US constitutional law that have been upheld, twisted, and breached over the decades of the prisons' existence. By contrast, both Cuba's Guantánamo Province and the US base itself have registered only lightly in Latin American, Caribbean, and even Cuban studies. Peter Hulme's wide-ranging *Cuba's Wild East: A Literary Geography of Oriente* (2011) traces the "literary geography" of Guantánamo and Cuba's other eastern provinces, from the first war for independence from Spain—the Ten Years' War (1868–1878)—to the detention camps opened in 2002. Hulme is one of very few to read detainees' writing together with that of Cubans, and his reflections on the camps' infiltration by Cuban animal life have been an inspiration for this book. Jana K. Lipman's definitive labor history of the US base, *Guantánamo: A Work-*

ing-Class History Between Empire and Revolution (2009), with its analysis of Cuban commuter workers' experiences in the years preceding and immediately following the Cuban Revolution of 1959, is unambiguously grounded in its claim that "Guantánamo is in Cuba" and is a cornerstone of my own study. The migrant crisis of the early 1990s, during which over thirty-four thousand Cubans and fourteen thousand Haitians were held at the base awaiting entry to the United States, has been the focus of considerable scholarship, notably by Elizabeth Campisi and Holly Ackerman. There has more generally, however, been a marked reluctance to extend the scope of Cuban studies, as practiced primarily outside Cuba, to Guantánamo. It is one of the more ambitious aspirations of this book that the compassionate relationships it traces, while unquestionably a product of the sui generis space that is Guantánamo, might offer models for understanding in a broader Cuba, rent apart as it has been by over sixty years of struggle—nominally revolutionary, but especially harrowing for those who have assumed positions of counterrevolutionary dissent.

A final asymmetry, and in many ways the one that is most ethically challenging, does not have the border between the base and Cuba as its axis, but rather has dividing lines intersecting throughout the region. This is the asymmetry—indeed, the incommensurability—of what I would name simply, echoing Judith Butler's reading of Guantánamo detainees' poetry, as suffering.[4] As has now been abundantly documented, in personal memoirs, legal briefings, leaked memoranda, and US government investigatory reports, many men held at Guantánamo, particularly in the first three years of the detention centers' existence, were physically and psychologically tortured—in ways that, despite contortionist attempts on the US government's part to tweak definitions of torture, were unequivocally just that. The myriad aspects of detention at Guantánamo that represent barely imaginable cruelty—indefinite detention without charge, restrictions and deprivations of what in one particularly dark period were termed "comfort items," no information or contact with the world outside the camps, even as distant family members despaired and, in many cases, passed away—appear orders of magnitude apart from the experiences of others in that same space. It is in some ways jarring, then, to see, for example, the cellblock guards being described as bored by their experience, reports on elevated rates of post-traumatic stress disorder among former Guantánamo guards circulating alongside investigative journalism about the long-term psychological trauma endured by released detainees, listings in the naval station's community newspaper for support groups directed at the nonetheless very real issues that deployed military personnel face, and, in Cuban poetry from the Guantánamo region, the no doubt well-meaning equation of the geographic and existential isolation of the poet to the experience of detainees.[5] More closely resonant with experiences of detainees at the base's camps are the reports of mistreatment and deprivation in the prisons of Cuba's Guantánamo Province that this book addresses, particularly when the latter are considered as part of longer history of the Cuban Revolution's repressions of its opponents that runs through decades of political imprisonment as recorded in the testimonial writings of, for example, Reinaldo Arenas, Jorge Valls, and Armando Valladares; to the Black Spring of 2003 in which seventy-five dissidents were jailed; to the more recent imprisonment of hundreds of citizens following public protests on July 11, 2021, on charges that Amnesty International has maintained are inconsistent with international law.[6]

With the fraught implications of Guantánamo's asymmetries, incommensurables, and opacities in mind, I hope to hold comparison in the balance for the coincidences, and indeed the sharing, it enlightens. It is around unanticipated commonalities among parties to vastly asymmetrical relationships that compassion forms in the Guantánamo region—commonalities sometimes recognized as such and at other times merely sensed or hoped for, sometimes discovered through direct and physical encounters, and at others through purely imaginary ones. It is the instances of compassion that grow from the rare common grounds of deeply asymmetrical relationships that, in my reading, sustain a Guantánamo that is fundamentally anti-war, in the specific senses in which war has converged on that space. Despite and because of the differences that constitute such relationships, therefore, and in the undergrowth of the intense hostilities that have long governed Guantánamo as a political space, there emerge small gestures of curiosity, kindness, and goodwill that are woven into the poetry, narrative, art, and photography of those who inhabit the Guantánamo region.

Crucially, and to return briefly to Adayfi's iguanas, gestures of compassion on the part of Guantánamo's human inhabitants take shape in an environment that, while it is governed at a political and rhetorical level by the divisions of warfare, is ecologically unrestrained. Not only is this an area shielded, like that around many military bases, from infrastructural development and consequently, in this very limited sense, unspoiled, it is also, and inevitably, one whose many man-made barriers—a mined fence line, cellblock walls, multiple checkpoints—are brazenly disregarded by the region's animal inhabitants and are minimal disruptions on the natural landscape writ large. As José Ramón Sánchez writes of the banana rats and iguanas native to this region, in his poem "Animal Planet," they are "oblivious to the President's orders" (*Black Arrow* 51). It is often the natural world that sparks compassion within Guantánamo's asymmetrical human relationships: just as wild animals who respect no borders, and the Caribbean Sea that encircles not the base but the entire island of Cuba, appear as figures of freedom and escape, they also model, and offer impetus for, understanding one's own experience in the terms of others who occupy the same space. It is in this sense that Guantánamo's compassionate asymmetries, as I want to call them, become part of a larger, ecocritical concern with how, as in Rachel Price's reading of contemporary Cuban art, the local bypasses the national to reflect, instead, the planetary.[7]

GUANTÁNAMO AND CUBA'S WAR ON IMPERIALISM

Between 1903, when land at Guantánamo was leased in perpetuity from the government of the new Cuban republic to the United States under the highly contested terms of the Platt Amendment, and 1959, when Castro took power at the head of Cuba's revolutionary government, Naval Station Guantánamo Bay grew from a coaling station to an active and well-supported base, housing large military and civilian populations. Jonathan Hansen's *Guantánamo: An American History* traces the base's development during this period, noting how the scant population of the first two decades of the twentieth century grew to a more stable community in the 1920s and 1930s, rising quickly in numbers, activity and infrastructure during World War II. By 1943, Hansen notes, "some ten thousand Cubans, Jamaicans and West Indians labored on the base alongside four thousand U.S. servicemen and civilians" (181), an expansion that "created the footprint of office buildings, warehouses, jetties, airstrips, magazines, and residential neighborhoods still visible today" (182).

The 1940s and 1950s represent not only the peak of the base's population and activity but also of its porosity in terms of contact with Cuba.

The base depended heavily on Cuban workers for much of its nonmilitary operation, via a contract labor force that, as Jana K. Lipman has studied, was obliged to accept precarious terms and low wages, and that significantly altered the economic basis of neighboring Cuban towns (*Guantánamo* 38–60). While fences and guard posts separated the US military zone from Cuba during this period, movement from one side to the other was nevertheless frequent and relatively unencumbered. Americans from the base often spent their free time in Cuba, with the result that in the 1940s and 1950s the border town of Caimanera and the city of Guantánamo gained reputations as hotbeds of prostitution and other forms of economic exploitation, ills that have since figured largely in local Cuban scholarship, particularly that of Guantánamo- and Caimanera-based historians José Sánchez Guerra and Ofelia García Campuzano.

The triumph of the Cuban Revolution in January 1959, however, put an end to most movement between the base and Cuba. It did not do so immediately, but after several years of increasing hostility at the local level that paralleled that within Cuba-US relations more broadly, with the base becoming a site of deep suspicion for Cuban government officials as they frequently suspected it of harboring potential counterrevolutionary insurgents and of facilitating armed attack. Lipman observes, "In the early 1960s, anxiety, suspicion, and military aggression defined U.S.-Cuban relations, and these tensions manifested themselves along the border between the base and Guantánamo" (182). Both the Cuban and US militaries "reinforced barbed wire fences, initiated military patrols, erected twin watchtowers, and planted massive minefields" (162), defenses that, as Cuban historians Felipa Suárez and Pilar Quesada have noted, would be supplemented in future decades as the threat of aggression from the base was supplanted by that of Cuban citizens attempting to reach it to claim asylum. After 1959, the Cuban government refused to cash checks it received for the lease of the base, and in 1961 it created an elite new unit of the national army termed "la Brigada de la Frontera," or the "Border Brigade," charged with guarding the increasingly fortified fence line between the base and Cuba. Nevertheless, until 1964, approximately three thousand workers continued to commute daily from Cuba to the base, under strict control by both sides. In that year, after a series of confrontations centered around the base as a result of which Castro cut off the water supply, the US government ordered that all commuter workers either return, unemployed, to Cuba, or remain on the base, although, as Lipman notes, "a final 750 workers retained their positions as commuters and remarkably did not have to choose" (183), a status quo that remained in place until the retirement of the last commuter in 2012.

Cuban hostility toward the presence of the US base at Guantánamo, perceived as an acute example of US exploitative usurpation, grew in tandem with the anti-imperialist stance that was to define the Cuban Revolution for most of its more than six decades in power, and with the power that a language of "war on imperialism" was to wield within Cuban political speech and society, permeating the discourse of social mobilization that underpinned the revolutionary endeavor. "War" as a rhetorical tool was at the forefront of the Castro brothers' efforts to build and sustain a revolution from 1959 on. In the climate of the Cold War, it was under the general rallying cry of a war on US imperialism that the particular political rhetoric of the Cuban Revolution evolved, underpinned by an expectation that citizens always be engaged in battle, mentally if not physically. That this war was at the core of Cuban revolutionary thought was proclaimed most resonantly in the closing line of Ernesto "Che" Guevara's 1966 address to the Tricontinental Conference: "Our every act is a war cry against imperialism" (362), although the stage had been set during Castro's first days in power. Speaking to audiences in the cities of Santiago, Camagüey, and Santa Clara in the first week of 1959, despite diplomatic relations with the United States still being in place, Castro made frequent mention of empire, although his referents were principally non-state-specific metaphors of empire such as "the empire of corruption, exploitation, abuse and injustice" ("Discurso pronunciado . . . el 4 de enero de 1959"). No matter their ostensible topic, Castro's speeches in the years after the Bay of Pigs invasion of April 1961—a turning point in the Cuban government's defensive stance, after it had successfully warded off, and publicly humiliated, US-backed Cuban counterrevolutionary attackers deployed to depose it—were liberally peppered with the words *war* and *imperialism*, and had defense against US aggression as their clear referent.[8]

In subsequent decades, the "war" against the imperial enemy, and readiness against an always imminent invasion, emerged as the pretext for the revolution's defense strategies, social innovations, and surveillance programs—and, indeed, for its very existence, as Antonio José Ponte has posited.[9] Differentiating between the various ways in which the idea of war operates in Cuba, Antoni Kapcia lists among the mechanisms that allowed the revolution's ideology to become persuasively meaningful "the sense of shared siege from 1961; the actual struggles (of 1961, the 1961–66 *lucha contra bandidos* and then Angola) and the imagined 'struggles' of repeated campaigns, defensive mobilizations and crises" (78–79). Richard Fagen sees the beginnings of the transformation of political culture in Cuba in the so-called wars on illiteracy and vice that opened the revolution's first decade. Fagen and, more recently, Ana Serra, draw attention to the military terminology and iconography with which Cuba's 1961 literacy campaign, in particular, was imbued: its volunteers were organized into brigades; its headquarters were in former army facilities; its motto was "Study, Work, Rifle." As Serra discusses, an iconic photograph from December 1961 shows literacy volunteers returning from the mountains, mission accomplished, holding giant pencils to stand in for guns (34–35).

The military genesis of the literacy campaign was, furthermore, an occasion for Castro not merely to orchestrate the performance of the relationship between war and language but also to authorize it for subsequent years. Mary Louise Pratt has located language at the core of violent military actions: "Where there is violence," she writes, "language is nearly always present, supplying meanings and alibis and inflicting injuries of its own" (1516). In a speech delivered as a Mother's Day address to the families of departing literacy volunteers on May 14, 1961, reprinted in translation in Fagen's *The Transformation of Political Culture in Cuba*, Castro made this move in reverse, placing warfare at the center of linguistic action, specifically in the case of the literacy campaign but by implication in the broader practice of revolution. Cuba, he declared, has two armies: "One armed with rifles and cannons to defend the work of the revolution, and one armed with books to advance the revolution" (Fagen 181). It is this second army that is "fighting a longer and far more difficult battle" (181), and, indeed, the vocabulary coined for this particular war was to have a long legacy in Cuba. In the rhetoric of its leaders, Cuba has been waging wars on many fronts for more than five decades, the campaign against illiteracy making way for the subsequent decades' metaphorical militarization of public speech and collective life, from the Revolutionary Offensive of 1968, designed to rid Cuba of the last vestiges of capitalism, to the Battle of Ideas launched in 1999 with the aim of renewing public commitment to the revolution, particularly in the areas of construction and education.[10] Until the end of his presidency—and, indeed, until his death—references to war with the "illegal empire" peppered Castro's writings and speeches. His successors Raúl Castro and Miguel Díaz-Canel, although less prone to long speeches, have deployed similar terms, with Raúl, for example, waging a "battle against crime and corruption" and Díaz-Canel urging Cuba to fend off "an intense and profound aggression on the part of the empire."[11]

The language of a "war on imperialism" that has provided terms for social initiatives in Cuba is intimately connected to the US occupation of the military base at Guantánamo, even though this occupation may have been invoked less insistently than other incidences of perceived imperialist aggression, such as the trade embargo on Cuba (the longest-standing target of Castro's outrage, and described on a billboard outside Havana's airport as "the longest genocide in history"), favorable migration policies for Cubans, and alleged Central Intelligence Agency support for Cuban dissidents.[12] Jana K. Lipman has argued persuasively, in fact, that between 2002 and 2007 the print version of the daily newspaper *Granma* reported on the prison camps with less frequency and ideological coherence than it did on Cubans, rather than foreigners, being harmed and unlawfully imprisoned at the hands of the United States (Lipman, "Where's Guantánamo in *Granma*?"). Accounting from a different perspective for what she considers to be "comparatively little discussion of the military base in public discourse in Cuba" ("There's Always Something about Cuba" 346), Dara E. Goldman has identified a paradox in which the affront that is the US occupation of the base is overshadowed by pervasive discourses of nationalist isolation that cannot accommodate the presence of the enemy on national soil (*Out of Bounds* 136). Cuban public discourse since 1959, Goldman continues, has defined the United States as a threat from outside, symbolized by the ninety miles' width of the Florida Straits that are a reminder of the distance between the two countries, and their separateness from one another. Having constructed Cuba as an "insular national space" (*Out of Bounds* 136), Goldman writes, this discourse cannot conceptually accommodate Guantánamo Bay Naval Base as a US presence within national borders.

The Castro brothers' reluctance to escalate tensions over Guantánamo, either by making it a priority in their anti-imperialist propaganda, or by initiating military confrontation, and to channel their political energies instead to other hostile positions held by the United States, has been read as largely pragmatic. Lipman notes that in the early 1960s, "despite international solidarity with anti-imperial, decolonization movements, Castro recognized that ousting GTMO was not worth a direct military conflict with the United States" (*Guantánamo* 146) and quotes Castro's predecessor as Cuban president, Osvaldo Dorticós, as dismissing concerns that Cuba would attack the naval base with "we are audacious and valiant, but we are not stupid" (146). This is consistent with the Statement by the Government of Cuba to the National and International Community issued forty years later, on January 11, 2002, in response to news that "enemy combatants" from the US invasion of Afghanistan would be held at Naval Station Guantánamo Bay. The Cuban government was initially and briefly supportive of this unilateral decision on the part of the United States and its statement, translated and reprinted in Castro's collection *Guantánamo: Why the Illegal US Base Should Be Returned to Cuba*, notes the "atmosphere of mutual respect" prevailing between each country's official at the border (155) and offers assistance with US efforts to deal with terrorism. In its statement, the Cuban government reiterates that "despite the fact that we hold different positions as to the most efficient way to eradicate terrorism, the difference between Cuba and the United States lies in the method and not the need to put an end to that scourge . . . we are willing to cooperate with the medical services required as well as with sanitation programs in the surrounding areas under our control" (157–58). Although the statement closes with the more familiar exhortation that "the illegally occupied territory of Guantánamo should be returned to Cuba!" (155), it makes clear that "a basic principle of Cuba's policy toward this bizarre and potentially dangerous problem between Cuba and the United States, which is decades long, has been to avoid making our claim a major issue, nor even an especially important issue, among the multiple and grave differences between our two nations" (155).

Cuban acquiescence to the US holding of detainees at the base was short-lived. In January 2005, after the exposure of abusive interrogation practices at the base's prisons, the Cuban Ministry of Foreign Affairs issued a public statement calling for the United States to end its torture practices at Guantánamo, reminding the US government that the treaty under which it leases the base, and which the Cuban government considers illegal anyway, allows for the base's use as a coaling and naval station but not the transfer there of foreign prisoners of war

(Castro, *Guantánamo* 160). The statement charges the US government with "a gross violation of human rights and numerous international treaties and conventions" (160), a claim consistent with over sixty years of unrelenting outrage at the occupation of the base. Just as in a November 1960 visit to address base commuter workers in the border town of Caimanera, Castro rehearsed the terms of the Platt Amendment that "curtailed our independence" ("Discurso pronunciado . . . el 13 de noviembre de 1960"), forty-seven years later, in a five-part essay titled "The Empire and the Independent Island," published in Spanish in the state-controlled daily newspaper *Granma* in 2007 and reprinted in an English version in *Guantánamo*, Castro retraces a similar script, drawing a clear line from the imperialist overreach of 1902, to the many acts of perceived aggression targeted at Cuba from the United States during the revolution, to the holding of detainees without charge at the naval base in the post–9/11 years. He concludes that Guantánamo is unnecessary to the United States from a military perspective, given that the United States' technical power is strong enough to transport war to "wherever best suits the empire" (49). Castro surmises that the United States needs the base to "humiliate" Cuba just as it humiliates men at the illegal post–9/11 detention camps, an attempt against which Cuba "will continue to be in a state of combat readiness" (49).[13] Speaking to the Cuban National Assembly a year later, Raúl Castro also condemned human rights violations at the naval base "on territory usurped from our country" ("Discurso pronunciado por el General del Ejército Raúl Castro Ruz"), nevertheless invoking the revolution's continuing victory against the embargo and other imperial aggressions, while on January 11, 2022, Díaz-Canel marked the twentieth anniversary of the opening of the detention centers with a condemnation on Twitter of abuses perpetrated there (@DiazCanelB). The Castro brothers and their successor have recognized, and condemned, the way in which consecutive US administrations have exploited Guantánamo Bay's anomalous legal status in the service of an egregious war on terror. They have, however, insisted on the consonance of this exploitation with a longer history of imperialist aggression of which the occupation of the naval base is one among several examples, and against which Cuba has long been waging its own war on imperialism.

Even though the Cuban government has shied away from direct confrontation with the United States over Guantánamo, it has been in the interests of its rhetorical war on imperialism to insist that the base is illegally occupied and to maintain it as a heavily patrolled military zone and the limit line of symbolic defense. Indeed, the Castro brothers' actions, speeches, and writings regarding the naval base demonstrate its importance to the genesis and perpetuation of a war on imperialism that has manifested itself primarily in language and has for decades served to fuel collective outrage within and outside Cuba. Even their pragmatic decision not to press their claim to the base either legally or militarily reflects, I would propose, their preference for keeping war at the level of rhetoric, and an understanding of this rhetoric's power to sustain the social project of a revolution: outrage has long been a staple of Castro speeches, and the contested lease on Guantánamo Bay Naval Base has since the first days of the Cuban Revolution given this outrage specific focus and force.

GUANTÁNAMO AND THE WAR ON TERROR

The so-called war on terror, although translated into milder terms during President Barack Obama's tenure and ostensibly brought to a definite end with President Joseph Biden's withdrawal of US troops from Afghanistan in August 2021, has a more recent and globally visible connection to Guantánamo than does Cuba's war on imperialism. It is, nevertheless, a term similarly dependent, for its power to define hostilities and mobilize support, on the war metaphors that Lori Hartman-Mahmud has read as organizing and simplifying cross-cultural contexts to the detriment of their nuance and complexity. Indeed, recalling George Lakoff and Mark Johnson's seminal work on metaphor as foregrounding similarity at the expense of difference, and James Geary's more recent revisiting of this, the term *war on terror* summarily displaced alternative languages and paradigms that might have constituted a response to the attacks of 9/11, just as Cuba's war on imperialism marshalled collective support for the revolutionary agenda along a binary of right versus wrong. And like Cuba's "war," scaled to a revolutionary temporality whose primary tense is a yet-to-be-achieved future of victory, the war on terror is embedded in temporal measures whose endpoints are unknowable: a lease "in perpetuity," the interminability of "terror," the "indefinite" time frame of detentions that in some cases have lasted more than twenty years.

The war on terror, as first invoked by President George W. Bush in a resonant speech to Congress on September 20, 2001, following the hijacking of four airplanes and attacks on the Pentagon and World Trade Center that claimed almost three thousand lives, was resolute in its zeal but gravely imprecise in its linguistic and temporal dimensions. Of the many categorical slippages that came to define this "war," one of the most striking is the abstraction of the designated enemy, severed from identification with either a state power or a group of human actors: within the course of Bush's address to Congress, the US enemy was first named as Al-Qaeda, expanding then to "every terrorist group of global reach" and, finally and most potently, to, merely, "terror" (68), diametrically opposed not to the people or territory of the United States but to "freedom" itself (65). Among the numerous scholars to have reflected on the warping of language in response to 9/11, Adriana Cavarero, in *Horrorism: Naming Contemporary Violence* (2008), remarked that the war on terror "mounts a direct challenge to the political lexicon of modernity" (2). Three presidencies and almost twenty years after the act of naming of this "war," in *Subtle Tools: The Dismantling of American Democracy from the War on Terror to Donald Trump* (2021), Karen J. Greenberg considers it the founding act in the "degradation of language" (4) that, along with other insidious practices, would systematically and perhaps irreversibly undermine American democracy for the twenty-first century.

Marc Redfield, in his study of a "rhetoric of terror" that that has marked political speech from the French Revolution to the Bush administration, notes that President Bush's invocation of a war on terror "respects and exaggerates the complications of conventional declarations of war and gives them an extra twist" (56). Not a formal declaration, the naming and inception of this "war" stand, rather, as a performative speech act that "troubles the difference between real and fictional, literal and figurative" (59), generating ambiguity on the US Supreme Court as to whether the United States was "actually 'at war' in the sense of Vietnam, Korea and the two World Wars rather than in the sense of the 'war on drugs,' which is, and always has been, primarily a law enforcement effort " (59).[14] Sealing its effectively undefeatable slipperiness as a category, the possibility of this war's ending stretches out indefinitely, as the enemy's indeterminacy rules out its definitive elimination. In Redfield's words, "The war, having no object except the abstraction 'terrorism' or 'terror,' is limitless and endless" (56).

Indeed, the war on terror extended through George W. Bush's presidential term and successive administrations, becoming known colloquially as a "long war," an "endless war," and a "forever war" (Greenberg, *Subtle Tools* 17). President Barack Obama began his first term in January 2009 pledging to close the Guantánamo detention camps, and made public efforts to change the specific terminology and the implicit temporal framework of the war on terror. His remarks at the National Defense University in May 2013 heralded a seemingly significant shift in counterterrorism policy and a renewed but ultimately doomed effort to close the Guantánamo prison. "Under domestic law, and international law," President Obama insisted, "the United States is at war with al Qaeda, the Taliban, and their associated forces," rather than with "terror" ("Remarks by the President"). Furthermore, he continued, "this war, like all wars, must end," rather than extending indefinitely as Bush-era terms and practices had appeared to permit. Even in posing an explicit challenge to the war's boundlessness, however, this speech allowed "terror" itself to persist at once as an entity and a threat, calling for the creation of "new tools to prevent terror." Ultimately, as Greenberg has traced, just as the Obama administration's new language of "overseas contingency operations" and "unprivileged enemy belligerents" remained "disappointingly imprecise" (21), so too were its aims of closing Guantánamo and fully withdrawing US troops from Afghanistan unrealized. President Donald Trump, in Greenberg's words, "revived the terms that his predecessor had attempted to excise from the national security lexicon" (*Subtle Tools* 25), revoked Obama's executive order to close the Guantánamo detention centers, and, in a memorable boast about Guantánamo immediately before being elected to office, promised to "load it up with some bad dudes" (25). While President Joseph Biden's withdrawal of US troops from Afghanistan stands as the largest-scale effort yet to end the war on terror, the last days of this "war" remain to be seen; in *Never-Ending War on Terror* (2021), Alex Lubin doubts that there will, in fact, be last days. Commenting on the global and seemingly intractable permeation of the language and insidious practices of the war on terror into twenty years of "policing, counterinsurgency, surveillance, and state violence" (115), and the absence of clarity as to "how to dismantle the war's meanings and feelings, which are so embedded in everyday life that they are hardly recognizable" (109), Lubin deems this war a story with "no conclusion" (109).

With the multiple ambiguities that cloud its location and legal status, Guantánamo Bay Naval Base lends itself peculiarly well to the rhetorical boundlessness and ill-defined reach of the war on terror as well as to its dubious standing in US and international law. Amy Kaplan, whose 2005 article "Where Is Guantánamo?" remains one of the more comprehensive and influential analyses of how legal anomaly and imperialist overreach have defined the site since the early twentieth century, has argued that "the temporal dimensions of Guantánamo's location make it a chillingly appropriate place for the indefinite detention of unnamed enemies in what the administration calls a perpetual war against terror" (837). Kaplan argues that "the legal space of Guantánamo today has been shaped and remains haunted by its imperial history" (833). She traces this history from the Platt Amendment, which in 1903 "legislated U.S. domination" (835) of the new Cuban republic, through the Insular Cases of 1902–1922, which allowed for "a two-tiered, uneven application of the Constitution" (841) in territories ruled by the United States beyond its national borders, to *Rasul v. Bush* (2004), where the US Supreme Court ruled that federal courts have jurisdiction over the US naval base even as it "carefully avoided the question of whether noncitizens in Guantánamo Bay have access to constitutional protections and rights" (841). Even as Guantánamo is not an anomaly but "one island in a global penal archipelago where the United States indefinitely detains, secretly transports, and tortures uncounted prisoners from all over the world" (831), it is intractably rooted in the United States' long-standing imperial enterprises in the Caribbean, such that "the global dimensions of Guantánamo cannot be understood separately from its seemingly bizarre location in Cuba" (831).

In *The Least Worst Place: Guantánamo's First 100 Days* (2009), Karen J. Greenberg traces the ostensible rationale that, as the winter of 2001 approached and prisons near Afghanistan's battlefields proved to be dangerously inadequate for the detention of captives, led to Guantánamo's selection from a number of possible holding sites. The interagency group seeking a new site judged Cuba's hostile relationship with the United States to be an advantage, as the base's perimeter was well-guarded and there was "no need to consider the opinions of a foreign government" (7). The notion of legal limbo was particularly attractive, for "it opened up the door to a much wider set of questions about the kinds of legal exceptions that might be permissible on the island base" (7). In the early years of the camp, before a series of Supreme Court decisions that established habeas corpus rights for detainees, beginning with *Rasul v. Bush* (2004) and ending with *Boumediène v. Bush* (2007), the US government considered itself bound, as Judith Butler puts it in *Precarious Life: The Powers of Mourning and Violence* (2004), "by no legal guidelines other than those fabricated for the occasion" (xv). The executive branch, Butler writes, had "effectively set up its own judiciary function, one that overrides the separation of power, the writ of habeas corpus (guaranteed, it seems, by Guantánamo Bay's geographical location outside the borders of the United States, on Cuban land, but not under Cuban rule), and the entitlement to due process" (63).

The hastily erected camps at the US naval base became an indefinite holding place for men and youths whose identities were unknown to their guards—for whom, Greenberg recounts, "the names of the detainees were a mystery, as were their countries of origin, their ages, the languages they spoke, and what they had done to warrant transfer to Guantanamo" (*Least Worst Place* 81). Over the years it emerged that the captives were of widely varying provenance and involvement in anti-US activities: far from all speaking Arabic, as the cue-card-equipped guards had anticipated (81), they spoke as many as seventeen different languages and were citizens or residents of forty nations (Kaplan 840). Of the 779 men to have been held at the naval base on suspicion of terrorist involvement from 2002 on, 39 remained twenty years later, with the majority of releases occurring during the presidencies of George W. Bush and Barack Obama. Many of the men released, as a series of memoirs by ex-detainees and statements by their former captors attests, appear to have been found in the wrong place at the wrong time. That a mission against "terror" should have yielded so broad and incoherent a haul of enemies should not surprise given the scope set for it from the outset, nor should the terminological contortions that the detentions at Guantánamo occasioned, most prominent among them the neologisms *enemy combatant*, *illegal enemy combatant*, and *unprivileged enemy belligerent*, that have occluded the "prisoner of war" status for which rights are clearly set out in the Geneva Conventions.[15] The lexicon of the war on terror is underpinned by the peculiarities of the Guantánamo Bay Naval Base, where jurisdiction and sovereignty are separate and, despite the trappings of American life that have sustained generations of military families, a hostile state—Cuba—lies at the border.

CREATING AT GUANTÁNAMO

Cuba's war on imperialism, and the United States' war on terror, at over sixty and over twenty years old, respectively, may seem increasingly obsolete in this third decade of the twenty-first century. They are, nevertheless, wars whose human collateral remains at Guantánamo—just as the Cold War anachronism of a fence line dividing versions of extreme state control (communism, socialism, the Cuban Revolution) from versions of freedom (the dream of democracy, political rights, and economic prosperity that draws migrants to the United States) lingers there, despite the glaring paradox of a US military that is "honor-bound to defend freedom" but oversees ongoing detentions without charge. The hostilities that have converged at Guantánamo have largely eclipsed its representation as a space of more positive affect, unsurprisingly given the reach and intensity of these hostilities and the very limited possibility for such expression, and yet the endurance, and the resilience, of small-scale gestures of compassion, care, and concern are a persistent undercurrent in the crushing tides of rhetorical posturing and antihuman violence. Such gestures are performed primarily by individuals distancing themselves more or less overtly from the rigid and forcibly collective patriotisms that have co-opted Guantánamo as a scene of war, and are largely manifest in creative expression broadly understood: poetry, fiction, art, and memoir, certainly, but also journalism, film, photography, oral history, advocacy taking the form of both legal action and public protest, and environmental activism. In the context of Guantánamo, these individuals are identified, with varying levels of coercion, as current and former detainees; cellblock guards, military linguists, and chaplains; newspaper reporters, photojournalists, and documentarians; artists, writers, and filmmakers in the capacities that Cuba's long-established professionalization of creative labor allows; and political prisoners, activists, and lawyers.

My attempt to elucidate individual gestures of care that push at the dominant narratives of war at Guantánamo builds on Barbara Harlow's "'Extraordinary Renditions': Tales of Guantánamo, a Review Article" (2011). Harlow assembled what was by then an already substantial corpus of works that stand as "extraordinary renditions"—her term for "a putative, self-styled literary sub-genre" (2) that "borrows ungenerously and paraphrastically from just one of the many euphemisms that emerged during the Bush administration" (2). Encompassing memoirs, stage plays, novels, documentaries, poetry, scholarship, and journalism, the driving interest of Harlow's essay is the role of the "literary," broadly defined, in serving "the aim of closing Guantánamo for good" (1). The "literary," she insists, "must assume . . . its own expanded sense of purpose, an advocacy, even adversarial, role" (3). My own reading not only expands Harlow's corpus to work published in subsequent decades but also addresses the specificity of gestures of care that while they may certainly contribute to a concerted, political effort to "close Guantánamo for good," and may, at times, be present in texts from the same corpus, unfold at a smaller scale, among individuals who rarely consider themselves to be agents of change. I also bring into this corpus work from Cuba, long neglected as a force in Guantánamo advocacy despite its physical proximity to and political stake in what happens at the base.

Writing and art by detainees is particularly rich in its recording of localized gestures of care. These have circulated increasingly outside Guantánamo since the mid-2000s, in the form of work produced at the camps themselves and made public, often in the face of seemingly insurmountable obstacles, by American and British lawyers working in a pro bono capacity on detainees' habeas cases, and of post-release memoirs of former detainees. The initial landmark publication in the first category is *Poems from Guantánamo: The Detainees Speak*, an anthology of twenty-two poems written clandestinely on the cellblocks, often on scraps of paper and Styrofoam cups in the absence of adequate materials, and passed through many layers of confiscation and censorship before their publication by the University of Iowa Press, in an edition edited by lawyer Marc Falkoff, in 2007. The second is *Guantánamo Diary*, the narrative account of Mohamedou Ould Slahi's abduction, detention, and torture, written for his lawyers Nancy Hollander and Theresa Duncan, shared in a heavily redacted version with editor Larry Siems, and published by Little, Brown and Company in 2015, which issued a version carefully "restored" after Slahi's release from Guantánamo in 2016. The third is artwork produced in programs of formal instruction at the Guantánamo camps in the later years of their existence, gifted by detainees to their lawyers. With the title *Art from Guantánamo*, this artwork was first exhibited under the curation of Erin Thompson for display at the President's Gallery of John Jay College of Criminal Justice in New York in late 2017, and subsequently reproduced in print and online formats. The archive of detainees' post-release memoirs, often produced in collaboration with journalists and professional writers, numbers over ten: dating back to British-Pakistani Moazzam Begg's *Enemy Combatant: A British Muslim's Journey to Guantánamo and Back* (2006) and with the publication of Mansoor Adayfi's *Don't Forget Us Here: Lost and Found at Guantánamo* (2021), it is still growing. Dispersed around the globe, often not repatriated but sent to third countries with which they have little linguistic or cultural affinity, former detainees have gained a scant if increasing presence as authors of op-ed pieces in major newspapers, and as the subjects of investigative reporting. While the writing and art of detainees, whether produced at the camps or post release, is unsurprisingly wide-ranging in its form, tone, and subject matter, it is striking for the almost total absence, across the corpus as a whole, of rancor, violence, or the strident hostility that has governed political languages at Guantánamo. It tends, rather, toward the pacific, conciliatory, and curious. As such, it is a powerful foundation of Guantánamo's alternative corpus.

Personnel posted to Guantánamo by the US military, either while part of the Joint Task Force that assumed operation of the detention centers there in 2002 or as members of the base's longer established US Navy community, have also recorded quiet gestures of compassion toward detainees, despite the rigid lines of rhetorical and physical separation that structure their respective roles. In 2005, military linguist Eric Saar and military chaplain James Yee each published accounts of their experience at Guantánamo, while civilian Pashtun-language translator Mahvish Rukhsana Khan published her *My Guantanamo Diary: The Detainees and the Stories They Told Me* three years later. Saar, Yee, and Khan each recount how the constitutive intermediacy of the roles of translator and chaplain was recast as a position of betrayal of the larger mission of American patriotism; a recasting in the face of which, nevertheless, none of them was able to renounce recognition of, and sympathy for, detainees' humanity and decency. A small number of cellblock guards, largely drawn from military police units and with little experience with ostensibly high-value detainees such as those held at Guantánamo, have placed on record the friendships and mutual respect they established with some of those they had been told would be the worst of the worst. They have done so in memoirs, magazine articles and, in the case of former guard Chris Arendt, in a collaboration with artists Amber Ginsburg and Aaron Hughes, the *Tea Project*, in which participants drink tea together from cups artistically engraved like those at Guantánamo. Guards' conversions to Islam as a result of their encounters with Muslim detainees as well as post-release reunions often filmed and posted online are part of a landscape of care that subtly undermines the more hostile scene of Guantánamo.

Although they are more transitory residents of Guantánamo, present there as observers of rather than participants in detention operations, many individual lawyers, journalists, and artist-activists have extended forms of care across power lines at the base, most particularly to detainees whose lives they are charged with representing in various ways. That pro bono lawyers have established trusting, respectful relationships with their detainee clients is evident not only in successful legal representation but also in a broader concern for well-being that has attended to physical comfort, contact with families, and friendships enduring after release. This is borne out, for example, in the memoir *Eight O'Clock Ferry to the Windward Side* (2007) by Clive Stafford Smith, British lawyer and founder of the London-based nonprofit Reprieve, and in the lawyers' stories collected in Mark P. Denbeaux and Jonathan Hafetz's edited volume *The Guantánamo Lawyers: Inside a Prison, Outside the Law* (2009). Similarly, the very act of keeping Guantánamo in the public eye over a more than twenty-year period is a gesture of care assumed by several journalists, unquestionably chief among them Carol Rosenberg, of the *Miami Herald* and subsequently the *New York Times*, whose articles were collected by the *Miami Herald* and published as *Guantánamo Bay: The Pentagon's Alcatraz of the Caribbean* (2016). Rosenberg has provided continuous, creative, and comprehensive coverage not only of prison operations and legal proceedings at the base but also of individual detainees in the daily rituals to which they have become habituated as they age in the more "open" environment of the late 2010s; of young US soldiers posted as guards to a tropical destination that in many cases turns out to be soul-destroying; and of communities already established at the base in the more tranquil years before 2002. Photographers and artists permitted to visit the base during the periods of lower entry restriction that preceded the Trump presidency have similarly participated in the generation of a compassionate Guantánamo, even as their work has been subject to strict oversight from military authorities at the base. Notable among these are Edmund Clark, whose *Guantánamo: If the Light Goes Out* (2011) is a series of plates documenting Guantánamo's different versions of home; Molly Crabapple who, following a visit to Guantánamo in 2013, published drawings of US Army personnel, detainees, courtroom scenes, and the abandoned cages of Camp X-Ray; and Janet Hamlin, the court artist whose *Sketching Guantánamo: Court Sketches of the Military Tribunals, 2006–2013* (2013) approaches detainees and families of 9/11 victims, in separate areas of the same courtroom, from similar perspectives. Distinctive in its geographical and conceptual reach is the work of Debi Cornwall, whose *Welcome to Camp America* (2017) photographs the spaces occupied by detainees, military personnel, and their families at Guantánamo, and individual detainees in their post-release environments. Cornwall extends the military-imposed restrictions on photographing faces at Guantánamo to images shot far beyond the base, as a commentary on the many levels of constraint that detention imposes, even in its aftermath.

Harlow broadens her corpus beyond work issuing from time spent at Guantánamo to the writing, art, journalism, and filmmaking of individuals who, although physically distanced from the base, have nevertheless engaged closely with the stories and plight of detainees. The ten-plus years since her article's publication have seen further collaborations with detainees, especially those whose post-release lives have proven to be deeply unstable. Among these is Mohammed el-Gharani, a Chadian teenager detained at Guantánamo for eight years and largely itinerant in the years following his release, whom New York–based artist Laurie Anderson "telepresenced" as a live image as part of her *Habeas Corpus* exhibit and performance at the New York Armory in 2015, and whose story French journalists Jérôme Tubiana and Alexandre Franc have told in the graphic novel *Guantánamo Kid: The True Story of Mohammed El-Gharani* (2019). *Life after Guantánamo: Exiled in Kazakhstan*, a documentary made for *VICE News* in 2015 and narrated by journalist Simon Ostrovksy, profiles Lotfi bin Ali, a Tunisian held without charge at Guantánamo for twelve years and resettled in Kazakhstan in 2014, where his inability to speak either Kazakh or Russian, to work, marry, or start a family, severely exacerbated the challenges of his existence, as did his unanswered requests for adequate healthcare for a heart condition, from which he died in early 2021. Mohamedou Ould Slahi's story, together with that of Steve Wood, Slahi's former guard and later friend and convert to Islam, has been retold in numerous forms, among them in Ben Taub's Pulitzer Prize–winning *New Yorker* essay "Guantánamo's

Darkest Secret" (2019); Laurence Topham's short documentary film *My Brother's Keeper* (2020); the feature film *The Mauritanian* (2021), directed by Kevin MacDonald and starring household names Tahar Rahim, Jodie Foster, and Benedict Cumberbatch; and the documentary *Guantánamo Diary Revisited* (2022), in which investigative journalist John Goetz sets out to find Slahi's former interrogators. Attentive engagements with detainees still at Guantánamo have become more numerous since the publication of Slahi's *Guantánamo Diary*, serving as willed endeavors to humanize lives that in official accounts are still recorded as numbers. The six-part Radiolab miniseries *The Other Latif*, for example, is journalist Latif Nasser's story of his Moroccan namesake Abdul Latif Nasser, detained at Guantánamo in 2002 and, despite having been cleared for release in 2016, held until his became the first Biden-era repatriation in July 2021. *A Ship from Guantánamo* (2021) is Dara Kell and Veena Rao's six-minute film about the intricate model ships built by Yemeni Moath Al-Alwi, one of Guantánamo's first detainees and one of the forty remaining there at the time of the film's release.

The lines of individual care extending to and from Guantánamo Cubans touch the lives of detainees more obliquely, with José Ramón Sánchez's poetry being by far the most explicit attempt to investigate, describe, and inhabit the experience of detainees. Despite being hampered by not only the scant and somewhat arbitrary nature of internationally available information about detainees but also by the vagaries of access to relevant reading materials, journalism, the internet, and mobility more broadly from his Guantánamo City home, Sánchez's poems extend their imaginative reach to the physical space of detainees' cells, their inner experience of captivity, and their relationship to poetry. Others creating from Cuban Guantánamo map different paths of compassion. Daniel Ross's award-winning independent film, *La espera* (The Wait, 2022), traces the acute pain of a lonely widower against a broader landscape of Cuba's border with the base, the protagonist's solitude disrupted by the explosions of land mines that migrants inadvertently detonate as they attempt to reach the base, the appearance on his doorstep of their discarded shoes, and the arbitrary acts of violence the Cuban Border Brigade perpetrates in its purported defense of the revolution. Compassion surfaces in short stories by Ana Luz García Calzada and Roberto de Jesús Quiñónes for the migrants who, since the mid-1960s, have risked and often lost their lives attempting to cross the heavily mined Guantánamo

Bay to seek asylum at the base; in the art of Alexander Beatón and Pedro Gutiérrez, for residents of the town of Caimanera, isolated and stultified by their proximity to the base; in a story by Leandro Estupiñán Zaldívar, for young soldiers charged with guarding the fence line between Cuba and the base, ostensibly against US attacks but more urgently against migrants from surrounding communities; and in editorials in the dissident publication *Porvenir*, for prisoners held by Cuban authorities in the province of Guantánamo.

This book traces the asymmetrical and unpredictable paths that individual gestures of care take at Guantánamo with a framework of five nouns, each accommodating differing interpretations, forms of engagement, and locations within what I understand as a tenuously cohesive region—a no-man's-land less in the sense in which British playwright Harold Pinter's 2005 Nobel Prize acceptance speech deploys the term with reference to the extralegal location of the detention centers, than as what Federica Pedriali, looking to the no-man's-lands of World War I, has called a "zone of exclusion managed by two warring sides" (150). "Borderlands," the noun heading this introductory chapter, represents a first attempt to reconsider Guantánamo as something more than two separate spaces, controlled by two mutually hostile governments, and physically divided by the fence line and the land-mined areas around it. Echoing the title of the widely influential work of Gloria Anzaldúa, *Borderlands/La Frontera: The New Mestiza* (1987), the chapter is, rather, an invitation to contemplate Guantánamo's fence line, as Anzaldúa does the Río Bravo del Norte/Rio Grande, from "both shores at once" (100), and to approach these shores—or the Cuban and US sides of the fence line—in terms of what Priscilla Solis Ybarra, reading Anzaldúa, has termed a "bioregion," whose subjects live in "direct connection to the animal world and the natural environment" (Solis Ybarra 286).

Chapter 1, "Translation," is motivated by a line former detainee Ibrahim al-Rubaish wrote during his time at Guantánamo in the poem "Ode to the Sea." "Doesn't Cuba, the vanquished, translate its stories for you?" (66) the poet asks, imagining Cuba, the Caribbean Sea, and a detention cell together as a Guantánamo in which stories—as experience, as narrative, as history—can be rendered intelligible in new languages. Al-Rubaish's poem was included in Marc Falkoff's English-language collection *Poems from Guantánamo: The Detainees Speak* (2007), its original Arabic subsequently remaining classified; it persists only in translated forms, with plausible alternatives for the word *vanquished* left to speculation. A second poem in Falkoff's collection, however, namely Mohammed el-Gharani's "First Poem of My Life," describes Cuba as "an afflicted isle" (39), and includes footnotes by the translator, Flagg Miller, who situates "afflicted" in relation to "a discourse of resistance that has a Palestinian tenor" (40). *Vanquished* and *afflicted* are expressions of political solidarity with Cuba that misalign in their correspondence to the future-orientated rhetoric of Cuba's revolution, which always anticipates victory. The sharing of experience that falls short in the form of political solidarity flows more smoothly, however, in namings of a natural environment common to Guantánamo's inhabitants, particularly the Caribbean Sea. The sea is the addressee of al-Rubaish's poem and assumes a complexly dominant, and deeply anthropomorphized, role in former detainee Mansoor Adayfi's memoir, *Don't Forget Us Here: Lost and Found at Guantánamo*, as well as in the collection of detainee art first exhibited in New York in 2017–2018, *Art from Guantánamo*. A sea that, in al-Rubaish's phrasing, "cruelly guards" ("Ode to the Sea" 66) while also offering what Adayfi calls "hope for our future freedom" (*Don't Forget Us Here* 63) reanimates the paradox of insularity that was central to Cuban poetry and cultural criticism in the twentieth century, and paves this alternative route toward a coherent regional unity. The two Cuban poets this chapter discusses have no direct familiarity with either detainees at the base or one another, and yet their writing, too, maps the contours of a Guantánamo whose natural environment defies its political divisions. In *The Black Arrow*, José Ramón Sánchez insists on proximity between detainees and the poetic subject in Cuba, imagining the spatial arrangements of a cell, the psychological toll of indefinite detention, and the physiological effects of torture. His most intensely liberating poem, "Secret//NoForn," is formatted as a redaction of a leaked US military intelligence document. In replacing once-classified information with lines from the most celebrated poetry of Cuba's Guantánamo province, Regino E. Botti's *El mar y la montaña* (1921), it overwrites justifications for confinement with the vast expanse, and implied freedom, of the region's land and sea. In the poems of *Con el alma cautiva* (2007), the oft-jailed Cuban dissident poet Néstor Rodríguez Lobaina looks out from his cell to seek comfort in a larger, natural world, and in doing so suggests uncanny continuities among experiences of detention, and sources of solace, in the Guantánamo region as a whole. Read together, these texts suggest that while the urgency of human rights abuses at the detention centers, and to a lesser extent the United States' continued presence at the base, have ensured a global reach for Guantánamo, local alliances and affinities, on a much smaller scale, have served to undermine large-scale hostility and secure solace for individuals.

Chapter 2, "Guards," explores the radical challenge to power structures imposed by US and Cuban military authorities at and around Guantánamo that is posed by certain guards, be these on patrol on the base's cellblocks or along the Cuban side of the fence line. Both the US war on terror and Cuba's war on imperialism established the "enemy" as a rigid category, and charged their militaries with defending against it. In the constrained space of the cellblocks at the base's detention camps, young men and women, often from military police units, spend their days and nights with the "enemy," and while some insist on maintaining the distinction between "us" and "them," or "good" and "evil," that governs the camps, others form slow, mutually respecting friendships with individual detainees. As reported in the memoirs a number of former detainees have published since their release, as well as in books and interviews by former members of the US military, these friendships often begin in the common ground of confinement—despite the immeasurably less restrictive circumstances of guards, they cannot depart at will—and develop more fully as shared interests, histories, and experiences come to light. Particularly in the memoirs of Moazzam Begg and Mohamedou Ould Slahi, encounters coalesce around interests in reading classical literature, generally posited as an uncontentious meeting place, removed from the realities and hierarchies of the camps; similar histories of colonialist and racist aggression that emerge in conversations detainees have with Black or Puerto Rican guards, whom they almost uniformly describe as the most compassionate soldiers on the cellblocks; and a deep respect on the part of some guards for the Muslim faith that they see sustaining many detainees, a faith to which some guards eventually convert. These intimate, compassionate relationships that form across deeply entrenched hierarchies extend as a model to relationships between guards and "enemies" on the Cuban side of the fence line, where border guards are on the alert for ever-less-plausible attacks from US forces at the base, and for Cuban migrants attempting the highly perilous escape route from Guantánamo Province to the base. Long figured by the Cuban government as "counterrevolutionaries," aspiring migrants expose the deep complexities of hostility within Cuban society and, in Cuban authors' and filmmakers' reluctance to condemn them, forms of compassion and acceptance akin to those that certain guards extend to detainees at the base.

Chapter 3, "Home," addresses the temporary, involuntary, or constrained nature of residency at Guantánamo for many people and its interplay with indefinite, short-term, and permanent temporalities, and traces the spatial, social, and aesthetic strategies with which the region's inhabitants have made home there. While in scholarship on incarceration the cell has been presented as a potentially domestic space, the leaked *Camp Delta Standard Operating Procedures* (2004) regulate this space and the so-called comfort items permitted in it in such a way as to approximate more closely the calculated defamiliarization of torture rooms that Elaine Scarry described in *The Body in Pain: The Making and Unmaking of the World* (1985). Memoirs by former detainees David Hicks and Ahmed Errachidi detail the spatial dimensions and living conditions of cells at Guantánamo through persistent contrasts with their distant homes and with what a human's—as opposed to an animal's—living space should be. Resisting this recalibration of home, however, Errachidi describes claiming a social space from which to extend hospitality to other detainees and beings, thus resituating the cell as a tentative, if much diminished, domestic space. Within the same forty-five square miles of the base, military families lead lives that have been touted as safe, close-knit, and traditional, harking back to ideals of small-town America. The archives of their community newspaper, the *Guantánamo Bay Gazette*, whose post-9/11 issues this chapter examines, convey concerted attempts to uphold ideals of home in the face of global scrutiny of Guantánamo, and the close proximity of ostensibly dangerous detainees. Despite its overwhelming focus on military families, the *Guantánamo Bay Gazette* sheds light on a small and ever-diminishing community of base residents with a particular claim to this space as home: "Special Category Residents," Cubans who commuted to work at the base in the early 1960s and chose to remain there when hostilities increased. The home this now-elderly community has created, with considerable economic assistance from the US Navy, bears much in common with Cuban exile communities in southern Florida, and yet is territorially continuous with the country left behind. In its final section, this chapter turns to figurations of home in and on behalf of the Cuban border town of Caimanera, whose status as "the first line of defense against imperialism" has rendered it exceptional in the national context, its proximity to the base overshadowing its communal and economic life. Documentary films about Guantánamo from the 1960s and more recently—José Massip's *Guantánamo* (1965) and Hernando Calvo Ospina's *Todo Guantánamo es nuestro* (2016)—reiterate the defiant stance of a home usurped, only to be rendered whole if the base is returned to Cuba. The artwork of Alexander Beatón and Pedro Gutiérrez, however, particularly the multimedia installation *El camino de la estrategia* (2013) (*The Way of Strategy*, 2014), explores less contestatory ways of living in the shadow of the base—under a rubric of *convivencia*, or living together, that I read as offering broader models for making home at Guantánamo.

Chapter 4, "The Future," looks to visions of a future at and for Guantánamo. More than 20 years into the establishment of the detention camps, more than 60 into the Cuban Revolution, and 120 since the initiation of the United States' lease in perpetuity, the question "what comes next?" still hangs in the balance. With the "indefinite" time frame of detention at the base's camps, and the ever-deferred fulfilment of the Cuban revolutionary project as its primary temporal references, this chapter explores contemplations of the future by and on behalf of the Guantánamo region's inhabitants, as it relates to their experience in a present of both the detention camps and revolutionary Cuba. Detainees speaking and writing from the camps have expressed fear that "indefinite" means "forever," and former detainees writing post-release—among them Murat Kurnaz, Lakhdar Boumediène, and Mustafa Ait Idir—describe various experiences of lingering in the present, hesitant, and mistrustful toward what might lie in a long-term future. Advocacy groups and investigative journalists have documented the post-release lives of former detainees as economically and socially precarious, often unfolding in countries to which they had no previous connection and wracked by the physical and psychological aftermath of Guantánamo, and the photographic work of Debi Cornwall, in *Welcome to Camp America* (2017), represents former detainees in their post-release spatial settings, as a tribute to their pasts and a gesture toward repair. The chapter's second section turns in part to textual material produced at Guantánamo before 9/11, in the two-year period between 1994 and 1996 when the base was used as a holding place for Cuban and Haitian refugees seeking asylum in the United States. *El futuro* is a handwritten journal produced by and for Spanish-speaking refugees at the camps as they contemplated a deeply uncertain future, their strategic translations into English of certain articles, and frequent inclusion of the Statue of Liberty among their detailed hand-drawings, attesting to their hopes for a future elsewhere. Alongside *El futuro* I read the almost-synonymous title *Porvenir*, a journal specific to the Cuban province of Guantánamo and initiated in 2008 as part of the politically dissident movement Alianza Democrática Oriental, charged with promoting independent, non-state journalism in Cuba. Through short and locally focused feature articles, open letters to Cuban authorities and international human rights organizations, reports on conditions in the prisons of Guantánamo Province and lists of those held there, *Porvenir* insists on a vision of Cuba's future rooted—like that of the earlier *El futuro*—in democratic principles. This chapter closes with three quite distinct imaginings of a post-conflict naval base, generated by artists and a scholar resident in the United States that stand as a form of anticipatory commemoration, or symbolic repair for conflict still underway. The first of these, *Reparations for Guantánamo's Torture Survivors*—written by Aaron Hughes and Amber Ginsburg in collaboration with advocacy groups HeaRT, CAGE, Witness Against Torture, and Chicago Torture Justice Memorials, and included in the 2022 DePaul Art Museum exhibit *Remaking the Exceptional: Tea, Torture and Reparations | Chicago to Guantánamo*—is a performative text that commands into being acknowledgement, apology, and reparation for abuses at Guantánamo. The second, American artist Ian Alan Paul's *Guantánamo Bay Museum of Art and History*, is a project that poses online as a museum and memorial to a defunct detention center, forcing into existence a present that is markedly more conciliatory and equitable than the current one. The third is a proposal by the conservation biologist Joe Roman to make the base an ecological research center, collaboratively managed by Cuba and the United States in an imagined moment of vastly improved relations. Together, these various perspectives on the aftermath of the present moment push at the urgent question of how to imagine, or better still inhabit, a future while acknowledging, and coming to terms with, what will then be the past; asking, in resonance with a much broader field of post-conflict contexts, what a repaired, restorative future might look like.

Alexander Beatón gave the title *Susurros* (Whispers) to his digital photography exhibit, shown by the Provincial Arts Council of

FIGURE I.2. ALEXANDER BEATÓN, *1898 . . . BONSÁI*. REPRINTED COURTESY OF THE ARTIST.

Guantánamo, Cuba, in 2021. Its twenty images juxtapose a small-scale replica of the watchtowers that line the perimeter of the base with everyday objects common in eastern Cuba but also present in US rural and popular culture: a baseball, a set of dominoes, a straw hat, a bale of barbed wire in the shape of a bonsai tree (fig. I.2). In lingering on these reminders of things that are mundane and shared, present with but not dominated by the symbol of vigilance that is the watchtower, the *Susurros* exhibit insinuated that, beneath the bombast and bluster of Cuban and American government rhetoric, there are simpler, more harmonious ways to experience the relationship between the base and Cuba. Even as actions at the US naval base have become notorious for their egregious departure from international concerns, such insinuations have grown in the creative expression of detainees and others at the naval base, and of writers, artists, and filmmakers in the Cuban province that surrounds it. Together, they trace a new "Guantánamo," a no-man's-land over which no state, and no lexicon of hostility, holds sway; one that is governed, rather, by curiosity, consideration, and a will to coexist.

CHAPTER 1

TRANSLATION

Guantánamo's moderate size and population, and its far-flung geographic location—on Cuba's southeastern coast, distant from the centers of government of Havana and Washington, DC—belie its geopolitical significance. As Amy Kaplan signaled in her 2005 essay "Where Is Guantánamo?," the base's territorial isolation, jurisdictional obfuscation, and clandestine military practices in fact place it frontally on the map of a "global penal archipelago where the U.S. indefinitely detains, secretly transports, and tortures uncounted prisoners from all over the world" (831). Rather than the effective nowhere that former secretary of defense Donald Rumsfeld purportedly had in mind when he sought to hold detainees in "the legal equivalent of outer space" (854), Guantánamo, Kaplan concludes, "is everywhere" (854).

It is this Guantánamo—legally nowhere but thereby potentially everywhere, with a pretext of exception whose ensuing human rights abuses have global reach and urgency—that has long been the focus of the many individuals and groups who have fought hard to keep its detention centers on the world map and in the public eye. And yet alongside unrelenting endeavors to draw Guantánamo out of its dislocation—to insist on it as a site with urgent moral ties to the United States, Europe, the Middle East, and the international community broadly defined—there have persisted smaller-scale gestures aimed at situating Guantánamo Bay Naval Base as geographically continuous with, and affectively connected to, Cuba and the Caribbean Sea, tracing for the base a local presence that complements and affirms, but does not conflate with, its global belonging. In the base's detention centers and in the Cuban lands that border it, writers and artists, speaking and writing in different languages and from vastly different subject positions, have crafted a vocabulary and images that, unlike the exceptional, divisive language waged at Guantánamo by the US and Cuban governments, acknowledges the sharing of land, space, and sea that takes place in this region. Guantánamo becomes not only a node in the globally extending network of black sites that Kaplan names; it emerges, at the same time, as a natural environment, shared experience, and sense of location that dissipates division among those who partake of them, despite the ostensibly insurmountable physical and political barriers that separate them.

The writers and artists whose work traces alternative contours for Guantánamo, extending from the base into Cuba and vice versa as a borderland region rather than as two bounded and mutually hostile territories, connect to one another in tenuous, and fundamentally asymmetrical, ways. Those that are the subjects of this chapter have little or no familiarity with one another's lives and work, have for the most part been involuntarily confined to discrete, enclosed spaces within the more expansive Guantánamo to which their work gestures, and led vastly different lives in the years before Guantánamo's detention camps opened. Writing in different languages and from experiences of isolation imposed under hugely different circumstances, these works together test the possibility of some form of commonality on divided, contested ground. This is in many ways an incommensurable gesture, in that the legality and conditions of detention at Guantánamo's camps that have profoundly marked the creative work of Mohammed el-Gharani, Ibrahim al-Rubaish, and Mansoor Adayfi—the poets and memoirists whose writing is the focus of this chapter's first part—differ significantly and in ethical gravity from the restriction experienced by the Cuban poets whose work I address subsequently, José Ramón Sánchez and Néstor Rodríguez Lobaina, despite the years the latter spent as a political prisoner of the Cuban state. I want to argue that these authors, each one aspiring to an experience of freedom denied to him by the particular version of Guantánamo to which he has been ascribed, remap a more hopeful, accommodating Guantánamo. Together they produce a peculiar form of regional culture, delineated not by linguistic or national boundaries but precisely by how fraught its legal and geopolitical mappings are.

Two of the five men with whose work this chapter engages, Ibrahim al-Rubaish and Mohammed el-Gharani, have authored poems included in *Poems from Guantánamo: The Detainees Speak*, a collection of twenty-two censored and translated poems by men then in detention at Guantánamo, edited by attorney Marc Falkoff and published to broad critical reception in 2007. Each poem is accompanied by a biographical note on its author, one of the many ways in which the collection seeks, as Falkoff puts it, to "attest to the humanity" (4) of these men. The note accompanying al-Rubaish's poem describes him as "a religious scholar who dislikes hostility and was once a candidate for a judgeship" (64). El-Gharani is introduced as "a fourteen-year-old Chadian national raised in Saudi Arabia," one of "as many as twenty-nine juveniles ... detained at Guantánamo in violation of international law" (37). Although their poems were written during detention, al-Rubaish was released from Guantánamo in 2006 and el-Gharani in 2009. After his release, al-Rubaish was noted in public record first as a suspected senior leader of Al-Qaeda in the Arabian Peninsula, and subsequently as having been killed in a US drone strike in 2015 (Shane). El-Gharani is reported to have led a precarious and itinerant life, one that became the subject of Jerôme Tubiana and Alexandre Franc's graphic account, *Guantánamo Kid: The True Story of Mohammed El-Gharani* (2019). A third former detainee, Yemeni citizen Mansoor Adayfi, is absent from *Poems from Guantánamo*, but, having remained at Guantánamo until 2016, he has had a central voice in the documentation and presentation of artistic work created at the detention centers. A text by Adayfi introduces the catalog for *Art from Guantánamo*, an exhibit of detainee art in which representations of the sea are abundant, and his memoir *Don't Forget Us Here: Lost and Found at Guantánamo* (2021) includes numerous passages about the vital importance, and deep symbolism, of the Caribbean Sea to those detained at Guantánamo.

The poetry of José Ramón Sánchez, who lives in the Cuban city of Guantánamo and has authored over one hundred poems in Spanish invoking the anomalous and oft ignored province of his childhood in its relation to the off-limits US base, maps the base as connected to Cuba by landscape and political history. Sánchez references detainees' experiences of isolation as resonant with those of the figure of the poet more broadly. He often privileges identification over disparity, even though he writes from relative security as a poet with access to information and mobility that would seem constrained in most other comparisons, but which are of a wholly different order from those of the detainees. The poetry of Cuban democracy activist and former political prisoner Néstor Rodríguez Lobaina, held numerous times in the 1990s and 2000s at Cuba's notorious Combinado de Guantánamo provincial prison, around twenty miles and a minefield away from the camps at the US base, traces more sinister parallels with detainees' captivity. Nevertheless, Rodríguez Lobaina's trial and sentencing, while sharply condemned by Amnesty International and other human rights organizations, were sanctioned by the Cuban Penal Code, providing a legal framework absent from the extrajudicial detentions of men at the base.

RENDITION, EMPIRE, AND CUBA

When Ibrahim al-Rubaish and Mohammed el-Gharani's poems were published, *Poems from Guantánamo: The Detainees Speak* was the only creative work produced at the base's prisons to be made publicly available, albeit in a form materially and linguistically determined by the demands of censorship.[1] Access to writing tools for the detainees had initially been restricted, and Falkoff has documented the many levels of interference that affected the production and publication of the poems, from their beginnings as inscriptions with pebbles or toothpaste on Styrofoam cups to the destruction or confiscation of many of them before they could be read by other prisoners or lawyers.[2] The volume's translation record is riven with impediments: its English-language translators were required to have secret-level security clearance, and most of the Arabic and Pashtun originals remained classified, the de facto source for subsequent translations being necessarily the English-language volume (3–5). What can be read in *Poems from Guantánamo* is only part of what was or might have been written, such that any critical approach to the project is marred a priori by the partial status of what appears on the page, and by losses in translation that are as literal as they are metaphorical. With the exception of those poems composed in English by British detainees and the very few nonclassified poems in Arabic, the originals to which comparatist readers might aspire remained classified for years after the publication of the translations.

Poems from Guantánamo has received considerable critical attention since its first publication. Judith Butler, for example, devotes a chapter of *Frames of War: When is Life Grievable* (2009) to the collection, reading it as offering "a different kind of moral responsiveness ... a kind of interpretation that may, under certain conditions, contest and explode the schisms running through the national and military ideology" (58). Approaching the poems from the perspective of precariousness, Butler observes that "war is precisely an effort to minimize precariousness for some and to maximize it for others" (54). Among the "others" in the war on terror are the detainee-poets at Guantánamo, whose lives have not been counted as human and yet have displayed a certain "survivability" (53). Butler asks, "What, if anything, accounts for the survivability of those who have been physically exploited?" (53), and finds one answer in the very enunciation of poetry: "The forming of words is linked with survival, with the capacity to survive, or survivability" (56).

Butler's reading exemplifies an approach to the collection that, as Erin Trapp has indicated, reads the poems primarily as "extensions of the discourses of human rights and political resistance" (2). Trapp instead proposes an initial reading of the poems from the perspective of their lyric subjects; while Flagg Miller, whose essay "Forms of Suffering in Muslim Prison Poetry" is included in Falkoff's volume as a second introduction, considers their place in literary and political traditions of the Arab world, situating them in a literary history in which poetry has long played a prominent role in voicing and resisting oppression. With this history in mind, Miller speculates that the poets have striven, precisely, for "a language that is more likely to win advantage: the discourse of international human rights" (15) rather than call upon "the vocabulary of radical Islamic militancy to defend themselves" (11). This assessment is necessarily based on those poems that have survived censorship sufficiently to have been included in the collection.

Elizabeth Weber reads *Poems from Guantánamo* in terms of legal and literary justice—the latter in Shoshana Felman's sense of a language that encapsulates that which cannot be closed—arguing that "the confiscation of thousands of lines of poetry from the inmates evinces that even the private possession of one's own poetic, literary writing is considered an intolerable threat" ("Literary Justice?" 424), silencing both forms of justice. Building to some extent on Weber's later claim that these poems can only be read "torn out of their cultural and especially linguistic and poetological context" (*Kill Boxes* 138), Rebecca Adelman has read *Poems from Guantánamo*, along with exhibits of detainee art, and a range of attempts at other cultural representations of detainees' experience at the base, in terms of the "affective and imaginative practices" (*Figuring Violence* xi) of those who approach this experience with a will to understand what they take to be the "pitiable detainee" (181). Adelman observes that "the project of making detainee voices heard by American audiences either presumes that they would be unintelligible or forces them into a preexisting grid of intelligibility" (187). Ultimately, she concludes, "The question is how we might respond ethically to detention in the absence of such intelligibility. The answer is not to pretend unintelligibility away" (187).

Despite their significant differences, critical assessments of *Poems from Guantánamo*, many of them written and published within the United States, tend to turn outward from Guantánamo as a place, to a context of US-led global war and an international community that opposes it, or to poetic and political genealogies known or assumed to be particular to the Middle East. Alongside these outward connections, however, some of the poems themselves appeal inward, across the base's border, to Cuba. In general, the poems name very few places, an absence that likely indicates as much about censors' fears of coded messages as about the poets' own interests.[3] Nonetheless, Cuba is named in three: "Two Fragments," originally written in Pashto by the Pakistani poet and essayist Shaikh Abdurraheem Muslim Dost, as well as el-Gharani's "First Poem of my Life" and al-Rubaish's "Ode to the Sea," both originally written in Arabic. "Two Fragments" names Cuba as a distant point on a map, from which a father has yet to return: "Eid has come, but my father has not / He is not come from Cuba" (36). El-Gharani and al-Rubaish, however, go considerably further, qualifying Cuba with specific adjectives that seem to seek a referent for their own experience within a local context.

El-Gharani's "First Poem of my Life" is a narrative poem that recounts being arrested by Pakistani police while praying in a mosque in 2001, spending long hours and days being transferred—or "extraordinarily rendered," in the language of the war on terror—first in a "transport truck" (38) and then "a warplane" (39) to a final, wholly unfamiliar destination. "They carried us, afterwards, to Cuba / Because it is an afflicted isle" (39) is one of the poem's final lines. Al-Rubaish's "Ode to the Sea," a more lyrically ambitious poem than many others in the collection, is an extended address to the Caribbean Sea as a promise of liberty as well as a captor, whose role is to "taunt us in our captivity" (65) and "cruelly guard us" (65). As the poem draws to an end it asks of this sea: "Doesn't Cuba, the vanquished, translate its stories for you?" (66).

"Afflicted" in el-Gharani's poem and "vanquished" in al-Rubaish's, Cuba is invoked by each poet as he seeks a causal logic for the absurdity of renditions from Pakistan to Guantánamo Bay, and a connection between his own experience and the land to which he has been confined. In el-Gharani's case, detailed footnotes by the poem's translator, Flagg Miller—the only such footnotes in *Poems for Guantánamo*, whose other translators remain unnamed—suggest such a connection. Miller explains that the Arabic word he has translated as "afflicted" is *mankuba*, which forms a pun with "Cuba" while recalling the nickname given by Arabs to their defeat during Israel's war of independence, "the Affliction." "The poet's choice of words," Miller writes, "evokes a discourse of resistance that has a Palestinian tenor" (40). Via Miller's interpretation, Cuba is linked to a larger political struggle in el-Gharani's poem. Although no such contextualization is offered for al-Rubaish's references to Cuba, similar historical resonances are nevertheless available for the word *vanquished*.

Drawing on Miller's footnote, Nicole Waller has read el-Gharani's poem as pointing "to Guantánamo's contested place on the global map and to Cuba's colonial and Cold War history" (366), and al-Rubaish's as appealing to "the colonial and postcolonial history of Cuba and to its literature" (366–67). Both poems, Waller argues, map Cuba "into global space as a site of both static imprisonment and dynamic resistance and connection" (367), an argument that, even as it engages with the base's location in Cuba and that country's own history, participates in the outward, global-oriented practices of reading *Poems from Guantánamo* that have marked much of the volume's critical reception. Indeed, from the early 1960s on, Cuba engaged "global space" by means of the language and political actions of its revolutionary leadership, whose internationalist agenda acknowledged the anti-imperialist imperatives of Latin America, Africa, and Asia. The revolution's relationship to anti-imperialist movements in the Middle East, as Eman Morsi has traced, has its roots in Cuba's alliance with Algeria, whose War of Independence, lasting from 1954 to 1962, was contemporaneous with Cuba's guerilla struggle; in power from January 1, 1959, Cuba's revolutionary government offered postindependence Algeria medical and military support in exchange for oil (Morsi 148). The Egyptian government of Gamal Abdel Nasser and the Palestinian cause were two further nodes cementing Cuba's relationships in the Middle East, Morsi writes: despite Nasser's initial hesitation toward Fidel Castro, the relationship between their two countries until the former's death in 1970 "can be characterized as one of mutual respect, occasional economic solidarity, and mentorship" (152), while Cuba's support for Palestinian liberation groups, and provision of scholarships for Palestinians to study in Cuban universities, was met with "widespread fascination among young Palestinians with the Cuban revolution" (151). Indeed, Robert Buzzanco writes that "few foreign leaders supported the cause of Palestinian liberation more than Castro" (276), and that "Cuba was the first nation to recognize the Palestinian Liberation Organization at its 1964 founding" (276). Raúl Castro and Che Guevara's visit to Gaza in 1959 was credited with casting the conflict there in global and anticolonial, rather than merely local, terms, as was a speech Fidel Castro delivered to the United Nations General Assembly in 1960. There, Castro drew an explicit comparison between imperialist exploitation in Latin America and in the Middle East, insisting that "the problems of Latin America are like the problems of the rest of the underdeveloped world, in Africa and Asia . . . the world is divided up among the monopolies, and those same monopolies that we find in Latin America are also found in the Middle East" ("At the United Nations General Assembly" 169). Cementing this alliance, Palestine Liberation Organization leader Yasser Arafat was invited to visit Havana several times, and he received Cuba's highest honor, the Bay of Pigs Medal, in 1974 (Hatuqa).

Morsi notes that, despite the political alliances of the 1960s, "the need to maintain political sovereignty and bridge the economic gap with the North in the new post-1945 World Order; and the linguistic barriers and top-down centralized control of cultural exchanges made it very difficult, if not impossible, for any lateral grass-roots interactions to take place, thus severely limiting the opportunities for the development of meaningful cultural ties" (146). As a result, she claims, "the Cuba that appears in Arabic was a vaguely defined and symbolic space for Third World political and economic struggle" (146), and representations of

Cuba that began in politically informed solidarity were assimilated into the Arab canon emptied of their "Cuban specificity" (146), a process whose legacy endures to this day. This legacy may account for the fact that the translated adjectives in el-Gharani and al-Rubaish's poems, whatever resonance they may have in a postcolonial global space, are not merely devoid of "Cuban specificity." They are also at odds with the language of the Cuban Revolution, such that the ultimately more sustainable, reciprocal connection must come through the environmental space of the island itself.

Afflicted and *vanquished* have little place in the revolution's long-established rhetoric of past and future victories and, although the Cuban leadership has termed the US embargo *genocidal* for its intent to stifle the country's economy and deprive its people of food and medical supplies, its political propaganda has in general drawn sparingly from a vocabulary of victimhood ("Proclamation by the National Assembly"). Even on the most public occasion on which Fidel Castro, like el-Gharani and al-Rubaish, drew a comparison between detainees at the base and the Cuban people, he did so in terms that carefully avoided naming the latter as having been successfully "overcome." Castro's three-part essay, "The Empire and the Independent Island," serialized in the Cuban national newspaper in August 2008 and later published in the English volume *Guantánamo: Why the Illegal US Base Should be Returned to Cuba* (2011), gives a detailed history of underhand legislation and increasingly aggressive uses of the base, including the post–9/11 creation of "a horrendous torture center" (47). It culminates in Castro's claim that "the U.S. naval base at Guantánamo was necessary in order to humiliate and carry out the dirty deeds that take place there" (49). This formulation allows for marked open-endedness regarding whether or not the purpose, "to humiliate," was fulfilled: Castro's final sentence, "Cuba will always be waiting in a state of combat readiness" (49), makes clear that there is an all-important breach between the United States' need to humiliate and a Cuba that refuses to surrender.

In its dominant mode, Cuban revolutionary rhetoric has been averse to assuming a position of weakness, favoring instead a language of valiant and ongoing struggle, in which Cuba is relentlessly strong, ready to fight, and an agent of its own destiny. In this context, *vanquished* is a term particularly antithetical to the narratives of struggle, invincibility, and deferred victory that have characterized the revolution's anti-imperialist language: although the Spanish-language edition of *Poems from Guantánamo*, translated by Ana Mata Buil from English in the absence of an Arabic original, renders *vanquished* as *derrotada*, an equally plausible translation would be *vencida*. This latter is a form of *vencer*, a verb that was ubiquitous in the speeches of Cuba's revolutionary leaders but was almost invariably conjugated by them in the future first-person plural. "¡Venceremos!" ("We will vanquish" or "We will overcome") is the coda to Fidel Castro's oft-repeated salute "Patria o Muerte" (Fatherland or death) and, among many other uses, a staple on government-directed billboards and the title of the official newspaper of Guantánamo Province. The unwavering projection toward the future accorded the idea of "vanquishing" or "overcoming" in post-1959 Cuba contrasts jarringly with the verb's attribution to Cuba as a past participle adjective in the English translation of al-Rubaish's poem.

Whatever common historical ground with Cuba el-Gharani and al-Rubaish may gesture at, and whatever the distance between their understanding of Cuba's history and the rhetoric of its revolution, as this is mediated by their translations and translators, naming Cuba also, and importantly, situates the poetic voice physically and affectively, generating a location and a network of sensory and compassionate connections that draw from the small-scale environment of the Guantánamo borderlands. That el-Gharani and al-Rubaish name Cuba at all appears, at the very least, as a significant act of self-location amid the practices of geographic disorientation instituted at Guantánamo Bay Naval Base. Karen Greenberg, for example, notes that newly arrived detainees were blindfolded for their first forty hours at Guantánamo and were not told where they were for some time, as total disorientation was considered an aid to interrogation, and the security of the base "might be compromised if the prisoners could somehow locate themselves and thus have knowledge of the terrain" (*Least Worst Place* 69). In a chapter based on interviews with Brandon Neely, a guard at Guantánamo from the day the first detainees arrived, Justine Sharrock writes, "The detainees weren't allowed to know which country they were being held in. Brandon and the others would mess with them, telling them a different location every time they asked: Russia, Iran" (16).

Cuba nevertheless announces its presence to detainees, allowing them to locate themselves though an ecological continuity that the camp complex cannot disrupt. Scenes of slow recognition appear in a number of detainees' memoirs. Former detainee Murat Kurnaz, for example, describes the process by which he came to realize that he was in Cuba. Pages after stating that "I didn't know we were in Cuba" (100), he describes the many creatures that made their way into his cage in Camp X-Ray. It is the sight of iguanas that first prompts him to wonder "Iguanas? Where were we?" (113). He then asks himself of the hummingbirds who visit him, "Weren't they native to the Caribbean?" (114) and, after hearing another prisoner say that the Americans have a military base in Cuba, he directs to one of his interrogators the question "We're in in Cuba, aren't we?" (114). Secure in the knowledge that he is in Cuba, his experience of place is mediated by the effect on his senses of the local environment: of the heat, smells, sounds, and sights that the naval base shares with Cuba and that, effectively, defy the dividing line between them. Similarly, Mohammed Ould Slahi's *Guantánamo Diary* (2017) explicitly associates Cuba—as climate and land—with pleasure, warmth, and comfort. There, Slahi recalls that, after a thirty-hour trip from Bagram Air Base spent blindfolded and shackled in "an ice-cold airplane" (32), "the warm Cuban sun hit me gracefully. It was such a good feeling" (32). Two months later his spirits are again lifted by his transfer to "a cell where I could see the plain" (47), which his editor's footnote takes to be a reference to "the Cuban landscape surrounding the camp" (47). Seeing Cuba's plain coincides with a renewed social existence for Slahi: in that cell, for the first time, he "was able to talk to [my] fellow detainees while seeing them" (47).

Peter Hulme, in a chapter on the memoirs of Guantánamo prisoners and guards that describes the base as "the most perfect colonial enclave that has ever existed inasmuch as it is [. . .] completely autonomous from its surrounding environment" (377), traces ways in which the Cuban natural world infiltrates even its most heavily protected spaces. Reading Kurnaz's memoir along with that of British detainee Moazzam Begg, he notes that palm trees are visible from certain areas of the camps, as they are more generally elsewhere on the base, and that insects, birds, and the ubiquitous *jutía*, or banana rat, cross the border freely. "The natural creatures of Oriente," in Hulme's words, sidle "through the fence that is supposed to isolate the base from Cuba, and through the walls and cages that are supposed to isolate the prisoners from the outside world" (394). Even as Cuba's people and political order are kept at bay, it is present as its fauna, flora, climate, sounds, and scents, and as an outside world that tempers the detainees' isolation.

Hulme notes that in a number of former detainees' memoirs the Cuban terrain, climate, and animal life provide a sense of location, comfort, and home. Mansoor Adayfi, imprisoned without charge for fourteen years before being transferred to a precarious existence as a stateless foreigner in Serbia, acknowledges these qualities gratefully in his own writings. In his memoir, *Don't Forget Us Here: Lost and Found at Guantánamo* (2021), he thanks the local cats, banana rats, hummingbirds, and woodpeckers "for your companionship and for bringing light into our lives in such a dark place as Guantánamo" (366), and expresses particular affection for an iguana he named Princess, whom he would entertain graciously in his cell (28). It is nevertheless the Caribbean Sea, invoked by al-Rubaish as a repository of Cuba's stories, that becomes for Adayfi, in his memoir, journalistic writing, and curatorship of detainee art, the primary symbol of ecological continuity with a larger world. Although neither Cuba nor the sense of political solidarity implied by el-Gharani's choice of the word *afflicted*, and al-Rubaish's of the word *vanquished*, figure explicitly in Adayfi's writing, the Caribbean Sea, at its coastline with the base and with Cuba, presents to him in a similarly promising way, allowing him to inhabit a Guantánamo that is more expansive, and more liberating, than the constrained space of the detention cells.

Adayfi's *Don't Forget Us Here* offers a nuanced, elaborately anthropomorphizing portrayal of that which he names, in his closing acknowledgements, "our friend the sea" (366). This is a friend who offers familiarity and comfort, vicariously manifests the anger that detainees themselves must suppress and, most capaciously, incorporates as many points on a map of the world as its beholder cares to imagine. Adayfi narrates arrival at Guantánamo in the second person, an urgent address that anticipates his closing thanks to himself as detainee number 441, "who fought so hard for my survival" (366), and the sea accompanies this frightened addressee, intervening as touch, movement, and smell to reassure him; offer friendship; silence his mind and transport it to his home in Yemen; and bear witness, just as it does in al-Rubaish's poem:

> You're moving now, across water and waves. You bounce and jostle and you feel the sea rolling below you. You know the salty air from your weekends in Aden with friends after you finished

high school. You're on a boat and you feel the sea receive you. The sea gives you comfort. The sea witnesses everything they do to you. The sea whispers in your ear, *I'm with you, friend.* You thank the sea, and it sings to you as they beat you. The sea shuts down your mind and that's good. You pray that the sea accompanies you for the rest of your journey." (18)

The sea is rarely visible to detainees in Camp Delta, despite, as Adayfi writes, "being only a few hundred feet away" (63). Stealing a glimpse of it, he traces it for a fellow detainee as an animate map, extending uninterruptedly from the Caribbean to other seas and finally to the Yemeni coast: "I see an endless body of blue," I said, "with a soul that courses through the Atlantic Ocean, the Mediterranean, and the Suez Canal, all the way to the Red Sea and the western coast of Yemen, where in the seaside town of Hudaydah, my father is at the market buying fish for a special meal" (63). The sea is at the same time of deep spiritual significance: it is both evidence of "the magnificence of Allah's creation" (63), an abiding source of hope, and evidence of a continuity between past, present, and future that rendition to Guantánamo has abruptly cut short: it "infiltrated our dreams, reminding us of our past and giving us hope for our future freedom" (64).

On a rare occasion when, due to an approaching hurricane, tarps obscuring detainees' view of the sea are removed, the sea's spiritual depths and geographic promise are overshadowed by a corporal immediacy and emotional agency, making of it a distinct persona that brings particular force to what Adayfi and al-Rubaish understand as its capacity to bear witness. Facing the sea in silence from the metal cages, newly exposed to the elements and to the sight of the coastline, detainees "watched him flex his muscles and bend the world with his strength" (185), and "listened to him howl and whistle and punch the rocks below with powerful waves (185). It is in response to these movements and sounds of the sea that Adayfi imputes to it a reciprocal, impassioned gaze that allies it with the plight of the detainees—"the sea saw us, too, and raged at what it saw: hundreds of men in metal cages" (185)—even as it inspires fear in them as well. "We were afraid," he writes, "that the sea wanted to carry us away with him. It was scary how mad the sea was and how loud the wind screamed and pulled at our roof" (185).

Although Adayfi's memoir did not appear in print until 2021, the scene of hurricane preparations at Guantánamo, and of detainees' short-lived but transformative contemplation of the sea, is anticipated in his earlier essay, "In Our Prison on the Sea," published first as an op-ed in the *New York Times* on September 15, 2017, and, a few months later, with an additional concluding paragraph, as the introductory essay to the *Postprint Magazine* catalog of detainee artwork in the exhibit *Art from Guantánamo*. Shown at the President's Gallery of John Jay College in New York in late 2017 and early 2018, this exhibit's display of detainee artwork beyond Guantánamo, like the publication of detainee poetry in *Poems to Guantánamo*, was subject to layers of military review and approval. Publicity surrounding the exhibit prompted a Department of Defense declaration that all art made at the base was government property, a further step in censorship that, until the declaration was reversed in early 2023, severely restricted the circulation of detainees' creative work (Rosenberg, "Pentagon Lifts Trump-Era Ban"). Kalyan Nadiminti has assessed how these restrictions' effective claim to state ownership of detainee art created "a circuit of total ownership over the detainee in spite of their continuing postcolonial citizenship" (356), and gave rise to a form of "detainee copyright," a "counterintuitive articulation of intellectual property where the protection being sought is not the artist's labor for economic sustenance and future progeny, but the production of artistic labor and political expression as forms of witnessing" (357).

Adayfi's "In Our Prison on the Sea," like his memoir, registers the sea's bounteous offerings of geographic and spiritual reassurance. He emphasizes that when detainees were first rendered to Guantánamo, not knowing where they were, the sea was a lone familiar element on a landscape that they could neither see nor identify with any precision: "We whispered: there is a sea around. We could feel it despite the marines hitting and kicking us" (2). As they made further efforts to determine where in the world they were, he and fellow detainees considered "the facts available," including the weather, the birds, and their own dreams. Although eventually informed by more recently arrived detainees that they were in Guantánamo, the name itself was both unrecognizable and unpronounceable to many of them, such that the sea remained the most reliable source of knowledge: "All we knew was there was the sea" (3).

"In Our Prison on the Sea," moreover, presents the sea as a force in the formation of community among detainees and in the brief but powerful levelling of the experience of detainees and guards, all subject to whatever destruction or clemency the hurricane-powered Caribbean and its attendant winds might mete out. Sharing knowledge of the sea's proximity bound and inspired detainees, even though few of them, Adayfi reports, had ever actually seen it. Afghan detainees, landlocked in their previous lives, contemplated the sea fearfully: all they knew "was that it was a lot of water that kills and eats people" (2); detainees from Arab countries, for some of whom the sea was a more familiar presence, wanted to share its wonder with the Afghans, even if explanations at first "made them even more afraid" (2). The hurricane opened all detainees' horizons, both figuratively and literally. With news of its imminent landfall at Guantánamo and the subsequent removal of tarps comes a sense of communion and possibility among those at the camp. "We all faced one direction: toward the sea" (4), Adayfi writes. Standing together, facing, and contemplating are reminders, if not assurances, of liberation: "It felt a little like freedom, to look at it" (4).

Don't Forget Us Here offers a detailed account of the art lessons offered to detainees in later years of the camp's existence, during what Adayfi calls, with thanks to their Iraqi art teacher, "a golden age at Guantánamo" (304). It is in his op-ed "In Our Prison on the Sea," however, that he draws an explicit connection between the sea and the production of art. Contemplating the sea leads, in his recollection, to detainees' desire to reproduce its image and invest in it "their dreams, feelings, hope and lives" (4). Having seen the sea during the days of the hurricane, he reports, detainees "started making art about the sea. Some wrote poems about it. And everyone who could draw drew the sea" (4). That the sea is the predominant image in detainees' artwork is what Erin Thompson, the exhibit's curator, first noticed when this art was shown to her by detainees' lawyers. "Everywhere, the sea," Thompson recalls ("What We Can Learn"). In some paintings, "storms thrashed apart the last plank of sinking ships," while in others, "boats were moored in safety at docks or scudded across vast expanses of water without a hint of shore in sight ... One detainee had even made elaborate models of sailing ships out of cardboard, old T-shirts, bottle caps, and other scraps of trash."

Commentary in the *Postprint Magazine* catalog for "Ode to the Sea" gestures at specific interpretation of individual paintings' representations of the sea. Next to Khalid Qasim's *Untitled (Fins in the Ocean)*, for example, is the comment that this piece "shows, perhaps most explicitly, the anxieties and fears underlying the surface of seemingly tranquil waters" (47). Text accompanying Muhammad Ansi's *Untitled (Black Shore)*, offers a less expansive interpretation, but nevertheless inscribes the specter of death into its description: "A coffin-like boat washes up on a shore under black skies" ("Art from Guantánamo" 54). Furthermore, the predominance and wide variety of seascapes in detainee art prompts curatorial speculation about specific locations that may have inspired the works. While some artists have insisted, in communications with their lawyers, that they were inspired only by their imagination, dreams, and images seen on television, catalog commentary accompanying their works frequently identifies the places depicted, with varying degrees of certainty. Muhammad Ansi's *Untitled (Statue of Liberty)*, for example, presents its subject relatively unambiguously, its accompanying text explaining that "because the guards at Guantánamo are American, almost all of the detainees have a functional knowledge of American culture" (55). Similarly, Ghaleb Al-Bihani's *Untitled (Blue Mosque)* is explained by a 2016 terrorist attack on Istanbul's Blue Mosque, which by that year detainees were able to learn about on television, although "the lush and idyllic landscape" incongruously surrounding the mosque is attributed to "the often optimistic way in which detainees combine images from various sources of locales they cannot visit" (43). Yemeni detainee Abdulmalik Abud, the catalog commentary states, "Frequently drew the complex architecture of Sana'a, Yemen" (37). Identification of other locales is more tentative: the bridge in Abud's *Untitled: Sunset With Bridge* "bears a resemblance to San Francisco's Golden Gate Bridge" (37), and Muhammad Ansi's *Untitled: Oasis*, with its low buildings and palm trees "may refer to a locale closer to Ansi's home" (53).

The *Postprint Magazine* catalog's curatorial commentary admits, nevertheless, that many of the seascapes in the exhibit are "completely unlocatable" (53), in a sense that comports with Adayfi's account of the sea as a sui generis locator—the mere knowledge of its presence a solace to those nearby even when they are ignorant of their precise coordinates—and accommodates a possible relation between these seascapes and the Cuban coastline that borders the camps. One image in particular, Ghaleb Al-Bihani's *Untitled (Two Palms)* (fig. 1.1), showing a darkened beach where two slender palm trees rise above a small hut, with the sea, moon, and low-lying hills in a blurred background, certainly resembles Cuba, and even Guantánamo Bay itself, no less than it does many a tropical coastline, and it is notable that the curatorial commentary reads

FIGURE 1.1. GHALEB AL BIHANI, *(UNTITLED) TWO PALMS*. REPRINTED COURTESY OF THE ARTIST.

this image in terms not of place but of a self-advocacy that would intertwine with dynamics of spectatorship and desire for the picturesque in which Cuba itself has long been embroiled. Al-Bihani, the commentary suggests, has produced "an image suitable for a postcard, hoping to contribute to his own advocacy" (45), knowing that his lawyers would distribute materials at public events.

The Cuban coastline and Caribbean Sea may be referents for detainee artwork, just as they are for Mansoor Adayfi's writing and, more directly in relation to Cuba as a political entity, for the poems of Ibrahim al-Rubaish and Mohammed el-Gharani. In this tenuous but nonetheless suggestive sense, in art and poetry by Guantánamo detainees, Cuba's presence as natural environment shapes an intellectual and sensory knowledge that bears the promise of diminishing detainees' isolation by extending the space they occupy—either inward, to the larger land mass that is Cuba, or outward, to the Caribbean and the Atlantic Ocean into which it feeds. While these paths inward and outward represent ways out of isolation as solitude and confinement, they at the same time resonate deeply with a long-established Cuban intellectual and poetic tradition that associates the figure of the island with both continuity and separation, cast as either cultural possibility or its opposite, limitation. Dara E. Goldman, in her study of islands and the demarcation of identity in Cuba, Puerto Rico, and the Dominican Republic, proposes that "the attachment to insularity, in and of itself, becomes the central trope of Antillean cultural discourse" (*Out of Bounds* 42). The Cuban poet José Lezama Lima is a dominant example of such attachment in its more optimistic light: in his "Coloquio con Juan Ramón Jiménez," he appeals to Cuba's condition as an island in order to "legitimize a unique poetic tradition" (Goldman, *Out of Bounds* 42). And yet there exists at the same time, in Cuban poetry, a parallel legacy of hostility toward the sea. Francisco Morán traces this legacy from the early nineteenth-century poet Manuel de Zequeira y Arango to the *modernistas* Julián del Casal and José Martí, describing the poet's circling of the city walls in Zequeira's "La Ronda" as prefiguring the impossibility of escape for Cubans, and inscribing the historical perception of the island as a trap (6). It is Casal and Martí, Morán claims, who definitively shed light on the island as a dead-end street; indeed, the title of Martí's "Odio al Mar" (I Hate the Sea) prefigures, in its sounds and in its sentiments, the Spanish translation of al-Rubaish's "Oda al Mar," a resonance likely to be clear to the latter's Cuban readers, at least. Most prominently in the history of antipathy toward Cuba's condition as island, Virgilio Piñera's long and polemical poem "La isla en peso" (The Weight of the Island), with its resonant opening line, "The cursed condition of water on all sides" (27), shares with "Ode to the Sea" its representations of the sea as an agent of confinement and powerful symbol of the impossibility of escape.[4]

The paradox that is the sea of al-Rubaish's poem, Adayfi's essays, and some detainee artwork in the *Art from Guantánamo* exhibition—a sea that, even as it reminds its beholders of their confinement, simultaneously promises an openness that is as compassionate as it is geographic—is one to which Cuban writers have long looked for their own articulations of solitude and connection. The natural environment—the sea, land, air, and animal life of eastern Cuba—stands as the experience most constantly shared among detainees and Cubans, and the most generative as they seek solace and community. The "afflicted" and "vanquished" Cuba of el-Gharani and al-Rubaish's poems manifests as an imagined, anachronistic and, ultimately, unrealizable political solidarity in the face of Cuba's impotence with regard to the US presence at Guantánamo and the rhetoric of victory that its ailing revolutionary leadership has prescribed for itself. It is Cuba experienced as an island that reveals the possibility of experiences shared beyond the Guantánamo of cells, camps, and guarded borders.

CUBA, THE CAMPS, AND THE SEA

"Don't the rocks tell you of the crimes committed in their midst? / Doesn't Cuba, the vanquished, translate its stories for you?" asks Ibrahim al-Rubaish, in "Ode to the Sea" (66). As well as attempting to locate the poet and stake a claim to political solidarity, these lines seek in Cuba the verbalization of a common experience; that is, they seek for a poem whose translation is itself marked by absence, translations of Cuba's "stories." The forms such stories might take are myriad, but José Ramón Sánchez, a reader of *Poems from Guantánamo* in its Spanish translation, rises to the task, albeit in a sui generis way. The land, sea, and animal life of the Guantánamo region feature prominently in his poetry as he, like al-Rubaish and el-Gharani, gestures toward those living on the other side of the fence line dividing Cuba from the base. Sánchez, however, has greater access to information and significantly more freedom to write than do detainee poets, such that his poetry's imaginings of experiences held in common are vastly more expansive and sustained.

Sánchez is one of few Cuban writers whose work addresses the presence in his country of the naval base and detention camps. His early poems on Guantánamo were published in *La noria*, the small and semi-independent literary journal that he and poet Oscar Cruz coedit in the city of Santiago de Cuba and distribute informally in and outside Cuba. As well as attempting to distribute *La noria* as broadly as possible, Sánchez has published his poems, in Spanish and English, in several other venues, and has included many of his poems on Guantánamo in the 2018 collection *Talibán*. His poems reflect on the history and continued presence of the base in Guantánamo Province, through actual, borrowed, and imagined knowledge of it. The archive from which he draws is vast, varied, and haphazard: it includes his own memories of a childhood in which light, sound, and broadcast signals from the base reached into the surrounding areas of Guantánamo Province, creating illusions of conviviality and worldliness particular to this region of Cuba; printed histories and maps, both obscure and mainstream; official records pertaining to the base's creation and development; oral reports from residents of Guantánamo Province, some of whom were former workers at the base; and copious, if sporadic, internet research. Incorporated in this archive are texts from the literary and political histories of the detainees, in the forms and languages in which Sánchez has encountered these. He draws on classical Arabic poetry, the Koran, Ana Mata Buil's Spanish translation of *Poems from Guantánamo*, and US government–authored documentation pertaining to the continued detentions at Guantánamo.

The sea that features most pervasively in Sánchez's *The Black Arrow* is Guantánamo Bay, the large, sheltered bay whose northern half is under Cuban jurisdiction while its southern section, opening to the Caribbean Sea, is controlled from the base, a division that has wrought havoc on the local fishing industry while offering a tantalizing—albeit extraordinarily dangerous—exit route for Cuban migrants. The animal life in which detainee writers have found consolation is present in this poetry in various forms, primarily occupying the fertile land that separates Cuba from the base at the edge of the border town of Caimanera, which is off-limits to the population of either place. It is here, in Sánchez's poems, that "the best-kept animals of the country live / Lodgers of the differential Imperialism / Revolution" (*Black Arrow* 47) and where banana rats and iguanas roam freely, "oblivious to the President's orders" (*Black Arrow* 51). While these same animals offer detainees models of companionship and community, and grounding in a sense of place, Sánchez's poems largely approach them with ironic envy.

The dividing line between Cuba and the base, cutting through Guantánamo Bay and marked on land by a system of wire fencing punctuated by surveillance towers and yet-to-be-detonated mines concealed underwater and underground, is a principal focus of Sánchez's poetry. The border has been closed since the 1960s, with the exception, until 2012, of the permitted daily crossings of a small number of Cuban base employees. As a result, despite their proximity, residents of Guantánamo Province can see and know little about life on the base. On the one hand, for a poet to write about the base is, as a line in Sánchez's poem "Impossible" declares, to submit to the authority of others when forming one's own knowledge and experience: the paltry assortment of materials and memories that are available to the poet must be supplemented by what others have reported, "images that others saw for me" (*Black Arrow* 21). On the other hand, several poems explore unperturbed border crossings that, at least during the poet's childhood, briefly and tenuously united residents of Guantánamo with those of the base. These come in the form of rays of light, sound waves, and television signals. The poem "Spotlight," for example, describes how light would extend into Guantánamo Province as "news from the base" (23). In "The Channel from the Base," Guantánamo residents receive television broadcasts from the base, allowing them to watch baseball games, including those in which Cuban Orlando "El Duque" Hernández starred for the New York Yankees, that were unviewable elsewhere in Cuba, showing these provincial Cubans that "there was an Outside World beyond our Socialist Republic" (23).

Sánchez's poetry is an exception to the small corpus of literature written in and around the city of Guantánamo that, as my next chapter addresses, has drawn primarily on a history of emigration via the base and largely occludes, or insinuates in imprecise terms, the presence there of detainees. What emerges from his writing is an ambitious attempt to imagine the border from both sides: the physical space of the base and, in certain poems, the lives of detainees at the camps. In the absence of any possible response, it seeks to acknowledge common ground in the sharing of a small area of land and an experience of isolation dictated by geographical and political circumstance. This imagining at times manifests as an articulation of proximity as comparison but at others as a farther-reaching, and by some measures overstepping, occupation of the place of detainees by the poetic voice.[5]

"Small Change," first published in Spanish as one of eight poems by Sánchez in a 2014 issue of *La noria* dedicated to the Guantánamo Bay Naval Base, sets out the mode in which he translates Cuban "stories," seeking to trace community and common ground between Cuba and the base. Its opening lines, referencing Sánchez's friend and fellow Cuban poet Oscar Cruz, insist on comparison as an inevitable practice for a poet writing about the base: "Oscar Cruz compares me to the prisoners at Guantánamo Bay: / isolation, scarcity, mistreatment and other endearments" (*Black Arrow* 31). These lines establish a working principle for Sánchez's Guantánamo poems, that one can only write about the base by comparing oneself to its victims, at the same time as they chart a broadly common ground for Guantánamo, opening the denomination of "victim" beyond the detainees currently at the base's camps. The poem offers an image of US Marines on leave in the towns around the base in the 1950s, throwing small change to impoverished Cuban children, victims of the base's economic impact on the region both before and after the Cuban Revolution. The base's victims, the poem implies, resonating strongly with the Cuban revolutionary leadership's claims to the base, are not only its current detainees but also those Cubans who have lived in its vicinity and outside its limits for over a century, subject to the designs of empire that infiltrated Cuban soil surreptitiously, as what the poem of the same name calls "A Trojan Horse in the Caribbean" (27).

The peculiarly spatial quality of being in another's place drives one of the more linguistically challenging poems of Sánchez's collection, *The Black Arrow*. It is written in the third person and opens with a scene in the cells of those named, in this poem, as "the Muslim prisoners" (15). The precision with which the detainees' location and the Mecca toward which they pray are charted in this poem in numerical coordinates, implying a calculated effort on the poet's part to know and recount their situation. The second stanza is composed largely of coordinates—"The Base is at 19°, 54,' 42. 95" North / and 75°, 09," 11. 75" West" (15)—rendering it visually strange and unwieldy to pronounce, in recognition of the many levels of defamiliarization to which detainees are subject and of the limits of verbal language in the context that is Guantánamo. The poem refers to the black arrows pointing to Mecca painted on the floors of detainees' cells and to the prayers that must travel "12 793 kilometers over the Atlantic / the Sahara and the Red Sea" (15) to reach their destination. The final lines of the poem, punctuated by a long ellipsis, ask, "And if the Americans / had not provided the arrows . . . then what?" (15). The poetic voice remains at a distance grammatically, but its detailed recounting of detainees' precise location and its imagining of the pain of literal and externally imposed disorientation—of not being allowed to know which way is east—imply an effort to engage intensely with their experience.

Sánchez's "Gitmo" poems rehearse different ways of being like, being with, and simply being a detainee at Guantánamo, the latter position being one that overrules qualitative distinctions between the sufferings of subjects who inhabit the Guantánamo region differently in favor of empathic approximations. His long, experimental poem "Secret//NoForn//20330602" performs a particularly ambitious identification as it moves toward calling into being a fluid, free, and inherently literary "Guantánamo," a common ground that knows no borders and scorns the linguistic and legal practices that have attempted to classify, contain, and censor lives at and around the base. Published in 2015, it is a graphically intricate poem that draws its title and format from a "Detainee Assessment Brief," a classified memorandum sent from Joint Task Force Guantánamo to US Southern Command, recommending either continued detention or release for a man detained at Guantánamo.[6] Sánchez accessed Detainee Assessment Briefs though WikiLeaks, which has released substantial classified documentation on former and current Guantánamo detainees.

"Secret//NoForn//20330602" is the heading of the Detainee Assessment Brief pertaining to Ahmed al Hikimi, a Yemeni national held at Guantánamo until April 2016, when he was released to Saudi Arabia. The "NoForn" of the heading is an abbreviation included in the US government classification system stating that no foreign national should view this document. Nonetheless, little of the text of al Hikimi's "assessment" survives in Sánchez's poem, beyond the first lines of letterhead and the subject heading, itself sealing al Hikimi's fate: "Recommendation for Continued Detention Under DoD Control (CD) for Guantanamo Detainee, ISN US9YM-000030DP (S)." The photograph of the detainee is absent from the poem, as is any information that might distinguish this detainee from others, although what passes for information in the brief itself is at once objectively questionable and of dubious internal logic.[7] Sánchez's poem empties out all the "information" fields in the Detainee Assessment Brief and, retaining their headings and subheadings, fills them with knowledge of a different order. The name in "subfield 1. (S) Personal Information, JDIMS/ NDRC Reference Name" is not one of the six of al Hikimi's aliases listed in the original brief, but "Regino Eladio Boti" (*Black Arrow* 57). Boti, born in the Cuban city of Guantánamo in 1878, is the region's most institutionally revered man of letters. A figure remembered in the history of Cuban poetry for straddling the modernist and avant-garde movements and reinvigorating lyric poetry with his *Arabescos mentales* (Mental Arabesques), it is his *El mar y la montaña* (The Sea and the Mountain), published in 1921 and rooted in the coastal and mountainous geography of eastern Cuba, that establish him as Guantánamo's literary founding father. In erasing al Hikimi's story and redirecting the genre of the Detainee Assessment Brief to a new poetic text that draws together the many subjects implicated by Guantánamo, Sánchez undermines the language, information, and construction of the enemy that have been so crucial to the base's use in the war on terror. At the same time, Sánchez overwrites the Detainee Assessment Brief with lines from Boti's *El mar y la montaña*, liberating its language from the rubric of what Joseph R. Slaughter has called contemporary counterinsurgency policy's "bloodless prose" ("Life, Story, Violence" 469) and reanchoring it in the elements of Guantánamo's natural environment that have offered solace to detainees and Cubans alike. "Place of Birth," for example, becomes "to the land of the Guayo tribal chief" (57) and "Date of Birth," "to my mother, to my sisters, to my nephews and nieces" (57–58)—both lines are from the dedication to Boti's collection. Innovative but not entirely illogical connections suggest themselves in several fields, subverting the premise and the language of the formulaic brief. "Reasons for Transfer" (60) is met with "somber and luminous rays" (60), countering detention with rays of light.

In the line entry for "Detainee's Account of Events," Sánchez draws not on accounts obtained during interrogation but on the impetus of al-Rubaish's "Ode to the Sea," reproducing the first lines of Boti's "El mar" (The Sea), which is the opening poem of *El mar y la montaña* and itself an extended apostrophe to the Caribbean. The "detainee's account" thus becomes an appeal to the sea as originary and nurturing: "Ancestor of the mountain/ nurse of the aged jungle / your entrails are still / marvelous" (59). In unmooring the generic Detainee Assessment Brief from its suspect bureaucratic language, Sánchez introduces an alternative Cuban sea, one that, like the anthropomorphized, angry, yet comforting sea whom Adayfi terms "our dear friend" (*Don't Forget Us Here* 366) allies and identifies with the writer. In Boti's "El mar," the sea itself is a "high poet, who symphonizes lamentations and barcaroles" (*El mar y la montaña* 23).[8]

As a response and challenge to the Detainee Assessment Brief, Boti's *El mar y la montaña* stands as a celebratory coda to the frustration, restriction, and impoverishment that Sánchez's other poems lament. Instead of dubious and damaging information, amassed to justify detention, Boti's lines claim a confident and intimate knowledge of Guantánamo, as a natural space rather than a legally contorted one. And yet even as new lines distance the poem from the intent of the Detainee Assessment Brief, visual markers that Sánchez adds reinsert it into the corpus of official and partly classified documentation of the post–9/11 years. Although the Detainee Assessment Briefs published by Wikileaks are not redacted, Sánchez's poem is scattered with black rectangles that obscure parts of lines, disrupting their flow and implying that certain words are not to be seen. These gesture toward the redactions overlaid on declassified official documents from the war on terror, which Joseph R. Slaughter has called a "textual bruising or scarring that signals the failure, impairment or death of narrative" ("Vanishing Points" 209).

Sánchez blacks out sparingly and with a critical intent that aligns his work with that of others whom Stephen Voyce includes in "an emergent poetics that counter-inscribes the redacted page and its pernicious cultural logics," among them Jenny Holzer, Trevor Paglen, and Philip Metres. And yet, reading "Secret//NoForn//20330602" alongside Boti's *El mar y la montaña* reveals an obscuring of words whose content can be considered incriminating or dangerous only insofar as it privileges creative thought and practice or provides situated reference points, criteria to which Falkoff attributes the censoring of poetry written by Guantánamo detainees. Attempting to account for the Pentagon's refusal to release many detainee poems, Falkoff cites the argument that poetry "presents a special risk" to national security because of its "content and format"—the fear, he writes, "appears to be that the detainees will try to smuggle coded messages out of the prison camp" (4). The first line of Boti's prologue, for example, reads, "This book cannot and should not be read by anyone who is not an artist or philosopher" (19): entering this as information in the "JTF-GTMO Assessment" field, Sánchez blacks out "artist or philosopher" as well as "poet" later in the section. In a final, critical gesture, "Secret//NoForn//20330602" obscures from its insertion of Boti's poem "Yo" (I) the lament that might resonate most closely with the experience of detainees at Guantánamo: "Because to exist is torture" (62).

In redacting the words *artist, philosopher, poet*, and *torture* from Boti's work, Sánchez effectively conceals the primary impetus for comparison between the base's "victims" and the poet himself that he advances in other poems. Similarly, in writing Boti's name over al Hikimi's into the Detainee Assessment Brief, he appropriates the brief's account of al Hikimi's life, condemning the detainee's name to yet further obscurity. And yet, each of these erasures can also be understood as part of a larger gesture of freeing the name *Guantánamo* from its associations with the war on terror and Cuba's long-standing anti-imperialist endeavors. In Sánchez's version, Boti's poetry regrounds the natural space that encompasses Cuban Guantánamo and the naval base, invoking a land, sea, and natural world that are unbound by the hostilities and limits that define the territory today.

In the Cuban Guantánamo from which Sánchez writes, and in a style that resonates with the lyric qualities of Boti's and al-Rubaish's poetry, Rodríguez Lobaina authored the collection *Con el alma cautiva* (With a Captive Soul). Like the biographical notes accompanying the poems in Falkoff's collection, the back-jacket text on Editorial Aduana Vieja's edition of the book positions its author primarily in relation to political repression and the language of human rights, introducing him as "a prisoner of conscience of the Cuban regime," prohibited from completing his training as an electrical engineer because of his political activism. Aligning Rodríguez Lobaina's political awakening with sweeping historical change, the text explains that "in 1990, transformations in Eastern Europe mark an important advance in the awakening to consciousness that for years had been gestating in the political thinking of this young opposition leader." It continues to recount that in 1991 Rodríguez Lobaina founded the dissident pro-democracy movement Movimiento Cubano de Jóvenes por la Democracia (Movement of Cuban Youth for Democracy), which would later become part of the larger umbrella organization the Plataforma Democrática Oriental (Eastern

Democratic Platform). "Beaten and incarcerated numerous times," Rodríguez Lobaina sought exile in Spain in 2011 and has since been a frequent speaker for human rights advocacy organizations in Europe.

Certain details of Rodríguez Lobaina's experience as a political prisoner correspond eerily to those of detainees at Guantánamo—who, as Padraic Kenney has argued, are themselves categorizable as political prisoners, given that in almost all contexts one person's terrorist is another's political prisoner (7). Although put on trial and convicted for set terms on charges that, however specious, are recognized in Cuba's legal code—for example, in 2000 Rodríguez Lobaina was sentenced to six years imprisonment for offenses that Amnesty International translates as "disrespect," "public disorder," and "damage"—reports of his having participated in hunger strikes and, while at the Combinado de Guantánamo Provincial Prison, of being "beaten and kicked, while handcuffed, by over 20 prison guards and then held naked and in darkness in a bare rat-infested punishment cell," resonate strikingly with more widely known accounts of isolation, constraint, and torture at the detention camps on the base ("Amnesty International Annual Report 1998" 150).

Rodríguez Lobaina's biography, and that of other political prisoners held at the Combinado de Guantánamo Provincial Prison during and immediately preceding the years of detention camps on the base, stands in more direct symmetry to those of post–9/11 detainees than do the life and poetry of Sánchez. While Sánchez is a lone voice tracing commensurability largely between the isolations of poetic subjects as such, Rodríguez Lobaina is one of a group of political activists whose incarceration and abuse at a Guantánamo prison run by the Cuban, rather than the US, government binds the region in ways that underscore the human collateral damage of national defense, or wars on imperialism and terror, on both sides. It is in the name of the defense of the Cuban Revolution (against the enemy that bears the face of US imperialism and its supposed internal ally, the Cuban counterrevolutionary) that the Cuban state has developed its network of semi-clandestine political prisons and a robust apparatus to discourage dissent among civilians, locating some of this network's infrastructure in the remote province of Guantánamo, where the US government has chosen to detain its own purported enemies.

Written in extreme physical constraint, Rodríguez Lobaina's poetry—like that of al-Rubaish, Sánchez and, indeed, Boti—maps the contours of both freedom and confinement onto the natural world. Many of his poems are odes that, like al-Rubaish's "Ode to the Sea," pose a direct address to elements of the natural environment that are largely impervious to restraint and stand as potential agents of liberation. "Conversaciones con la luna" (Conversations with the Moon), for example, opens with the poet confined to "this humid room," illuminated only by "the lucidity of hate" (40).[9] It is the unattributed verb, "you appear" (40) closing the first stanza, that introduces a feminine presence to soften the harsh contours of the cell and cast a new, caring light, returning the poet to kinder times. The moon passes softly through the cell bars, "Invited to the gentle / narrowness of the bars" (40); its light, unlike that of the poet's hatred in the opening stanza, rekindles his childhood, "illuminating the joyful pupil / of my childhood" (40). The moon cannot mitigate the poet's sense of his own impotence, incarcerated for having chosen to live in opposition to the Cuban Revolution and its tired symbols of guerrilla rebellion, and for leading "this warrior's life / with no jungle, no red knapsacks / weighed down with utopias / and stupid guns" (40). It can, nevertheless, return to him nightly, assuaging for him the terrain of absence, "this vast territory / of absent and shadowy springs," as a calming, light-bearing firefly (41).

The island—the figure for both liberation and constraint in al-Rubaish's ode as in a long tradition of Cuban poetry—is a similarly ambivalent force in Rodríguez Lobaina's "La indignidad del hombre" (The Indignity of Man). The poem begins as a meditation on the futility of life and the weariness to which humans are condemned: "Among shadows and solitudes / Man is trapped / in his perennial weariness" (75). Symbols of defeat include those with clear political reference, as do the warriors, utopias, backpacks, and rifles of "Conversations with the Moon." Here, it is "a red painting of hammer and sickle" (75) that lies in a corner, like an epitaph and "grey relic" (75). However, the more unifying force, and the one that guarantees survival, albeit bleakly, is the island with its stones, shadows, and dawns. It is "the stoic soul of an island" (75) permeating "every stone / every shadow / every dawn" (75) that survives, ultimately, to perpetuate the human indignity of the poem's title.

Each of Rodríguez Lobaina's poems bears the name of the location where it was written, tracing a map of imprisonment and forced labor that, even as it recalls the map of "black sites" known to many detainees at the base, extends Guantánamo's prison complex more locally, across the fence line into barely charted carceral territory. Between 1993 and 2002, Rodríguez Lobaina wrote many of his poems from the Combinado de Guantánamo Provincial Prison, the primary prison complex in the Guantánamo province of Cuba, situated on the outskirts of the city of Guantánamo; others are signed from the Aguadores Provincial Prison, in the neighboring province of Santiago de Cuba. Yet others are signed from sites that are much more clandestine—El Granadillo Forced Labor Camp; El Corojo Manuel Tames Forced Camp, Cuba; and La Bamba Forced Labor Camp, Guantánamo Provincial Prison—all of which indicates the persistence into the early 2000s of a system of forced labor camps that became notorious in Cuba in the late 1960s when, as Abel Sierra Madero has documented, men perceived as counterrevolutionary for their sexuality and religious beliefs, as much as for their politics, were sent to camps known as Military Units for Assisting Production (UMAP). In recent years, scrutiny of state-sanctioned forced labor in Cuba has focused primarily on the international medical missions into which numerous Cuban doctors claim to have been conscripted, with very little on record about the camps that Rodríguez Lobaina's poetry names.[10] Nevertheless, to the extent that these coordinates are traced as necessary to each poem—its last word, as it were—and at the same time incidental to the much larger experience of an unconstrained natural environment in which al-Rubaish and Sánchez also find hope and frustration, Rodríguez Lobaina's poetry joins theirs in mapping Guantánamo as a region unified by its geography and literature.

FEAR, FREEDOM, AND COMMON GROUND

As Mansoor Adayfi remembers, it was only when a hurricane was hurtling toward Cuba that tarps were removed and detainees could finally share the sea, with one another and with military personnel at the base, an episode that brought with it an indiscriminate extension of the extreme discomfort and threat of destruction with which the detainees lived daily. This was a brief time of connection in which all at the base were vulnerable, the sudden interruption of a scenario in which subjugation, constraint, and brutality are meted out to some by others. It was also, however, a time of shared vulnerability with residents of Guantánamo Province, who no doubt also braced themselves for whatever the elements might dispense, as they had many times before. In such moments, the small isolations into which the region has been divided of necessity collapse: all those who inhabit Guantánamo, in the camps, the military facilities of the base, and the entirety of the Cuban province, face the winds and rising tides together.

The global in its many dimensions—Nicole Waller's global mapping, Amy Kaplan's Guantánamo that is "everywhere"—defines in large part the "Guantánamo" in which el-Gharani, al-Rubaish, Adayfi, Sánchez, and Rodríguez Lobaina find themselves as they write, as do the detainee contributors to *Art from Guantánamo* as they paint. It is, indeed, to a readership that reaches far beyond a small area of eastern Cuba that each of these figures must appeal, if they are to be received within the frameworks of testimony and universal rights in which many readers of *Poems from Guantánamo* and viewers of *Art from Guantánamo* situate this work. Similarly, it is within the history of global imperialism, and the covertly authoritarian maneuvers with which Cuba's leaders have defended the revolution, that both Sánchez and Rodríguez Lobaina have lived, and that they reference, albeit from different political standpoints, in some of their poetry. Another, smaller-scale version of Guantánamo, one that underlies and sustains its "global" counterpart, emerges, nevertheless, from this work when it is read together as a peculiarly regional literature. It is a version in which the sea, the land, and a sense of profound and brutal isolation—an experience of island-ness that is environmental and psychological—are imagined to be held in common on both sides of the fence line in such a way as to undermine, on a small scale, the legal separation of the naval base from Cuba and the multiple languages of political hostility that have mapped Guantánamo.

CHAPTER 2

GUARDS

In the dead of night, two guards are on patrol. One is Chris Arendt, a former guard for Joint Task Force Guantánamo, walking the cellblocks of Camp Delta while detainees are asleep. The other is the fictional narrator of Cuban writer Leandro Estupiñán Zaldívar's 2014 short story, "Abducción" (Abduction). This narrator is a military service recruit to the Brigada de la Frontera, the unit of Cuba's Armed Services charged with guarding the border with the US naval base—ostensibly against American attacks but, in practice, against migration attempts by Cuban citizens. For both, nighttime solitude brings on a ruminative state of mind as they contemplate the possibility of moving across supposedly inviolable dividing lines. Arendt finds peace in the night—it is during the day that he feels pulled to cross a line that is anathema to his role in the war on terror: to dignify, and apologize to, detainees. He tells his interviewer at *Esquire* magazine: "I liked working night shifts. Whenever they were awake, I wanted to apologize to them. When they were sleeping, I didn't have to worry about that. I could just walk up and down the blocks all night." Estupiñán Zaldívar's narrator, in contrast, feels a persistent sense of unease, as he imagines being transported extraterrestrially in a fantastic version of the abductions and illicit border crossings that have taken place in the borderland that is Guantánamo Bay Naval Base.

At and around Guantánamo, encounters with the supposed enemy are neither uniform nor fully scripted, whether this is the enemy combatant—so-called in one of the better-known neologisms of the war on terror, and held at the base's detention centers—or the two-pronged enemy, the US military and aspiring Cuban refugees, against whom Cuba guards its border with the base. These encounters have been performed differently by defenders in varying relationships with their adversaries: just as hostility, violence, and a categorical separation of "us" from "them" mark the act of guarding, so, in many instances, do vulnerability, curiosity, and care. Former translators and guards at the detention camps have written about the impetus for such relationships, which have been cast in the memoirs and accounts of former detainees as engendering connections deeply destabilizing to the hierarchical structure of the camps. In the Guantánamo that lies beyond the perimeter of the base, around the fence line, and in the watchtowers that mark the edge of Cuban territory, encounters with ostensible enemies have produced similar scenes of unexpected connection.

This chapter explores scenes, at Guantánamo's detention centers and along the Cuban side of the fence line, in which a guard becomes not a representative of his or her commanding authority, but rather an interstitial figure—a representative of the military as an institution, but at the same time an individual engaged in a mundanely intimate friendship with the figure cast as enemy. This is a friendship that, while largely below the radar of military authorities, threatens to destabilize the unanimity, and therefore the reach, of these higher authorities' power. Like the late nineteenth-century anticolonial friendships that Leela Gandhi has explored, it is friendship as a form of "innovative border crossing, visible in small, defiant flights from the fetters of belonging toward the unknown destinations of radical alterity" (6–7). It is intimate for the unavoidable physical proximity from which it evolves and for its place on the map of uneasily aligning experiences that constitutes Guantánamo as a political space: a map which I propose considering, in Lisa Lowe's terms, as "a constellation of asymmetrical and unevenly legible intimacies" (18) that overlays contexts otherwise read as discrete. Guantánamo, as the base and the Cuban borderlands that surround it, is a site of shifting guard-guarded relationships and crossings of territorial and interpersonal boundaries, played out in a region that is itself an in-between, claimed and contested from multiple perspectives. Rather than the bounded, isolated, and exceptional site that the US base has been cast as politically and legally, the relationships that take shape at Guantánamo inscribe it as a space whose landscape, geography, and human experience produce coincidences among the various people—detainees, military personnel, military families, contract workers, border guards, and aspiring migrants among them—who constitute the Guantánamo region's permanent, transitory, and "indefinite" populations.

CELLBLOCK INTIMACIES

Guantánamo's detention camps were chaotically assembled and haphazardly populated, the improvisations of the first three months that Karen Greenberg has documented having been streamlined only erratically over the subsequent twenty-plus years (*Least Worst Place* 1–22). Over the course of the 2000s, 780 detainees from over forty countries were rendered to Guantánamo—some from battlefields in Afghanistan and others, as Anne McClintock has documented, captured by bounty hunters seduced by the US military's generous rewards program—together constituting what Amy Kaplan has called "a transnational population" speaking "as many as seventeen different languages" (840).[1] Once at the base, detainees were confined to spaces of varying sizes and degrees of isolation, from the notorious outdoor cages of Camp X-Ray to what Australian former detainee David Hicks has called the "technological marvel" of the Haliburton-designed Camp Five (355). Hicks distinguishes between the cellblocks based on the social interaction they afforded: while some placed detainees within earshot of each other, others were designed for punitive isolation. As a consequence, for many detainees in the early years of Guantánamo, the closest and most frequent human contact was with cellblock guards. Also entering the camps' cellblocks with some frequency were interrogators and military linguists; detainees' meetings with medics, civilian defense lawyers, and members of the International Committee of the Red Cross took place in designated spaces elsewhere on the base.[2] US Navy personnel and their families, a population unconnected to detention operations, reside in a Guantánamo of schools, baseball games, and McDonalds, on the same forty-five square mile base but, as Jonathan Hansen has observed, effectively a world away (233–64).

The experiences of detainees and of guards, interrogators, and translators have made their way into the public domain in various ways, in many cases reflecting on the interpersonal relationships that cross and distort power lines on the cellblocks. A number of former detainees published book-length, first-person accounts of their experience at Guantánamo after their release, Mohamedou Ould Slahi's heavily redacted *Guantánamo Diary* being to date the sole example of a memoir written and published during detention. Josephine Metcalf has proposed that these detainee memoirs stand as a literary subgenre, "peculiar" in its relation to the American prison memoir and to what Barbara Harlow, reading accounts of Guantánamo by former detainees, journalists, lawyers, filmmakers, and fiction writers, has termed "extraordinary renditions literature" (Metcalf 67). While their accounts differ significantly, each memoir has among its structuring events unexpected and inexplicable detention, rendition, disorientation, interrogation, and, often, torture, underpinned by a reiteration of innocence that was eventually corroborated in all cases. There is a smaller number of published writings by, and interviews with, former guards and linguists. Those former military members who have written full-length accounts of their time at Guantánamo are, in most cases and perhaps unsurprisingly, the disaffected: those who, in the words of former military linguist Erik Saar, consider the US government's actions at Guantánamo to be "morally inconsistent with what we stand for as a nation" (247).

Reading accounts from the camps together for their depictions of relations between detainees and individual representatives of the US military and government, the most prevalent image is of a deeply entrenched opposition between captor and captive, a replication of the language of "good" versus "evil," or President George W. Bush's "either you are with us or you are with the terrorists," with which the war on terror was inaugurated. Despite the insistence in Joint Task Force Guantánamo's leaked *Camp Delta Standard Operating Procedures* (2004) that military personnel must "respect all detainees as human beings and protect them against all acts of violence" (1.4), former guards report categorical oppositions in the daily operations of the camps, with detainees being introduced to them as "some of the worst people the world had to offer" (Center for the Study of Human Rights in the Americas), "hate-filled, evil, terrorist dirt-farmers" (Holdbrooks, *Traitor?* 29) and, indeed, "not people" (29). Mohamedou Ould Slahi reports being reminded by a guard that "You are not one of us. You are our enemy! . . . If I speak to you, I speak to my enemy" (*Guantánamo Diary* 304–5). Detainees recall experiencing these designations in human and nonhuman versions: they are called, and treated as, "lethal" (Hicks 218) and as the iconically evil Hannibal Lecter (Begg, *Enemy Combatant* 236), or as animals either caged to protect human life, hunted for the slaughter, or tormented for sport.[3] In an ontological hierarchy that spirals ever downward, some detainees report being treated as less than animal and thereby, as Terri Tomsky has argued, excluded from the sphere of rights altogether, just as they are denied the legal protections afforded to certain wildlife species on the base (101).[4]

And yet, beneath the arc of the events structuring detainee memoirs, and interspersed with their accounts of the physical deprivation, psychological suffering, and intolerable monotony of days and nights on the cellblocks, lie snapshots of compassionate interpersonal relationships, acknowledged succinctly in former detainee Murat Kurnaz's admission that "over the course of time I did meet some soldiers who treated us like humans" (193) and Mustafa Ait Idir's memory of one soldier who, unlike others, "had always treated me like a human being" (Boumediène and Ait Idir 151). Similarly, the accounts of former military personnel, even as they know that asking unscripted questions, doubting the wisdom of one's superiors and showing curiosity about detainees' experience are serious transgressions of the interpersonal codes in place at the base, record an evolving sense of care and respect toward those designated as enemies and a forging of engagements that undermine the physical and ideological premises of Guantánamo. Certain roles lend themselves more easily to such engagement by virtue of their constitutive mediatory function, among them the roles of chaplain and translator. It is an engagement that has aroused suspicion from those in more clearly oppositional military roles, as was clear in the cases of Captain James Yee and Senior Airman Ahmad al-Halabi, a chaplain and a linguist, respectively, both Muslim servicemen charged by the United States with espionage in 2003 (Rivera). The memoir Eric Saar co-authored with journalist Viveca Novak describes an increasing recognition that his ability to converse with detainees in their own language, while for them a "primary source of hope" (Saar and Novak 75), arouses in the guards "a special loathing for linguists" (75). Guards tended "to think of us as sympathizers, a term at Gitmo that included anyone who betrayed signs of compassion or empathy for the captives, or talked to them a little too long" (72). Saar eventually petitions for removal from Guantánamo, recognizing that translating, a practice to which mutual understanding is crucial, is ethically incompatible with continued loyalty to the military in that context.

Some cellblock guards, those charged with explicitly treating the enemy as such, also begin to trace the contours of an intimate friendship that represents a radical troubling of who the enemy is and of what purpose is served at the detention centers and in the war on terror more broadly by the division of entities into friends and enemies. Cellblock guards have often been drawn from the military police units of the US Armed Forces under the command of Joint Task Force Guantánamo, and in the early years many had experience as military police officers in Iraq or Afghanistan. Their work in detainee operations at Guantánamo differed significantly from the correctional work they would undertake outside the context of the war on terror, in both the national security significance attributed to those whom they guarded and the isolation of their deployment.[5]

Despite the base's Caribbean location and the leisure pursuits ostensibly on offer there, guards work long shifts on the cellblocks in a frequently hostile environment; Carol Rosenberg has written of the excessive eating, body building, or drinking to which guards turn—the option to become "chunks, hunks or drunks" (*Guantánamo Bay* 2), as she puts it. The fear of an extended term at Guantánamo, even as it looms far more gravely for detainees, haunts guards too, to the extent that mental health concerns among current and former guards have raised red flags in the military, and in "Guard Duty," an essay published six years after the first edition of *Guantánamo Diary*, Mohamedou Ould Slahi describes episodes of substance abuse and aggression among guards that underpinned their troubled and deeply imbalanced interactions with detainees in solitary confinement at Camp Echo.[6] Nevertheless, guards have also found familiarity and closeness in their long hours spent with detainees, relationships that former detainee David Hicks has read as inevitable given the mundane interactions and physical proximity of their time together: "When two people are locked in a room together every day for months on end," he writes, "it should be no surprise that they will come to know each other on a personal, profound level" (296). In the highly charged context that is Guantánamo, this reciprocal knowledge lays bare a broader set of shared experiences, ones inherent to and deeply entrenched in the various crisscrossing circuits of power that meet in what Amy Kaplan has called the "imperial location" (854), "haunted by the ghosts of empire" (854), that Guantánamo stands as today.

Of the detainee memoirs published to date, three—Mohamedou Ould Slahi's *Guantánamo Diary* (2017), Moazzam Begg's *Enemy Combatant: A British Muslim's Journey to Guantánamo and Back* (2006), and Ahmed Errachidi's *The General: The Ordinary Man Who Challenged Guantánamo* (2013)—together offer a framework for reading the corpus of accounts from Guantánamo's cellblocks as punctuated by deeply subversive intimate friendships between detainees and their interrogators. These memoirists' reflections on friendship cohere around three areas of shared, rather than oppositional, experience: a political history of imperial and racist aggression that precedes and surpasses the space of the Guantánamo base but also accounts for its very existence; a critique of the military's understanding of female sexuality as it pertains to the camps' predominantly Muslim detainees, which in Slahi's and Begg's cases presents as friendship grounded in a shared appreciation for literature; and curiosity and respect for the other's religious faith. Each of these becomes a meeting point where the detainee manifests to the guard as also and equally human, leading to reciprocal gestures of humility and caring.

Slahi's *Guantánamo Diary* is the best-known text by a Guantánamo detainee, both for the circumstances of its publication—the only memoir to date to be published while its author was still in the detention camps, and released first in 2015 in a heavily redacted edition whose blackouts were, as Joseph P. Slaughter has written, "Untelling that is telling nonetheless" ("Life, Story, Violence" 469)—and for the violence and relentlessness with which its author was subjected to torture. Held without charge at Guantánamo from 2002 to 2016, having been initially detained in his native Mauritania, Slahi wrote his narrative in an English learned at Guantánamo and revised it, in a "restored version," after his release. Begg's *Enemy Combatant* is written as a memoir of his upbringing in a Muslim community in Birmingham, England, and of the relocation to Afghanistan with his wife and young children that led, in 2002, to his arrest and detention at Kandahar and Bagram Air Bases and, eventually, Guantánamo, where he was held for three years, often in solitary confinement in Camp Echo, before being released to the United Kingdom. Errachidi is a Moroccan citizen and fluent English speaker who worked as a chef in London prior to his capture in Pakistan in 2001 and subsequent detention at Guantánamo from 2002 to 2007; his account of his rendition and detention, *The General: The Ordinary Man Who Challenged Guantánamo*, references the nickname he earned for his role in organizing effective protest among detainees.

Even as these three memoirs dwell on the pain, inexplicability, and injustice of the experience of detention, and on the inner strength to which each author turned to survive it, each is closely bound up with reflections on the lives of others, and on what they and the authors share. *Guantánamo Diary* is attentive to the broad spectrum of personalities with whom Slahi crosses paths at Guantánamo and before. Indeed, Alexandra S. Moore has proposed reading this memoir "for the ways in which it documents [Slahi's] interrelationship with and responsiveness to fellow detainees, guards, interrogators, medical personnel, staff psychologists, and so forth" ("Exception as Alibi" 83), and his surprising statement that his cell and guards are his "new home and family" (*Guantánamo Diary* 310) as demonstrating "the terms through which Slahi constructs a social matrix for himself within the very context designed to destroy him as a social being" ("Exception as Alibi" 84). Similarly, paying tribute to the individual guards who ran the risk of befriending him, Begg positions his relationships with them in particular as foundational to his experience of Guantánamo and to the finding of "some common ground between people on opposing sides of this new war" that the book's prologue lists among its primary aims (*Enemy Combatant* xvii). Errachidi's interactions with members of the US military are somewhat more skewed toward the political and toward illustrating his de facto leadership in negotiating rights for detainees. Nevertheless Errachidi, like Slahi and Begg, references some interactions with guards that depart from the general binary governing the camps.

In tracing the nuances of their close relationships with members of the US military, Begg and Slahi look to racial, postcolonial, and neocolonial hierarchies common to the contexts from which detainees and guards alike originate, and which are so deeply ingrained that they derail the captor-captive power binary underpinning the detention camps. That *Guantánamo Diary* is a text whose own location in a global experience of colonialism's aftermath is central is the proposal of Yogita Goyal, who addresses its potential contribution to unresolved questions in the field of literary studies, among them "the place of the United States (especially for the study of contemporary postcolonial literature, much of which emanates from or is entangled with the United States) and the theorization of race in a truly global context" (77). Elizabeth Swanson and Alexandra S. Moore have read Slahi's post-release confinement to Mauritania, as well as his initial abduction from his home country at the behest of the United States, as demonstrating "the still powerful reach of U.S. empire" and "the perhaps unavoidable deference of Mauritania to that empire" (40). Slahi directs considerable ire at this particular figuration of racial and colonial power imbalance, of which he himself is victim, but also draws attention to inequities of similar historical origin within Guantánamo's guard force, drawn from a US military of whose enlisted personnel roughly one third identify as nonwhite (Congressional Research Service 20). He observes, for example, that the one Black guard permitted to deal with him "had no say" (*Guantánamo Diary* 283), despite being higher in rank than his associate, "a younger, white army specialist . . . who was always in charge" (283). He also makes note of the distinctive kindness of the Puerto Rican guards he encountered: "They were different than other Americans; they were not as vigilant and unfriendly . . . Everybody liked them . . . But they got in trouble with those responsible for the camps because of their friendly and humane approach to detainees" (229). Although Slahi does not directly connect the Puerto Rican guards' relative affinity with detainees to their own precarious status in the United States, nor to their standing among other guards, there have been reports of what an experienced Puerto Rican National Guardsman has termed "prejudice against Puerto Ricans in the operations of the base" (Morales Blanco). This is a prejudice that Manuel Avilés-Santiago, in his study of media representations and self-representations of Puerto Ricans in the military from World War II to the war on terror, reads in relation to "complex, layered histories of imperialism, racism, heterosexism, and second-class citizenship" (26).

Begg, however, directly addresses the racial and colonial hierarchies operating among guards at Guantánamo, clarifying in no uncertain terms their origin in histories and experiences similar to those of detainees. These common histories and experiences become, for Begg, the primary framework within which to posit alternatives to Guantánamo's structuring us-versus-them relationship. His interactions with Black and Hispanic American soldiers—in which he presents himself as a detainee and a dual British-Pakistani citizen, raised in the racially divided England of the 1970s and 1980s—urge these soldiers to read beyond their own local experiences and primary identifications, to recognize broader commonalities. He effectively invites them to what Lisa Lowe has called a "practice of reading across archives" that "unsettles the discretely bounded objects, methods, and temporal frameworks canonized by a national history invested in isolated origins and independent progressive development" (6). Begg's interactions with these guards trace a broader understanding of Guantánamo as a space that is Caribbean, American, African, and European, and thereby transatlantic, postcolonial, and neoimperial—one whose very resistance to a simpler, sui generis division between US soldiers and non-US detainees, or between good and evil, produces unauthorized identifications and transgressive affective bonds.[7]

Begg remarks on the amenable presence of Hispanic guards, distinguishing one in particular as "decent and empathetic" (*Enemy Combatant* 240), and he befriends a number of Black guards, engaging them with his reflections on Booker T. Washington and W. E. B. Du Bois (181). He is sensitive to how race situates these individuals among other guards, despite their ostensible unity as members of the US military. He notices that white guards "were pretty scornful and racist towards their fellow soldiers from the U.S. Virgin Islands . . . seeing them as not really American" (247). One Virgin Islander confides to him that race, rather than captivity, is the ultimate regulator of hierarchy at Guantánamo: "To the other guards we're in a lower category even than you detainees, because you're still lighter-skinned than us . . . we're black, and they just hate us" (247). With regard to the Haitian American guard whom he befriends, Begg writes—resonating with centuries of what Michel-Rolph Trouillot, Sibylle Fischer, and others have read as the willful, fear-driven exclusion of Haiti from modernity—that "many soldiers saw Haitians as the lowest of all in the Caribbean" (252).

In what is by far the most nuanced analysis to date of racial identifications and misidentifications among the detainee and guard populations at the Guantánamo detention centers, Darryl Li has cautioned against superimposing US-derived understandings of Blackness on the very different contexts from which individual detainees originate. Slahi, for example, Li writes, grew up in a Mauritania in which both slavery and Blackness are coded in very specific ways, and in which Slahi himself identifies as neither Black nor a descendant of enslaved people but is "in local terms, white [*bīḍānī*]" (26). In Begg's account, however, any higher status that may be accorded to detainees with lighter skin has little overt manifestation in the context of the cellblocks. He reports that whatever may be the pitfalls of conflating locally specific experiences, detainees and nonwhite guards find solace and connection in seeing their respective histories of discrimination and territorial usurpation reflected in one another. He writes of some of these guards that "when they looked at the detainees, they couldn't help seeing some of their own history" (248). Other guards learn from Begg's self-assumed role as analyst and didact: he instructs one Caribbean guard to "study a bit of your roots and your origins and try and work out how that relates to the situation that we're in. If you can't recognize the parallel, then I think you're blind to history" (249). In the physically intimate setting of the cellblock, Begg reports guiding the guards in mapping experiences that constitute uneven historical intimacies among colonial and neocolonial practices and experiences in Pakistan, the Middle East, the Caribbean, and the United States.

A transcontextual history of racial and imperialist aggression, while it structures not only interpersonal relations on the cellblocks but also accounts for the very existence of the detention camps on leased land at Guantánamo, can only be the basis for friendships with certain guards. An appreciation for literature and natural wonder, for tenets of humanist culture that promise to transcend the locality and disparities of the detention cell, is a second area around which encounters, conversations, and friendships coalesce, and it stands as an ostensibly more generally available interest, despite the uneven distribution of free time, reading material, linguistic competence, and formal education across the guard and detainee populations.[8] Although in the first years of the camps, as Begg comments, the recreational offerings for detainees were "brain-numbing" (218), offerings improved over time. These included increased access to library materials in numerous languages and, in the detention centers' second decade, art classes that yielded drawing, watercolors, and sculpture that detainee-artist Moath Al-Alwi, whose intricately carved model ships were exhibited in New York in late 2017, has described as a way to "open a window in the cell" (*Art from Guantánamo* 33).

Both Slahi and Begg write of the pleasures of reading and creating not only as solitary pursuits but also as a basis for the close and trusting relationships with the members of the military with whom they spend most time. Offered a historical novel as reading material by Sergeant Mary, an interrogator who looms large in Slahi's account and "was the one who came with most ideas related to literature I was given to read" (314), he "received the book gratefully and read it hungrily, at least three times" (314). Later, his first encounter with Sergeant Amy, another of his interrogators, begins with a greeting in Arabic and moves quickly to her offer to help him plant a garden, which she does expertly, helping him to "grow sunflowers, basil, sage, parsley, cilantro, and things of that nature" (347) in what he calls "the aggressive soil of GTMO" (347). In addition to assuring that he got an adequate diet, Sergeant Amy also supported Slahi as he learned English and "worked hard on that, especially on [his] pronunciation and spelling" (349). It is partly on the basis of the shared experience of gardening that Slahi names a relationship to Sergeant Amy that counters the hostility with which their interactions should be governed, according to the structure of the camps: "Amy treated me as a brother," he writes, "and I as if she were my sister" (348).

Begg's recollections of his relationships with a guard, Jennifer, and his principal interrogator, Kim—warm, nuanced relationships in which an appreciation for aesthetic pleasure figures prominently—similarly run counter to his hostile interactions with many guards. He recalls of Jennifer that "the very first time I spoke to her was about Dickens' *Bleak House*, which I was reading" (236); from that initial encounter, he anticipated having "some rare, erudite discussions with her" (236). She eventually confesses that she prefers Begg's company to that of her fellow soldiers, despite having been primed to expect the worst when she was first assigned to his maximum-security isolation block. "The unique circumstances," Begg writes, "produced a somewhat unique friendship" (236), grounded in a range of common interests as broad as it is unanticipated: "Studying jujitsu, flying lessons, sword collections, affinity for the English language, poetry, a taste for classical literature and ancient history" (236).

Boredom, inactivity, and the isolation to which Begg is confined mean that the closest company he keeps, "the person I saw most" (207) while in isolation at Camp Echo, is his interrogator, Kim, who, he insists, takes it upon herself to redirect this proximity toward a level of care and solicitousness that befits a friend more than an interrogator, sitting in his cell while he is unshackled, a gesture of trust shown by few in her position. "No previous interrogator, in Kandahar or Bagram," Begg writes, "had spent more time, showed more compassion, or appeared more impartial, than her" (208). It is with Kim that he shares not his reflections on literary works he has read but a more personal engagement with writing: a poem he has composed (222). In a later epilogue to artist Debi Cornwall's book *Welcome to Camp America: Inside Guantánamo Bay* (2017), Begg again invokes the empathic texture of his friendship with Kim, recalling a moment at Guantánamo when she sought special permission for him to leave his cell to contemplate, alongside her and other guards and detainees, "something quite marvelous that was happening in the Cuban sky," namely "a perfect circular rainbow that had formed around the sun" (Cornwall n.p.).

Although the focus of the connections Slahi and Begg report with Mary, Amy, Jennifer, and Kim is one that may appear especially capacious, as a coming together around reading and creating rather than around more divided histories, their relationships with these women are deeply subversive of Guantánamo's defining power structures not only because they cross the soldier-detainee divide. By forming and reporting close relationships with female members of the US military, they undermine a secondary binary forcibly brought to bear at Guantánamo in the service of the detention operations' governing separation of American from enemy, captor from detainee. This is the binary underpinning one of the enhanced interrogation techniques authorized by the CIA and various branches of the US military in the war on terror: sexually provocative behavior, including physical contact, directed toward a usually shackled detainee by a female member of the military. This is acknowledged in the military-commissioned Schmidt-Furlow Report of 2005 (*Army Regulation 15–6*), one of a number of US government–commissioned sources that artist Coco Fusco brings to bear in her violently satirical intervention *A Field Guide for Female Interrogators* (2008), an "exploration of the role of female sexuality as a weapon in the 'war on terror'" (107). [9] It is also the subject of Jane Meyer's investigative work, initially for the *New Yorker* in 2006, on the technique known as "Invasion of Space by a Female," and it was acknowledged in the 2014 report of the Senate Select Committee on Intelligence on the CIA's detention and interrogation program, known as the Feinstein Report.

It is, however, Slahi's *Guantánamo Diary*, published ten years after the Schmidt-Furlow Report, that gives the most searing testimony of sexually abusive enhanced interrogation techniques: heavily redacted in the first edition, a scene "restored" in the second edition describes "an afternoon dedicated to sexual molestation" (222) with precisely the "SSG Mary" who later offers Slahi reading material. In a performance orchestrated and watched through a one-way mirror by the consistently cruel, male, senior interrogator "Sergeant Shally," SSG Mary takes off her uniform, rubs her body against Slahi's, and threatens to rape him (223). The rationale behind this particular form of abuse reinscribes what Safiyah Rochelle has described as a racing and gendering of the detainee body that "is also shaped by an understanding of religion—specifically and especially the Muslim religion—as adhering to the body in particular ways" (216): detainees subjected to this treatment are asked to be "men" in a carnal sense that is explicitly meant to undermine their fitness for prayer and shake their faith. While Slahi is being abused, Sergeant Shally yells at him, "Stop the fucking praying! You're having sex with American whores and you're praying? What a hypocrite you are!" (228); similarly, in Eric Saar and Viveca Novak's *Inside the Wire*, as a female interrogator abuses a detainee, she says to him, "I can see that you are starting to get hard. How do you think Allah feels about that?" (224). Compounding the enormously troubling implications of these incidents for the roles available to women in the war on terror—implications that Fusco, Meyer, and Mary Ann Case have addressed in some detail—there is in this practice a clear message: to be a man, in the sense dictated by these forced encounters, the detainee cannot also be a Muslim, and if his commitment is to his faith, then he is not a man. Thus, the detainee is neither sufficiently man in his sexual inclination nor sufficiently human in his standing within the governing ideologies of the war, reinforcing his categorization within the camps' warped logic.

While Slahi's report of his relationship with Sergeant Amy is straightforwardly positive, even as it defies the norm of how he, as a male, Muslim detainee at Guantánamo, should engage with her, his efforts to justify his friendship with Sergeant Mary are more strained. Although she is a perpetrator of physical and psychological abuse, who lies to (230) and bribes (226) him, he has some pity for her when she starts to remove her clothes, "hoping," he suspects, "I would crack and relieve her from the pain of humiliation she was inflicting on herself" (223). Later, he admits to himself that "I know I am looking for excuses to acquit SSG Mary" (312), exonerating her because he knows that, despite her actions, she "doesn't believe in torture" (312). Ultimately, despite the pain and degradation to which she, unlike Sergeant Amy, subjected him, Sergeant Mary was, he claims, "the closest person to me; she was the only one I could relate to" (276).

Begg records no direct experience of the abuse so graphically documented in Slahi's account, nor does he indicate awareness of this form of interrogation either while he was detained at Guantánamo or when he wrote his memoir. Rather, his account is remarkable for its insistence on close and mutually respectful friendships with women. Begg's interactions with Jennifer and Kim—who enter his cell, engage with his mind, share his interests, and find ways to cast him as a friend and equal rather than a prisoner—radically undermine the prescribed soldier-detainee and male-female relationships at Guantánamo; indeed, he largely lets pass as unexceptional the fact that his closest interlocutors are women. Shared interests in literary classics and one's own poetry, ostensibly among the broadest and most open areas of potential common ground at Guantánamo despite the layers of suspicion under which even the simplest forms of writing fall there, become, in Slahi and Begg's sharing with female soldiers, deeply subversive of the camps' established power structures.

Women stand in Slahi and Begg's memoirs as the entry point to a third area of connection between detainees and guards—namely, a connection around religious faith. Although it is his guard Steve Wood who, after leaving Guantánamo, quietly converts to Islam—as reported in Ben Taub's Pulitzer Prize–winning *New Yorker* essay, "Guantánamo's Darkest Secret" (2019), as well as in Laurence Topham's short documentary film *My Brother's Keeper* (2020)—it is with Sergeant Amy that Slahi reports having extended conversations about religion. They question one another seriously about the doctrines of, and differences between, Amy's Christianity and Slahi's Muslim faith, with Slahi seeking an understanding of the Holy Trinity (352) and Amy curious as to whether Islam allows her, as a Christian, to go to heaven (351). Begg's memoir includes no such discussion, but refers to two soldiers, "a young black woman from the South" (220) and a Puerto Rican (220), whose conversions to Islam at Guantánamo he appears to relate to the histories of racial subjugation that they share with detainees. He describes, too, his friendship with "a young woman from Maine" (220), a military police guard who approaches him with her interest in Islam and subsequently orders books on the topic (220). Unlike the mutual recognition of histories of discrimination, guard-detainee encounters that lead to an embrace of Islam are not presented as a sharing of past experience; rather, they develop from a growing interest on the part of certain guards in the power of faith in the face of suffering, and from their observations, corroborated by the detainees with whom they engage, that Islam anchors detainees in a way that is unavailable to non-Muslim soldiers, despite their relative freedom. The interest, admiration and, indeed, envy on the part of guards leads in some cases to a full embrace of Islam and, in others, to a form of respect and willingness to learn that is crucial to a broader landscape of resistant recognitions and intimate friendships emerging from the detention camps as from Guantánamo more broadly.

The detainee for whom guards' interest in Islam figures most prominently is Ahmed Errachidi, who, in addition to his political protagonism, stands as a spiritual leader to other Muslim detainees and to those guards who are drawn to Islam during their time at Guantánamo. Guards' interest in, and occasional conversion to, the detainees' faith stands as an asymmetric meeting: the guard, who wields the power to inflict pain and withhold comfort, and who represents the larger incarcerating authority, seeks to learn from the detainee who rarely, in the corpus of writing from Guantánamo, shows reciprocal interest in the guards' faith and other sources of inner strength. At the insistence of certain guards who claim to be "amazed at how well we withstood adversity" (136), Errachidi agrees to guide them in their acceptance of Islam. "There were some," he writes, "who promised me that they would accept Islam after they left Guantánamo and there were others who uttered the Shahadah prayer that there is no god but Allah and Muhammad is his messenger" (136).

Errachidi has a prominent role in one of the more notable conversions to Islam at Guantánamo, that of military police guard Terry Holdbrooks, for whose memoir, *Traitor?*, he wrote a prologue in both Arabic and English. This self-published memoir, neither co-written with a journalist or professional editor, nor taken up by a major press, as are many detainee memoirs, is singular among the corpus of first-person writing by military personnel at Guantánamo. Although not precisely a conversion narrative, in the sense that Karin van Nieuwkerk defines as a story in which "past events are reinterpreted in the light of current convictions" (2), *Traitor?* concords with van Nieuwkerk's insistence that an entirely introspective turn toward "the constitution of a pious self... often expressed as 'peace of mind,' 'calmness,' or 'finally feeling at ease'" (15) is often as important to contemporary Western subjects' embrace of Islam as are prior social experiences, or the "crisis theory" of conversion that she attributes to Monika Wohlrab-Sahr (7). Having initially chosen to enlist in the military police as a way to "find a purpose in life" (12), Holdbrooks was deployed to patrol cellblocks at Guantánamo, passing first through what he terms "reprogramming" efforts to persuade him and other recruits that detainees there will "stop at nothing to kill you" (29). He nevertheless becomes curious about detainees' experience and, although ostracized by fellow guards for what they term his attempts at "bridge-building" (49), he makes efforts to learn Arabic, and finds in his interactions with detainees "an escape, at least in my mind" (49) from the grim realities of his surroundings. Taking advantage of the solitude and minimal supervision accorded most soldiers working in the camp, he is inspired by the strength that Muslim detainees derive from their faith, and approaches them with an increasingly detailed list of questions about Islam. "No matter how simple or bothersome the questions were," he writes, "the prisoners always treated me with respect... They did not present Islam as the only way, or even the right way, but simply their way, answering my questions with gentle grace" (55). One prisoner lends him his Koran and, although Holdbrooks approaches this with skepticism, expecting it to be "a book of nonsense, like other religious texts I had read" (55), he discovers instead that reading it "was like seeing a huge light-bulb of logic, illuminating the dark world of ideas that had previously clouded my mind" (55). He subsequently spends long hours talking to Errachidi, eventually approaching him in order to "embrace Islam in his presence" (128). Errachidi transliterates the Shahadah for him, wakes a neighboring detainee and, through the wire mesh of his cell, witnesses the conversion (130). Looking back on his experience in an article written for *VICE News*, Holdbrooks relates it specifically to the magnitude of detainees' happiness relative to his own and to his desire to be their equal in this. "The detainees," he says, "with their living faith were happier than I was. They had nothing, but they were still happy. Their religion was holding them together. I wanted the peace that they seemed to have" ("My Time as a Guard" 7). A photograph of Holdbrooks by Debi

FIGURE 2.1. DEBI CORNWALL, *TERRY, AMERICAN (UNITED STATES)*. © DEBI CORNWALL, REPRINTED BY PERMISSION.

Cornwall (fig. 2.1), facing away from the camera as are all the subjects in her *Welcome to Camp America*, shows him in a post-Guantánamo, post-conversion moment, contemplating a desert landscape and apparently at peace.

CUBAN GUARDS, COUNTERREVOLUTIONARIES, AND MIGRANTS

There is no Terry Holdbrooks to embrace the perspective and faith of his assumed enemy along the Cuban side of the fence line that separates the country from the US base. There are still fewer analogues for detainee memoirs at this site: Cuba's own prison system, including the notorious Combinado de Guantánamo, about fifteen miles away from the base, holds petty criminals together with political prisoners, some of whom have been detained for activities related to the base. Information on their existence and experience is tightly regulated by Cuban authorities, and it has fallen to independent journalists and dissident activists, such as those producing the clandestine journal *Porvenir*, a subject of my final chapter, to maintain lists of the incarcerated and the charges against them.

The fence line has been heavily fortified since the United States and Cuba broke off diplomatic relations in 1961. Sown with landmines, dotted with watchtowers, and patrolled by soldiers on both sides, there is currently no legal way to cross it in either direction. It is consequently a site of little person-to-person engagement aside from scheduled meetings at a designated point between the commanders of the base and of the Cuban Border Brigade to ensure cooperation on certain issues of common concern as well as between base personnel and retired Cuban former employees who collect their pensions monthly at its north gate.[10]

Cuban border guards' encounters with the enemy at this site are less structured than similar encounters at the base, and there is no counterpart on the Cuban side to the base's highly publicized detention camps. And yet, Cuban border guards share with US prison guards across the border a rigorous national ideology of good versus bad, one that is invested with particular force in the figure of the soldier, and, at the same time, a pervasive troubling of who and what the enemy is. The troubling in this case begins at the source, in the Cuban government's own construction of the enemy. Rather than enforce an unyielding binary of us against them, like the one to which American guards at Guantánamo are subject, the Cuban Revolution has, since its inception, armed its defenses against two distinct enemies. The first is the United States and what Cuba has cast as its doctrine of imperialism, while the second is the Cuban "counterrevolutionary," whose manifestation at the border with the naval base is the aspiring migrant, for whom the United States beckons as a refuge.

Like US soldiers guarding at the detention camps, Cuban guards at Guantánamo are often young, low-ranking, and on short-term deployments (in their case as part of the military service required of all male citizens over the age of sixteen and available on a voluntary basis for women of the same age). They are assigned to the Brigada de la Frontera (Border Brigade), a specialist unit of the Revolutionary Armed Forces established in 1961 to defend and monitor Guantánamo's fence line at all times, in response to the perceived threat to the newly triumphant Cuban Revolution from American military forces concentrated within the base. In their history of this unit, Felipa Suárez and Pilar Quesada describe its growth from a small battalion, charged with not retaliating to provocation from the base or allowing passage to anyone other than base workers, to a well-structured organization that drew elite military professionals and military service recruits, known for the extreme physical and psychological demands made of its members (104). As Jana K. Lipman has noted, the Border Brigade "came to symbolize unblinking resilience and preparedness against U.S. imperialism" (*Guantánamo: A Working Class History* 167) and over the course of the 1960s, particularly in the wake of the 1961 Bay of Pigs invasion from which Cuba emerged victorious while also legitimately perceiving itself as under threat, individual acts of aggression and suspicions of support for larger plots were recorded on both sides of the fence line. In a speech given at the United Nations in 1964, resonant for its expressions of anti-imperialist solidarity with nascent states and nationalist movements across the globe, Ernesto "Che" Guevara, then Cuban minister for industry, protested that the Guantánamo base "has become a nest of thieves and a launching pad for them into our territory. We would tire this Assembly if we were to give a detailed account of the large number of provocations of all kinds" ("Create Two, Three, Many Vietnams" 335).[11] It has never, however, been in the foreign policy interest of either the United States or Cuba to seriously escalate tensions at the border: the base is of strategic use to the United States, and Cuba is under no illusions about its own relative military strength. As Hal Klepak observes, "There has been a clear interest on both sides to avoid incidents and solve problems before they became serious" (132).

Symbolically, however, the Border Brigade defends something much greater than a forty-five-square-mile naval base. As Cuba's only land border and site of its closest encounter with the United States, the fence line at Guantánamo looms large as a figurative battleground, for military forces and Cuban citizens alike, in the war on imperialism that has motivated the Cuban Revolution since its beginnings. In its historical roots and rhetorical reach, this imperialism is the same oppressive force that Begg identifies as common to the experiences of detainees and nonwhite US soldiers; it is, in fact, a further experience in the network of intimacies that enmeshes Guantánamo, as Amy Kaplan and Nicole Waller have observed.[12] Named and targeted by a ruling power that claims to have broken the chains of oppression, imperialism has in Cuba become a deeply entrenched enemy that, to this day, justifies an ambitious international agenda and broad-scale militarization of society and collective language. In the climate of the Cold War, it was in the service of a war on US imperialism that the particular political language of the Cuban Revolution evolved, underpinned by an expectation that citizens always be engaged in battle, mentally if not physically. Fidel Castro's speeches laid the ground for this war and unleashed it vehemently as hostilities with the US government become more pronounced. That it was at the core of the Cuban Revolution's self-assumed role in the world is manifest in Che Guevara's 1967 address to the Tricontinental Conference: "Our every action is a battle cry against imperialism and a call for the unity of the peoples against the great enemy of the human race: the United States of North America" (362).

The Border Brigade's guard posts, like the fence line itself and the towns bordering the naval base—among them the fishing town of Caimanera, officially designated "the first line of defense against imperialism"—have long been a principal stage for the performative dimensions of the war on imperialism. Fidel Castro spoke at the border on many occasions, each time reiterating Cuba's objection, on anti-imperialist grounds, to what has persistently been named as an illegal occupation of Cuban territory and to the ensuing threat the US presence poses to Cubans' sovereignty and safety.[13] Cultural activities were incorporated into the brigade's regular programming from its inception and, with the establishment of its own Commission on Culture in the 1970s, the border became an arena for popular gatherings and concerts. Drama, music and dance groups, and literary workshops were formed in each of the brigade's small units, with the aim of performing in the nearby communities, which were already well-versed in Cuba's particular brand of anti-imperialist rhetoric thanks to its domination of the national media and education system. On the international level, the Border Brigade and other institutions in Guantánamo Province have since 2012 collaborated with the US-based nonprofit Witness for Peace to stage an annual protest rally at Cuba's border with the base.

The role of the Border Brigade in Cuba's war on imperialism, as well as that of the civilian citizens of Guantánamo Province, is the focus of Hernando Calvo Ospina's 2016 documentary, *All Guantánamo Is Ours*. Calvo Ospina, a Colombian journalist with long-standing personal ties and political loyalties to the Castro brothers, was granted an unusual level of access to military facilities and members of the Border Brigade as well as to schools and cultural institutions in Guantánamo Province, and his documentary traces an unambiguous history of violation both preceding and following the Cuban Revolution. Local residents and historians recall the moral ruin perpetrated on the region by its de facto function as a weekend playground for US Marines in the 1940s and 1950s; fisherman tell of the devastation to their industry caused by the US Navy's control of the most resource-rich half of Guantánamo Bay; former Cuban base workers remember the humiliating prejudice with which they were treated by Americans; and schoolchildren and university students alike declare their outrage that this territory has been illegally taken from Cuba. José Felipe Cisneros, a lieutenant colonel who served in the Border Brigade for twelve years, speaks of his time as a member of the air defense unit when US aircraft would frequently break the sound barrier as well as windows and buildings in Cuba as they violated Cuban airspace. Cuban forces, he insists, "were educated on the principle of not allowing ourselves to be carried away by provocations" (*All Guantánamo Is Ours* 00:20:40). A unit of female soldiers offers perspectives on femininity and combat readiness that resonate with the difficult integration of women into the military in other contexts, as Stephanie Szitanyi has studied. One soldier proclaims her patriotism and reiterates Fidel Castro's metaphor of the US presence at Guantánamo as "like a dagger in my heart, like in the heart of all Cubans" (00:27:25) while another insists that "we can perfectly be combatants, crawl on the floor, take up arms, stand firm, and combine that with our beauty" (00:27:41–00:27:51). All voices in the documentary unite in their condemnation of the US presence at the naval base and their identification of the enemy of the Cuban people: the United States and its imperialist designs. Together, they resonate as the voice of a collective border guard, situating the imperative to defend at the core of the Cuban Revolution.

In Guantánamo Province as well as in the broader Cuban context there also exists a significantly less adversarial model for engaging with the United States and its military, political leaders, and citizens. Government-level rapprochement has ebbed and flowed, with President Barack Obama's 2016 visit to Cuba and cordial diplomatic negotiations with President Raúl Castro as a high point. And, as many scholars of Cuban migration and transnational ties have shown, very few Cubans express animosity toward Americans, whether these be Cuban-born US citizens whose ever-growing numbers have forged strong and economically indispensable bonds between the two countries, the thousands of tourists who have flocked from the United States to Cuba during the past quarter century, or the Americans whom Cubans see as they participate with increasing frequency in the global consumption of US media.[14] All this notwithstanding, there is a vested interest on the Cuban government's part in continuing to define its revolutionary project against the imperialism of the United States and in maintaining the border at Guantánamo as a site of imminent confrontation. It is this antagonism that the soldiers of the Border Brigade are charged with upholding, and this the enemy against whom they defend the border and, by extension, the nation.

Cuban soldiers at Guantánamo's border also, however, guard against a second, more insidious, and barely nameable enemy, one whose proximity to their own lived experience, as opposed to that of the more abstract American imperialism that they have learned to contest, makes this a particularly difficult relationship to understand and perform as a hostile one. This enemy is the Cuban migrant, for whom the land and sea border between Guantánamo Province and the US naval base has for decades represented a route out of Cuba, albeit an immensely hazardous and barely survivable one. Despite its founding mission to defend Cuba from aggressive incursions from the base, the Border Brigade soon focused its efforts more urgently on escape attempts from Cuba. Cuban fortifications of the land border were amplified with this enemy in mind, and Suárez and Quesada describe the network of trenches, wire, and landmines that was completed in 1971 and effectively put an end to migrants' attempts to reach the base solely by land. The primary escape route, they acknowledge, then shifted to cover the swamp- and mine-ridden land around Guantánamo Bay and the bay itself, where the Cuban military subsequently introduced underwater mines and barriers (101–2).

Suárez and Quesada, Cuban military historians whose account of the Border Brigade is published by the press of the Revolutionary Armed Forces, describe those attempting to flee Cuba for the base as "unscrupulous citizens, at times accompanied by young children who suffered the dire consequences of their own crazy recklessness" (102). This profile draws heavily on the figure of the child, a primary vessel for rhetorical articulations of the future of the Cuban Revolution, as Lillian Guerra has noted ("Feeling like Fidel"), and the figure of the "counterrevolutionary," whose presence in the Cuban political imaginary dates to the early years of Fidel Castro's leadership and has demonstrated considerable elasticity over the more than sixty years since his rise to power. Even as the term initially referenced only US-backed Cuban exiles and a rural resistance explicitly loyal to the previous government, by the end of the revolution's first year in power Castro had extended its applicability widely through what Guerra calls "a new slate of counterrevolutionary laws that implied guilt by sympathy, association and . . . class affiliation" (*Visions of Power* 91). Many of the principal landmarks in 1960s political speech reiterate the rigid model of inclusion and exclusion on which the revolution would depend for its endurance. Speaking to an assembly of writers and intellectuals in April 1961, for example, in the wake of both victory at the Bay of Pigs and the banning of the short film *P.M.*, widely considered the first act of artistic censorship in revolutionary Cuba, Castro made the ominous and resonant pronouncement "within the Revolution, everything; against the Revolution, nothing" ("Words to Intellectuals" 220). He thus initiated decades of social intolerance and insidious censorship largely because, as Par Kumaraswami has commented, "within" and "against" "were necessarily unstable concepts that, far from establishing the rigid parameters of the permissible in cultural practice over nearly 50 years, are unresolved to this day" (539).

Intellectuals were long under suspicion for their supposed bourgeois class affiliation but while early exiles were presumed to share this affiliation, and to support armed attack on Cuba, the desire to leave Cuba was insistently translated as a counterrevolutionary act even as the class basis of migration changed and the likelihood of armed attacks from the United States dissipated. Leaving Cuba in the first three decades of the Castro era was layered with a language of rejection and carefully orchestrated spectacles of public humiliation. *Gusanos* (maggots) and *escoria* (scum) were Castro's preferred epithets for those who chose exile over revolution. As María Cristina García recounts, seeking an exit permit was a "long and tedious affair" (17) riven with seemingly arbitrary obstacles, during which the confiscation of one's property and harassment by neighbors and government officials alike were guaranteed. The mobilization of rejection toward would-be migrants reached its low point in organized acts of repudiation, open and violent hostilities staged at homes and workplaces, encouraged by the government, particularly during the large-scale migrant crisis of 1980 known as the Mariel exodus.[15]

Following the fall of the Berlin Wall in 1989, and the economic crisis and political isolation that Cuba endured as a result, the act of leaving the country, and, particularly, of returning with financial support for family members, became less clearly counterrevolutionary within government-directed rhetoric. In the 1990s, the toughest decade of what was termed Cuba's "special period in times of peace," gusanos of previous decades returned as what were jokingly termed *mariposas* (butterflies), bringing or sending the remittances that would become the country's most important income source, forming close-knit transnational communities and family units and, as Ariana Hernández-Reguant has outlined, reshaping a Cuban nationalism that could accommodate rather than reject its diaspora (87). Nevertheless, even as economic migrants replaced political exiles as the embodiment of those who had left Cuba, and returned frequently to a homeland that accepted and needed them, migration out of Cuba was heavily restricted: until 2013 Cubans were required to seek exit permits for foreign travel, and the crime of attempting to leave the country illegally has remained in Cuba's Penal Code.[16]

Despite the extraordinarily high risks involved, attempts to leave Cuba illegally have persisted, even beyond President Barack Obama's effective relegation of Cuban migrants to a legal par with those from most other Latin American countries, rather than as beneficiaries of the highly preferential treatment that, as Susan Eckstein has documented, they had been accorded since the 1960s.[17] Although the most highly publicized route for these attempts was for decades across the Florida Straits on perilous makeshift rafts—with President Obama's policy change significantly increasing Cubans' transit attempts through Central America and Mexico—the US base at Guantánamo, coterminous with Cuba and thus functioning as the country's only land border, long coexisted alongside this as a clandestine, if no less dangerous, migration route. Getting to the base does not guarantee entry to the United States: even under the migration accords that preceded Obama's policy change, migrants who successfully reached the base, like those apprehended at sea, were returned to Cuban authorities unless they were able to demonstrate a legitimate fear of persecution. This is the proviso in which migrants placed their hopes, knowing that if they could convincingly demonstrate such a fear, they would be taken to Guantánamo Bay's Migrant Operations Center, the lesser-known and considerably less restrictive of the base's detention centers, while their claims were assessed (Parmly 72).

Reports and records of migration attempts via the base are scarce. Within Cuba, they in many ways form part of a specifically local history, its contours and pains harbored closely by the Guantánamo Cubans who live in far greater proximity to the US naval base, and to a borderland of mines, searchlights, barbed wire, and watchtowers, than they do to their own capital city of Havana. In the US press, reports about such attempts have appeared sporadically over past decades, with a particular concentration in 1993, when the Clinton government filed a formal protest with the Cuban Foreign Ministry about numerous incidents in which the Cuban Border Brigade shot and killed civilians as they tried to reach the base (Kempster), and again in 1994, when the detention at the base of over thirty thousand Cubans who had been intercepted at sea impelled hundreds of others to take what William Booth termed "the direct route" to the base, swimming across Guantánamo Bay.[18] More recently, in February 2019, Cuba-focused news outlets in Spain and Miami carried the story of fourteen young men who attempted to enter the base, two of whom successfully crossed the minefield and swam across the bay but were returned to Cuba by US authorities; in one of the many sinister parallels that haunt the Guantánamo region, they were then imprisoned in Cuba on an extended sentence, which they protested with a hunger strike.[19] In July 2022 the Miami-based television channel AméricaTeve featured a video interview, direct from Guantánamo Bay Naval Base, with Yariel Alfonso Puerta, a young Cuban who had been imprisoned for his involvement in anti-government uprisings and had subsequently left the country on a raft, only to be intercepted by the US Coast Guard and taken to the base for assessment of his asylum claim ("Desde la base naval de Guantánamo").

Press reports have rarely included accounts from migrants themselves, the July 2022 interview with Yariel Alfonso Puerta being a rare exception. The archive of testimony from these particular "enemies" of the Cuban Revolution—which I consider analogous, in the structure of hostilities governing Guantánamo Bay Naval Base, to first-person accounts of detainees—is a fragmentary one, its corroboration fraught by the many obstacles that Cuban and US authorities have posed. One of the best-known first-person accounts of an attempt to leave the base is that of dissident writer Reinaldo Arenas, whose memoir *Before Night Falls*, published ten years after his exile from Cuba in 1980, records his determination to swim to the naval base, which he renounced at the onset of rapid-fire searchlights and the sound of machine guns (163–64). Among the most concerted efforts to gather testimony, and at the same time the most chilling records of Cubans' migration attempts, are the independent journalism compiled locally in Guantánamo under the umbrella of the dissident organization Alianza Democrática Oriental and the register of the deceased maintained by Cuba Archive's Truth and Memory Project, an initiative of the Washington, DC–based Free Society Project.

While the purview of *Porvenir*, Alianza Democrática Oriental's publication for Guantánamo Province, is pro-democracy activity and government repression within the Cuban province, migration attempts via the US naval base feature among its pages because of the custodial sentences these have incurred under Cuba's Penal Code and because of the suffering and conflict with border guards that such attempts entail.[20] The fourth issue of *Porvenir* includes a contribution by Claro Sánchez Altarriba, a political prisoner and prisoner of conscience incarcerated as part of the March 2003 "Black Spring" crackdown on Cuban dissidents, recounting the stories of several Cubans who have attempted to escape via the naval base, only some of whom have survived.[21] Sánchez Altarriba names a twelve-year-old boy, a resident of the town of Caimanera, whose attempt to swim to the base to join two uncles already there was disrupted by the explosion of a land mine; seriously injured, the boy was initially refused assistance by members of the Border Brigade, although they eventually picked him up, threatened, and mistreated him (7). Others mentioned by Sánchez Altarriba were less fortunate and perished in their attempts to flee.

Cuba Archive's scope is broader: it aims to document deaths believed to have resulted from the Cuban Revolution, based on accounts from family members. The project's director, Maria C. Werlau, has called the separation barrier between Cuba and the naval base "the tropical version of the Berlin Wall," comparing the loss of life, or time spent in prison, of Cubans who have attempted to reach the naval base to the experience of East Germans who tried to scale the Berlin Wall before it was brought down in 1989. The Cuba Archive includes testimony from relatives of several people either shot by Cuban authorities or killed by land mines during attempts to reach the base as well as a report that the San Francisco cemetery in the city of Guantánamo has an area set aside for victims of land mines planted around the base.[22]

While testimonial accounts from both migrants and guards in Cuban Guantánamo are much scarcer than they are for the analogous enemy-defender relationship across the fence line at the detention camps, there has emerged in recent decades a small corpus of fictional representations produced and set in Cuba's borderlands, in which the perspectives of these two figures are played out as a deeply violent human drama.[23] Short stories by Ana Luz García Calzada and Roberto de Jesús Quiñónes have depicted migrants as ordinary people driven by a common desperation for a better life, rather than as traitorous counter-revolutionaries; while guards, usually a distant threat to migrants as part of a more generalized landscape of surveillance and potential violence, appear in Estupiñán Zaldívar's "Abducción," as themselves vulnerable, afraid, and empathic toward those trying to flee. It is, however, Daniel Ross's 2022 film, *La espera* (The Wait), that most cohesively weaves together the stories of aspiring migrants and soldiers charged with guarding the fence line with the base, drawing these into a wrenching portrayal of the violence, despair, loneliness, and delusion that have marked lives in Guantánamo's borderlands. Winner of the Luciole D'Or award for Best Drama at the Cannes World Film Festival in March 2023, *La espera*, as Reynaldo Lastre has written, is singular within Cuban cinema for the dramatic density with which it imbues the frequently neglected border zones near the base.

Ana Luz García Calzada, a longtime resident of the city of Guantánamo and a fixture on its literary scene, includes two short stories with aspiring migrants as protagonists in her 1995 collection *Heavy Rock*. Although in the introduction to the recent English translation of these stories, by Jessica Adams, García Calzada describes her migrant characters as "so-called illegal emigrants, who jeopardize others' lives while risking their own to reach the base" (174), her fictional portrayal of these characters is deeply sympathetic. The first story, "Breathing Room" is a third-person account of a young man who attempts to swim across Guantánamo Bay to the naval base under the cover of a total, blinding darkness. Long before he reaches the base, his sudden movement triggers a mine, a searchlight, and a siren. He makes a quick and terrified retreat at the sound of approaching border guards: "Warning shots," and then "the cars, the guns, and the dogs barking" (179). Assuming that he is being pursued, he lifts himself through a sewage outlet into the bedroom of an unsuspecting woman who agrees to cover for him when soldiers and dogs enter the house, such that he escapes arrest for his attempt to leave. "Kites," García Calzada's second story about attempted migration to the base, ends more grimly. The Guantánamo fence line here is a site of extreme physical violence: not a crossing point but an end point where the migrating body is blown apart. The story opens with two brothers, Luis and Raúl, who plan to follow their emigrant parents to the United States by crossing illegally to the naval base. Hiding near the border at nighttime, waiting to launch their escape, their bodies are transformed by fear of the soldiers whom they know are nearby. Raúl becomes highly agitated, losing self-control and risking discovery; to keep him quiet, Luis knocks him to the ground and then falls asleep dreaming of a kite flying away to freedom. The dream recurs horrifically in the reality to which Luis awakens: Raúl, in his impatience to complete the migration attempt, has advanced to the fence that marks the border and is being blasted apart by a mine, his limbs rising then falling to the ground, like "a bloody kite, destroyed" (178).

Similar fates befall the main characters in a story by Roberto de Jesús Quiñónes, who has been on PEN International and Amnesty International's watch lists as a dissident journalist, lawyer, and writer and, as documented in a report by the Inter-American Commission on Human Rights, in 2019 was imprisoned for a year by the Cuban government for unauthorized reporting on a trial at the Guantánamo Municipal Tribunal ("Resolution 24/2021"). In Quiñónes's 2015 story "La fuga" (The Escape), the border is once again the place where the migrant body and the language to narrate it fall apart. The story follows the travails of an engineer, Arsenio, and an old friend (the narrator), both imprisoned in Cuba because of unsubstantiated allegations that they have attempted to leave the country. In anticipation of the difficulty of rebuilding their professional lives after their release, and having heard of others' success in escaping via the base, the two concoct a plan to cross the fence line themselves. They flee the prison and after an arduous trek through the no-man's-land at the edge of the base, watching the movements of distant border guards, they see lights they believe to be from the base. As Arsenio reaches toward the narrator for a celebratory embrace, he is blown up by a mine. The narrator's senses are overcome by the horror of the spectacle: "A rough, horrific sound arose from the water as Arsenio flew through the air in pieces" (29). Paralyzed by what he names as terror, the narrator swims toward the base; there the story ends. There is no clear way out for this migrant, whose psychological disintegration, like that of Luis in García Calzada's "Kites," mirrors the physical fragmentation of his companion, and who appears as a victim of both his immediate circumstance and a larger historical context.

"Kites," "Breathing Room," and "The Escape" depict migrants who, although their movements are under surveillance by border guards and their attempts to leave are illegal and "counterrevolutionary," do not figure as anyone's enemy. Rather, they are frightened, traumatized characters with close ties to their immediate families and local communities. Against this context, one of the more striking stories in the corpus of Guantánamo borderland fiction, for the identity of the protagonist as much as for the elaboration of his fears and compassions, is Estupiñán Zaldívar's "Abducción." Told from the perspective of a border guard, introduced only as "the Soldier," the story casts defense of the border as an experience of isolation and intense psychological pressure. The Soldier is a scared and homesick young man on military service, stationed with an equally fearful colleague at a point on the border where migrants often attempt to escape, which is therefore known to be particularly dangerous for guards. The initial fear to which he and his fellow guard succumb is that they will fail in their duty to intercept migrants and that they will themselves be sanctioned as a consequence. They exchange hearsay about a previous incident in which border guards who were unable to prevent an escape were effectively construed, and punished, as enemies of the revolution, and briefly jailed for their failure. They are most afraid that, despite being assigned to vigilance of the border, they are themselves under surveillance: "Someone is watching us at this very moment" (30). Exacerbating their fear is the bleak landscape around them, a sterile scene of cement and barbed wire that, in seeming devoid of life, renders their own sense of humanity fragile. They imagine that they are being watched not by other Cuban soldiers, nor by US guards, nor even by "enemy" migrants, but by extraterrestrial forces that they can neither see nor control and that threaten to abduct them at any moment. Acutely aware of, and terrified by, their own vulnerability, they accept that it makes little difference whether they are threatened by "ill-doers or aliens" and that the role of "enemy" at the border is as available to them as it is to anyone else (64).

Ross's *La espera* was filmed over a four-day period in late 2021, in the house formerly inhabited by Guantánamo's most prominent poet,

Regino Eladio Boti y Barreiro (1878–1958), and now the home of his grandson, Regino Rodríguez Boti, who plays the film's eponymous main character. The house's interior and verdant patio are its setting, and this restricted spatial focus buoys the intensity of the film's primary drama: the loneliness and bare brutality of Regino's life as a widow, as he lives through days of monotonous routine and nights of delusional but heartbroken fantasy. The human tragedy of *La espera* has another specific location, however, marked visually by the panoramic shots of Guantánamo Bay Naval Base that open the film and punctuate it throughout, alternating Cuban military watchtowers with US ones, and marked aurally by a soundtrack that poses a violent alternative to the carefully curated sampling of regional Guantánamo music that accompanies most of the scenes. This second soundtrack is composed of loud explosions that shatter the quiet of Regino's house and sleep and occur when land mines are detonated by migrants attempting to cross from Cuba to the base. These lives lost to mines or migration have a makeshift memorial on the rooftop of Regino's home: each explosion coincides with his discovery of migrants' discarded shoes on his doorstep, which he then throws up to his roof. In the absence of public acknowledgement within Cuba of lives lost this way, the assemblage of shoes—their permanence attesting to the transience of the beings who once wore them—is reminiscent of more formal collections of the shoes of the disappeared, like those in Colombian artist Doris Salcedo's *Atrabilarios* (1996) or preserved at the Auschwitz-Birkenau Memorial and Museum.[24] Migrants, the alternative and unseen protagonists of *La espera*, are further acknowledged by matchstick models Regino builds in reference to the work of Cuban artist Geny Jarrosay; Ross has claimed in interviews that each matchstick represents a Cuban migrant, such that the lighting of a matchstick replica of Cuba in one of the film's later scenes is a powerful symbol of the country's own destruction.[25]

The Border Brigade wields its presence in *La espera* in ways that reveal both its uncompromising violence as a collective entity and the vulnerability of the individuals who comprise it: as a force defending the Cuban Revolution, it destroys indiscriminately, even as its own soldiers, compassionate in their own right, become its victims. Aside from the hallucinatory appearances of his deceased wife that come to Regino at night, he has three regular visitors. The first is Moya, played by the Cuban artist Ramón Moya, depicted as a free spirit who sits for Regino to draw his portrait and leads him in ungainly meditation sessions. The second is an unnamed and always uniformed soldier of the Border Brigade, assigned to watch Regino for suspect activity but instead a loyal friend who borrows books of poetry. The third is a dog, whom the soldier entrusts to Regino's care as his colleagues who once harbored her now consider her a traitor to the fatherland for having crossed the border to the base, where she was fed by US soldiers. Each of these visitors is lost, one by one, to the violence of the Border Brigade and the hostility that underpins the Guantánamo borderlands. Moya is killed by soldiers who see him playacting with an old gun he finds at Regino's house. The dog, mirroring an incident of extreme violence rumored to have taken place in the 1960s, is hanged as a traitor by the Border Brigade, left to rot next to the base's fence line as an example and deterrent to others, human or not, who might be tempted to cross.[26] Finally, the soldier himself—relieved of his duties for refusing to kill the dog, too ashamed to return to his hometown, and leaving his boots along with a note at Regino's door—decides to attempt to cross the minefield and seek asylum at the base. The soldier, no longer able to defend the revolution against those whom he knows are not its enemies, whether they are stray dogs or desperate human beings, himself becomes the migrant.

On the Cuban side of the Guantánamo fence line, guards—be these the commanders and foot soldiers of the Border Brigade, or the Cuban citizens who, marshalled to protect the revolution, fulfill a similar role—are superficially united by a bellicose rhetoric that has underpinned their leaders' political speech for over sixty years. The fracturing of their "enemy" into two quite distinct adversaries, however, fractures and undermines the possibility of defense itself. For all its abstraction, US imperialism is a more coherent and easily externalized enemy than the enemy within, namely the fellow Cuban taking extraordinary risks in order to migrate from a country in which an entrenched culture of sacrifice of civil liberties and material comforts has worn thin for many. Fictional representations have approached this latter enemy's fear, torment, and destruction: in the case of Quiñónes, in tandem with a broader public life of dissidence and journalistic activism and, in that of García Calzada, retroactively retracting support for the figure of the migrant when her stories were published in the United States. Estupiñán Zaldívar's story and Ross's film, meanwhile, in their portrayals of the interchangeable vulnerabilities of the migrant and the border guard, lay bare the fragility, and ultimate unviability, of hostile person-to-person engagements on the Cuban side of the fence line.

ENEMIES AND APOLOGIES

Unlike Estupiñán Zaldívar and Ross's soldiers, Chris Arendt, the former cellblock guard at Joint Task Force Guantánamo quoted at the beginning of this chapter, discovers peace on his nighttime patrol as well as an impulse to apologize that is a step toward the conciliation that the intimate friendships formed between guards and detainees implicitly impel. Terry Holdbrooks, for example, follows through on a similar impulse, reporting that he apologized to a prisoner and begged "please do not hate me" (*Traitor?* 71); former guard Brandon Neely wrote a letter of apology to detainees he had watched over at Guantánamo (Stetler). Former detainee David Hicks, too, recalls guards issuing a broad, collective apology to him in the name of the authorities that they serve: "Some soldiers," he writes, "apologized on behalf of their government for what was happening to me and the other detainees" (298).

Indeed, in the absence of any public gesture of atonement on the part of the US government for abuses at Guantánamo—and in a murky context of undisclosed repatriation and resettlement deals for former detainees, often with countries unable to guarantee even the most basic level of stability—it has been left to individual former guards and detainees to effect small-scale reconciliation and repair.[27] A primary example is Chris Arendt, who, having admitted in his interview with *Esquire* that "one thing I miss is the cups"—Styrofoam cups that detainees would write and draw "lots of flowers" on, before seeing them confiscated and sent to military intelligence as potential evidence of conspiracy—joined with fellow veteran Aaron Hughes and artist Amber Ginsburg to enact repair through art and ritual in the Tea Project. The project has staged a series of gatherings in which participants drink tea from cups carved and decorated to resemble those that detainees made on Guantánamo's cellblocks, a practice that "reveals our personal and collective entanglements with current and inherited patterns of violence and resilience" (Hughes and Ginsburg 17). Central to the exhibit *Remaking the Exceptional: Tea, Torture, and Reparations | Chicago to Guantánamo*, shown at DePaul Art Museum in Chicago in 2022, the Tea Project's gatherings spurred *Invitation to Tea*, an archive and recipe book authored by

Hughes and Ginsburg that reflects on tea-drinking rituals in the countries where current and former Guantánamo detainees hold citizenship.

Other guard-detainee friendships have been renewed in post-release contexts, with roles sometimes jokingly reversed for media appearances: Brandon Neely reunited with former detainees Ruhal Ahmed and Shafiq Rasul in London, courtesy of Facebook and the BBC, and was photographed being restrained by them (Stetler); when former guard Albert Melise visited Moazzam Begg's home in England, Begg reminded him that, this time, "I got the keys" (El). Mohamedou Ould Slahi's post-release friendship, and reunion in Mauritania, with his guard Steve Wood has been subject to particular attention, in both a *New Yorker* investigative report by Ben Taub and the short film *My Brother's Keeper*, made by the *Guardian* journalist Laurence Topham. Forgiveness is an implied response on the part of former detainees in each of these encounters but nowhere with more candor, and what Martha Nussbaum has termed "unconditional forgiveness that lies very close to unconditional love and generosity" (77), than in the brief address Mohamedou Ould Slahi gave to the American Civil Liberties Union soon after his release from fifteen years of isolation and torture at Guantánamo. "I wholeheartedly forgive everyone who wronged me during my detention," Slahi said, "and I forgive because forgiveness is my inexhaustible resource" ("First Video of Author Mohamedou Slahi").

Such gestures of apology and forgiveness, private in the sense that they play out between relatively powerless individuals but public in the attention they have garnered, have few counterparts in the broader Guantánamo region that extends across the base's fence line into Cuba. Apologies issued by the Cuban government have been ambiguous and extremely rare, and directed at neither the imperialist nor the counterrevolutionary enemy.[28] State control of the military, including of the movements and interactions of junior recruits, is such that an apology on the part of a soldier, in his or her capacity as such, is barely conceivable. Nevertheless, apology and forgiveness are gestures that model and resonate with existing conciliations within Cuban culture, at their most commonplace and their most vulnerable in the figure of the migrant, who, despite being cast as the enemy at the Guantánamo fence line, is barely distinguishable, in many familial and communal contexts, from the revolution's citizen defenders. These encounters with and proximities to enemies—played out in a space that is, paradoxically, at the margins and the political forefront in Cuba and the United States—nevertheless trace an intricate and local network of intimacies, where power imbalances are addressed, if not redressed, through small-scale ways of finding common ground. Guantánamo as a region emerges from a scene of troubled and uncertain hostilities, on both sides of the base's fence line, as a stage for low-level engagements that disrupt the hierarchies and physical dividing lines imposed upon it; as a stage, that is, for uneven intimacies and fraught symmetries, with too many opportunities for recognition to stand coherently as hostile territory.

CHAPTER 3
HOME

"Nobody has chosen to live in this place," says artist Debi Cornwall of Guantánamo Bay Naval Base; more ominously, former detainee David Hicks hears an interrogator describe the base as "a place where even dogs won't live" (206).[1] And yet, despite the compromised, constrained, or coerced nature of many people's residency at and around Guantánamo, traces of the affective, spatial, and social strategies that make a home mark the accounts of even the most dispossessed of the base's occupants, as they do for those Cubans who live near the border. Detainees held at the base's high-security cellblocks, their belongings confiscated, chart in their memoirs geographies of the familiar. The community journalism of US Navy servicepeople and their families subscribes to an image of the base as small-town America even as it hosts one of the world's most notorious prisons, and Cubans living on the base tend nostalgically to their houses, the country of their birth visible in the distance. Artists working in the border town of Caimanera draw on the traditional materials of local labor—fishing nets, driftwood, salt—to reflect on the subtleties of their cohabitation with the US base. Reading these expressions of home together, this chapter proposes that, despite its starkly different manifestations, "home" has a necessarily provisional and fractured quality at Guantánamo: a quality, precisely, around which the Guantánamo borderland coheres.

"Home" at Guantánamo depends on a complex interplay between the indefinite, the short-term and the permanent—the temporalities in which detainees, members, and families of the US military, and Cubans, respectively, dwell there. These temporalities dictate the making of home in all its dimensions, beginning with the experience of the immediate environment that provides the basis for Yi-Fu Tuan's distinction between place and space: "Place is security, space is freedom. We are attached to one, and long for the other. There is no place like home" (3). The experience of home as shelter, comfort, and familiarity, forged through a relationship with the home's physical structure and the objects that furnish it, on the one hand, and with the community and environmental locale around it, on the other, is similarly shaped by the temporality of residency at Guantánamo as well as by the starkly differing degrees of restriction keeping one there, as, too, are the more interpersonal inflections of living at home. The presence of family and the ability to extend hospitality at Guantánamo—to invite others to enjoy one's home or, in Jacques Derrida's rendering, to allow guests to "take place in the place I offer them, without asking of them either reciprocity (entering into a pact) or even their names" (Derrida and Dufourmantelle 25)—is largely governed by why one lives there. The same can be said of experiences of home that draw one dwelling place into contact with others as community or, most stridently for the Cubans who inhabit Guantánamo, as homeland.

British photographer Edmund Clark has offered a sustained reflection on the idea of Guantánamo as home in his 2010 exhibit and book *Guantánamo: If the Light Goes Out*. Clark describes his project as "a study of home, of a very particular home at a very particular time in our history, and the lives of people whose paths crossed on 45 square miles of Cuba, cut off from the rest of the world by razor wire and water" (n.p.). The sixty-seven plates in his book are drawn from three different spaces with claims to "home": Guantánamo's detention camps, the living and recreational areas provided for members of the US military at the base, and, as a third rendition of "home," the rooms, houses, and gardens, primarily in Europe and the Middle East, to which released detainees returned after their time at the base. The plates are thematically nonsequential—for example, plates 4, 5, and 6 show a bedroom in a post-release "Home," an isolation unit in Camp 1, and the screen of the open-air cinema for naval base personnel and their families, respectively, and Clark accounts for this "disjointed narrative" as an attempt "to convey the sense of disorientation and dislocation central to the daily experience of incarceration at Guantánamo." Sixteen of the plates are titled "Home," and, while all appear to be taken in residential spaces beyond Guantánamo, their subjects are off-kilter as a group—sunlight shining through a closed curtain, a child's plastic toy in the corner of a carpeted room, a neatly mown lawn in a yard with a shed, a fence, and a modest-looking brick house—leaving no consolidated impression of what even this "home" is. Images shot at the base have more varied and descriptive titles, those taken at the camps implying austerity, surveillance and pain (a bare bathtub at Camp 4, a call button for interrogators and guards in Camp 5, a mobile force-feeding chair), while there is more range and, implicitly, more comfort, in the military spaces.

Absent from all Clark's images are human faces; indeed, the one image of a human body is exemplary for the scene of corporal disempowerment that it implies: it shows the legs and torso of a detainee lying on a bunk, taken through glass in which are dimly reflected the torso and legs of a prison guard. Among the tight restrictions on reporting from Guantánamo is a prohibition on human faces, and it becomes key to the disjointed quality of Clark's narrative that all versions of "home" are depopulated: people leave their traces in less frontal ways (a neatly made bed, rumpled sheets, a toothbrush). Nevertheless, there is a corpus of narratives in media other than photography—memoir, newspaper journalism, documentary film, and installation art, for example—that offer a broader range of perspectives on the relationship between Guantánamo and "home." These are the focus of this chapter and they form a corpus whose third space is not the vastly distant countries to which detainees return post-release, but rather the area just across the fence line whose faintly twinkling lights illuminate the final image in Clark's series. The Cuban province of Guantánamo has, arguably, as much a claim to the base as "home" as do those who regulate the residency of current inhabitants, namely the US government, a claim that itself affects what it is to live in close proximity to the base, in the border towns of Caimanera and Boquerón. While the materials that I bring to bear from this third space are substantively different, and scant, in relation to those from the base, they are nevertheless a crucial piece of an archive whose very unevenness speaks to the fragile cohesion of Guantánamo as a region and as a home.

HOME AND THE CELL

To be imprisoned—or "detained," as per the specific euphemism in use at Guantánamo—is, by design, to be deprived of the liberties and comforts of home. And yet, as Jennifer Turner and Victoria Knight observe in their edited collection *The Prison Cell: Embodied and Everyday Spaces of Incarceration* (2020), the prison cell is a de facto living space, whatever its qualities, and "policy-makers often diminish the significance and individuality of the embodied and everyday practices that are critical to the lived experience of carceral space" (6). In her contribution to Turner and Knight's collection, Irene Martí notes that the prison cell, as a place to sleep, "spend unobserved time" and "experience privacy," affords some of the features of a home and is likely the only space within a prison complex to do so. Her research on incarceration is mindful of the spatial and temporal dimensions of home-making, as she explores "how prisoners sentenced to indefinite detention in Switzerland *inhabit* the prison cell" (122) and how they "use, appropriate and (re)arrange the institutional spatio-temporal order that defines the prison cell through individual practices and thereby create personal and intimate space" (126). Consistent with Ben Crewe and colleagues' studies of adaptation and agency among long-term prisoners in England and Wales, Martí finds that some prisoners resolutely consider the cell "as a place to be, but not to live" (127) while others inhabit it as a "home," a practice that takes shape through a spatial domestication, via the inclusion and arrangement of personal items, and through "domestic patterns of movement and activity" that include social interactions and the receiving of guests (127).

It goes without saying that the detention centers at Guantánamo afford little of the legal, psychological, and physical infrastructure that permit the creation of a "home" in the Swiss and British prison cells that are the subjects of Martí and Crewe's studies. The refusal of the designation as "prisoner of war," in favor of the term *detainee* that persists as one among many lexical neologisms of the war on terror, was predicated on a denial of legal rights, and the same impulse to deprive has dictated the space as much as the interpersonal dimensions of the Guantánamo cell, particularly during the early years of the detention centers' existence. Camp Delta, for example, one of the first and largest areas of the detention center to be installed, what the *Miami Herald* has termed the first "housing improvement" for detainees after the open cages of Camp X-Ray, was constructed by Halliburton as a complex of shipping containers welded into over seven hundred individual cells, ranging in size from around eight to ninety-six square feet into which were fitted a toilet, a sleeping shelf, and, in some cases, a window slit.[2]

The *Camp Delta Standard Operating Procedures (SOP)*, issued in 2004 and publicly leaked in 2007, stipulated that detainees were to be provided with "basic needs." Detainees would not, they stated, "be deprived of adequate shelter, food, or water at any time" (*SOP* 8–2). The *SOP* also regulated the additional items permitted within a cell to support basic needs as well as personal care, religious worship, and entertainment, all of which can be understood, to quote Turner and Knight, as "embodied and everyday practices" (6) in the inhabiting, and potential homemaking, of a cell. It is, however, in the context of their restriction and potential confiscation that most personal items are listed in the *SOP*. A "Detainee Classification" System instituted at Camp Delta distributed privileges, listed generally as "items and activities," to the detainees in accordance with their degree of compliance, rated from levels 1 (high compliance) to 4 (low compliance). Items issued to compliant detainees under this system included additional toilet paper, pen and paper, and shampoo; among authorized activities were saving a meal for later, performing approved exercises in the cell or in the yard, and cold water after exercise (8.7). Confiscations were overwhelmingly targeted at "comfort items," a term used frequently in the *SOP* and including soap (a regular-sized bar was allowed only on level 1), a mattress (confiscated at level 4), an additional blanket (permitted at levels 1 and 2), and a Styrofoam cup (allowed at all levels except the most severe, unless a detainee had written on it, in which case it was to be retained as "evidence"). Prayer beads and a prayer cap were also classified as comfort items, despite their central place in the religious practice of many detainees (B.15).

Although the cells in which Guantánamo detainees have described living are different from the interrogation and torture rooms that Elaine Scarry discusses in *The Body in Pain: The Making and Unmaking of the World* (1985), the objects they contain are nevertheless conscripted into a form of what she calls "the mime of uncreating" the prisoner's world

(20). In normal contexts, Scarry argues, the room is "the simplest form of shelter" and expresses "the most benign potential of human life" (38). It is both a "magnification of the body" (38), in that it "keeps warm and safe the individual it houses" (38), and a "miniaturization of the world, of civilization" (38), its walls standing also as "independent objects . . . which realize the human being's impulse to project himself out into a space beyond the boundaries of the body" (39). In the torture situations that are Scarry's focus, however, not only is the world "reduced to a single room or set of rooms" (40), but the room, "in its structure and its content, is converted into a weapon, deconverted, undone" (41): chairs and beds become objects of pain rather than solace when tortured victims are chained to them for hours, as do soft drink bottles when they are beaten against a victim's head, and bathtubs when, in a chilling prefiguration of Guantánamo's waterboarding, they are used not to soothe but to scare (40–41). The comfort items distributed and withheld at Camp Delta in accordance with its Standard Operating Procedures are not weaponized in this same way but their categorization in relation to reward and punishment, rather than as supports that the body can take for granted, is a significant impediment, alongside the involuntary and indefinite dimensions of detention, to inhabiting the cell as home. Consonant with Scarry's reading, certain comfort items—the pillow, in particular—become endowed with significance in the cell's regulation of reward and punishment. Mohamedou Ould Slahi records the moment in which, having broken after months of torture and given a false confession, he was given a pillow, which he received "with a fake overwhelming happiness, and not because I was dying to get a pillow," but rather, "because I took the pillow as a sign of the end of physical torture" (*Guantánamo Diary* 289). A pillow, moreover, is one of the items that for Lakhdar Boumediène would affirm the humanity that his detention has denied: "I want a pillow and a real mattress . . . a mattress for human beings" (199).

Detainees' accounts of their experience at Guantánamo cast the idea of home with suspicion, skepticism, and despair. In his 2010 memoir, *Guantánamo: My Journey*, David Hicks, an Australian captured in Afghanistan and held at Guantánamo from 2002 until 2007, connects the cruel excuse for a home that are his various cells at Guantánamo specifically to their spatial dimension. He is first held in one of the outdoor wire enclosures at Camp X-Ray, a space that does not afford even the minimal protections of a cell: "They were open to the wind, sun, dust and rain and offered no respite" (214). When he is moved to Camp Delta, he notes that "the most obvious fact about this facility was how small the cages were: one step wide, two steps long" (236). Equipped with a sleeping shelf, a sink, and a hole in the floor for body waste, "the entire enclosure must have been no bigger than an average suburban toilet" (236–37). The "worst realization" for Hicks as he occupies this space at Camp Delta is that he is being "housed" (237) in a shipping container, a space designed for cargo rather than human habitation. When he is moved to Camp Echo, to a windowless and punitively overchilled cell that, at four steps long, was "the biggest living space I had been kept in yet" (291), he is deeply reluctant to acknowledge that "this green, painted metal cage was probably going to be my new home" (291). *Housing*, *home*, and *living* are words and modes of being that Hicks's memoir insistently overrides with designations antithetical to human habitation: "cage," "container," and "forest of diamond wire" (237). Indeed, in a long passage that describes the torment of ants and mice invading his cell in search of food, and the derision levied at him in the media for his violence toward these creatures, he redirects attention to what constitutes a human home: "The question that should have been asked," he insists, "is what were mice doing in my living space?" (251). The so-called comfort items meted out in the camps' warped reward system, Hicks recognizes, have little relation to the comfort one's home, or even one's own body, provides: "Anything more than a pair of shorts was now classed as 'comfort items' . . . even guys with false limbs had them taken away on Levels Two, Three and Four" (262).

Hicks's memoir includes a central, glossy insert whose stark division between Guantánamo and "home" is notable in format and content. The first half of the insert consists of maps: first, a stock map titled *Guantánamo Bay and Surrounds*, whose smaller frame locates Guantánamo Bay in Cuba and the Caribbean while its larger detail situates each of the camps in which Hicks was held within the boundaries of the US naval base. The following eight pages are four pairs of more schematic diagrams: in black and white, they appear as grids within grids, the diagrams of Camps X-Ray and Echo zooming in to the single cube that Hicks marks as his. Diagrams of Camp Delta denote the camps and blocks within this large complex as well as a less angular, more animated illustration that includes a shadowy human shape, captioned

"Camp Delta cages. A cage is one-sixth of a shipping container—my home for years" (n.p.). The second half of this section is a burst of color photographs populated by the often smiling, active figures of Hicks and his companions in a life before and after Guantánamo: it begins with Hicks in primary school and as a teenager in Australia and ends with a post-release wedding portrait and a group shot with his large extended family. In the middle section are similarly vibrant photographs that trace his unusual but, he insists, noncriminal path to and from his Australian home: scenes from his time training with the Kosovo Liberation Army in Albania, widely circulated photographs that falsely identify Hicks as a combatant in Afghanistan, aiming a gun at US or Australian troops; protests by Hicks's father and fellow Australians, demanding his release from Guantánamo. The implication of this graphic insert in Hicks's memoir is that detention facilities at Guantánamo are of an entirely different order—spatially, visually, and affectively, from his home or any human home; the former is "home" only in derisive, terrified, quotation marks, and to consider it a true home would be the ultimate admission of defeat. "The most dangerous thing to do is adapt," Hicks is advised by one of the few visiting members of the International Committee of the Red Cross to whom he is allowed access, "because you will keep adapting until there is nothing left" (219).

Ahmed Errachidi, a Moroccan citizen and former British resident held at Guantánamo from 2002 to 2007, is similarly derisive toward associating the word *home* with Guantánamo, and attentive to the spatial abuses that render this association impossible. His recollection of his arrival at Guantánamo is accompanied by a detailed description of Camp Delta's layout, a verbal map that corresponds to Hicks's visual documentation of the camps, cellblocks, and cells: "Each cell measured about nine by seven foot (some were bigger than others by a foot or two) and they were made out of a diamond-patterned metal mesh, save for the back walls which, being the walls of the container, were solid metal in which a slit window had been cut, almost like a postbox" (76). The cells are minimally furnished, with a metal sheet and thin mattress, a latrine, and a sink; there is nothing inside them to support the function of preparing or consuming food, as food was "pushed" through a slot in the door that also served as an access point for applying handcuffs (77). The space, once again, seems unwelcoming and antithetical to the presence of human life and the possibility of home: "This metallic environment—the only thing non-metallic were the human beings—was to be my home for years" (76).

Even as he describes the sparseness and restricting size of his cell, however, Errachidi acknowledges a second social, rather than spatial, notion of home, one in which he can find solace. He recalls how on most cellblocks "breezes would bring in the sea's salty moistness" (75) and how from his first cell he saw "Guantánamo's endless blue sky, across which a giant white cloud floated" (76). Describing the interior of his cell, he includes the black arrow on the corner of the bed provided to orient detainees toward Mecca, with an inscription reminding them that it is ten thousand miles away (76). Nevertheless, this surreptitious admitting of the outside anticipates Errachidi's holding of two compatible but different notions of home simultaneously and of finding some solace in one of them. The Swiss prisoners whom Irene Martí describes make "home" in their cells by rendering it domestic in its physical and social aspects; while the first option is foreclosed to Errachidi, he embraces the second.

The title of Errachidi's memoir, *The General: The Ordinary Man Who Challenged Guantanamo*, refers to the nickname he earned at Guantánamo through de facto political leadership as a negotiator with military authorities. He was, at the same time, a spiritual leader for other detainees as well as for certain guards. There are also moments in Errachidi's memoir in which he assumes a social centrality on the cellblocks, subversively extending hospitality from his cell and inhabiting it as a home in this sense, even as he cannot do so in others. With references to Jacques Derrida's essays on hospitality, and to the work of Emmanuel Levinas, Moroccan writer Tahar Ben Jelloun has written of the powerful act that opening one's home to a guest represents: "The act of entertaining a guest is something that both honors and humanizes the host. But as well as filling the heart, it does something more. It makes the guest recognize me, the host, as someone capable of sharing" (2). To the space that he has named as dehumanizing in its physical presentation, Errachidi, a cook who achieved some success in London's restaurant world with his gift for livening up bland dishes, introduces hospitality as an alternative way of making home. He writes in his memoir of how, despite their limited social interaction, he would nevertheless "love to entertain" (125) those near him by re-creating the hospitality he would extend to them were he really at home. He would call out from his cell, and "they would listen to me as I used words to paint delicious meals for them. I'd ask them to imagine they were guests at my house in Morocco sitting around a large dining table. I'd begin to describe different types of seafood meals ... For a moment we'd forget where we were" (125).

Interviewed by Tim Wild for an article titled "The Restaurant at Guantanamo Bay," published in September 2020 in the somewhat unlikely venue of *Bon Appetit* magazine, Errachidi expands on the effects of the hospitality he extended to others on his cellblock: "They all had a good time sitting around the table, eating all those beautiful dishes and desserts and juices and chocolates" (125), and he would then "bring them back to reality ... in a nice, gentle way" (125). What Wild names as "Errachidi's desire to feed and care for people"—or to care through food, as a form of hospitality—extends, in fact, beyond people, in one of the most startling and nurturing episodes in his memoir. Having recalled the imaginary feasts he would concoct for his fellow detainees, Errachidi continues, "In addition to these moments of humor and conversation in the standard blocks, I became aware that I was not entirely alone when I was in punishment either. Visitors would come in their dozens, three times a day, after every meal. I'd sit with them and enjoy their company" (126). Visits to detainees are heavily restricted, and would have been unlikely to include anyone outside the US military aside from authorized and rare meetings with defense lawyers and members of the International Committee of the Red Cross. The "dozens" of visitors whom Errachidi receives, however, are ants, whom he feeds and protects from the heavy boots of angry guards. While for David Hicks, animal life in the cell is further proof of his forced removal from humanity, Errachidi finds a different perspective. Consonant with Ben Jelloun's understanding of a humanizing hospitality, Errachidi sees the ants reciprocate his generosity by restoring to his life a "sense that normal life still existed" (126). Their presence, he writes, "made me smile and it comforted me" (126). In the absence of a home that can offer physical comfort—indeed, confined to a cell where comfort items are explicitly restricted—he finds some security in a highly inventive form of hospitality, in reshaping "home" as a social space.

NAVY LIFE AT GUANTÁNAMO

In close proximity to the detainees at Guantánamo's camps, but vastly different in their level of domestic comfort, the base's military and military-affiliated population inhabits a space of neatly ordered houses, baseball fields, playgrounds, movie theaters, and what has often been touted as Cuba's only McDonald's: an entirely contrasting scene to which visiting photographers and, particularly, the *Miami Herald* and *New York Times* journalist Carol Rosenberg, have paid considerable attention.³ The oldest of the United States' overseas bases, Naval Station Guantánamo Bay had sheltered US Navy personnel in varying numbers since its lease from Cuba was established as a term of the Platt Amendment in 1903. As Jonathan Hansen recounts, by 1921 the base "housed roughly eleven hundred marines and laborers on a regular basis and could accommodate up to twenty thousand sailors when the fleet pulled in" (147). Its residential infrastructure was developing, with "hospitals, clubhouses, canteens, tennis and handball courts" (147). A 1921 article in *National Geographic* that included these details and others, Hansen writes, effectively introduced American readers to "a new thing: the colonization of the nation's overseas bases and the cultural contact and social interaction that this entailed" (147). In the following decades, navy personnel and their families continued to enjoy tennis, swimming, bridge, and moderately quiet lives (Hansen 164) at Guantánamo until the onset of World War II and an ambitious infrastructural project that was drawn close to completion in a hurried three years. By 1943, "some ten thousand Cubans, Jamaicans and West Indians labored on the base alongside four thousand U.S. servicemen and civilians" (181), an expansion that "created the footprint of office buildings, warehouses, jetties, airstrips, magazines, and residential neighborhoods still visible today" (182). The 1940s and 1950s represent the peak of the base's population and activity as well as its porosity to Cuban and Caribbean labor, via a contract labor force that, as Jana K. Lipman has studied, was obliged to accept precarious terms and low wages, and that significantly altered the economic basis of neighboring Cuban towns (*Guantánamo* 38–60). Cuba's break in relations with the United States in 1961 isolated the base and dramatically diminished its population: the expulsion of the majority of Cuban commuters in 1964, in retaliation for Fidel Castro's cutting off of the base's water supply, left contract work open principally to Jamaicans and Filipinos, and navy personnel and their families led quiet lives—often stiflingly so—aside from evacuations during major political disruptions, among them the Cuban Missile Crisis and the Haitian/Cuban Rafter Crisis of the early 1990s. For the remainder of that decade and into the 2000s, the base remained a low-key place, of little notoriety: Captain Robert Buehn, its commander from 2000 to 2003, remembers arriving for what "probably looked as though it would be a quiet tour" (Evans 1). This was a quiet dramatically disrupted by the rendition of almost 780 detainees and an expansion of the military-affiliated population from 2,600 before January 2002 to over 10,000 by 2005 (Byington, "Housing Town Hall" 1).

Those US Navy families who have lived at Guantánamo over the past century have inhabited a place with similarities to the many other military bases that have dotted the globe during that time period, set up to provide basic but comprehensive support for residents' professional, community, and family lives in ways that, as David Vine observes, "often replicate self-contained American towns" (2). Like a small town in the United States, Guantánamo Bay Naval Base has a school, a hospital, a library, a baseball field, a drive in movie theater, places of worship, and opportunities for recreation that recruiters have touted liberally.[4] The base, though, has the added anomalies that come with there being no "off-base" recreational options since the break in relations with the Castro government and its own set of Cold War anachronisms that spill over, as it were, from Cuba. Architecturally, commercially, and in terms of the willfully idealized strength of its community, the base maintains a certain aesthetic of slowness that harks back to the 1950s. The "Mayberry" of *The Andy Griffith Show* is a moniker frequently and affectionately adopted by the base's current and former residents for its associations with a small-town America of close-knit families and wholesome activities.

For military families, "home" is inevitably defined by the particularities of the large military community of which they are part. In his interviews with the children of US military personnel who lead the itinerant lives of multiple postings, Edward Queair records many as reflecting that, as a "military brat," you "don't have a home to go home to" (185). Several interviewees describe themselves as holding onto certain places "emotionally, or metaphorically," in the absence of a physical home to which to return (184–85). Others, Queair observes, define home as "the place they eventually returned to in the U.S." that "already possessed a long history of generational family attachment," while still others "saw *Home* as where they were in the present—"where, with their families and careers, they invested in and established roots" (199) or "only in its abstract, in its quality as a container for things held dear, a kind of visceral evocation of the proverb 'Home is where the heart is'" (199). The affective associations of the "small-town" community, attributed to Guantánamo Bay Naval Base throughout much of its history, often emerged in Queair's interviewees' recollections of living on military bases, which was to them "representative of an iconic, beneficial, small-town world that succeeded in providing a positive (despite acknowledged irritations), unique environment within which to grow up" (213).

To portray Guantánamo Bay Naval Base as "home," and to maintain it as such against all odds and evidence, is the apparent project of the naval station's weekly community newspaper, the *Guantánamo Bay Gazette*, whose issues from 2002 to 2017 are the basis for my reading in this chapter.[5] Although produced as part of the US Department of Defense's Defense Media Activity operations, with journalists primarily drawn from the American Forces Press Service until its closure in 2015, the *Gazette* shares much of the general animus, and many of the specific features, of community newspapers more generally, including the transition from print to digital-only format that has marked the latter in the twenty-first century. Drawing on Benedict Anderson's foundational work on the role of print capitalism in allowing "rapidly growing numbers of people to think about themselves, and to relate themselves to others, in profoundly new ways" (Anderson 36; quoted in Funk 576) and hence to form imagined communities that laid the groundwork for modern nationalisms, Marcus Funk finds in contemporary scholarship on community newspapers a tendency to "retain a special connection with local readers" (577) via "more locally focused content" (577), with sections such as obituaries being of particular importance for reiterating the identity and history of a local community. The *Guantánamo Bay Gazette* does not have a regular Obituaries section—one of many tell-tale signs that this is a demographically unusual community, with a very small population of elderly residents—but birth announcements are frequent, and the newspaper includes regular sections designed to shape a sense of regularity, neighborliness, and close-knit community. Among these are the schedules of worship services for the various religions and Christian denominations represented at the base, meetings of the Single Parents Support Group and the Spouses Organization, movie listings for the base's three outdoor cinemas, the Career Counselor's Corner and "Gitmo Shopper," and the classifieds section that offers cribs, dining sets, and diving suits for sale or announces the loss of a quiche dish, with four-digit contact phone numbers reiterating the simplicity of communication at the base. Shorter-lived sections include the monthly "Best-Kept Yard" award announcement, the "Favorite Places" column that introduces hidden corners of the base, and the "Gitmo Gab" column in which select interviewees answer questions about life on the base. These regular weekly or monthly sections are punctuated by a reliable annual calendar of holidays and events: the Easter Egg hunt, the Fourth of July fireworks, the Halloween parade, Veterans' Day commemorations, the community Thanksgiving dinner and the Christmas lights, and an annual garden party, introduced by the wife of the base's lieutenant commander as a "new tradition" to honor the hospitality of "the ladies of Gitmo" ("A Garden Party" 8). Other annual contributions reflect the population and location of the base more narrowly: preparations for Military Family Appreciation Week and for the hurricanes that inevitably sweep through the base in early fall. Predictable in their occurrence but varying in their content are reports on the concerts and spectacles coordinated by the Morale, Welfare, and Recreation service, whose Guantánamo coordinator in 2005 received a humanitarian award at the LA Music Awards for bringing Los Angeles–based entertainers to the base, among them well-known bands, cheerleading squads and, in 2006, the Vamphear Circus, whose performers produced their own short film, *Guantánamo Circus*, about their visit (Byington, "Basel to Receive").[6]

In addition to the regular sections and reports, whose regularity, as Anderson notes in his discussion of "calendrical coincidence" (33), is in and of itself important to the imagining of community, the *Guantánamo Bay Gazette* makes explicit and frequently reiterated investments in the "small-town America" dimension of the base's community, drawing on this for its construction of the base as home. A notable example is the farewell letter of the *Gazette*'s departing editor, JO1 Amy Kirk, in the October 1, 2004, edition. "One of the things I will miss most about Guantanamo Bay," Kirk writes, echoing the long-standing association of the base community with the Andy Griffith show, "is its 'Mayberry' feel" (Kirk, "Farewell" 10). She further elaborates, "I love that many of the residents know my name (if not my face). I love being able to say hello to most of the people I pass on the street or at the NEX, and I love having a name and a phone number already in my head when I need information"

(10). The "lack of variety" inherent in such a setting, though, is something she "will not miss" (10).

Junior Officer Kirk's depiction of the base as a small-town home is picked up in various headlines whose referents for "home" speak only to a very local readership. A call to "Keep Gitmo Beautiful" implores readers to "remember that Gitmo is not only a base, but also our home" (Schoenfeld 9); schoolchildren on a visit to the Lighthouse Historical Museum "learned a little bit about the place they call home" ("Teaching the Past" 5); when one of the two ferries that shuttle between the Windward and Leeward sides of the base returns from maintenance in February 2002, a month after the arrival to the base of the first detainees, the *Gazette*'s cover headline is "Home Sweet Home" (fig. 3.1). The *Gazette* reports frequently on homes in various forms. The idea of home propagated in the *Gazette*'s pages can pertain to individual housing units, some provided for military personnel posted alone and others for families, on which there is practical information from the base's housing office along with more community-oriented renderings, as in the Holiday Homes tours of festively decorated houses. "Home" is also deeply anchored in the institutions that sustain the community, primarily through its families: features on events and programs at the W. T. Sampson School, which serves elementary through high school students, appear almost weekly, and coverage of the Boy Scouts and sports teams are similarly staples. It is largely through an ideal of family life that the pleasures of living at Guantánamo are filtered in the *Gazette*, as they are in many recruiting strategies deployed to attract personnel to the base. The reopening of Ferry Landing Beach in April 2004 is announced with "Enjoy a day at the beach with your family at the newly renovated Ferry Landing Beach . . . This is a family beach—no alcohol is permitted" ("Ferry Landing Beach" 3). The extent of the affective associations of the base as home is further evident in its capacity to produce nostalgia in those who have left, as indicated by the *Gazette*'s reporting on the "reunion" visits of former residents, whose GitmoBay Association has organized trips to the base since 2014. For these visitors, most of whom lived on the base between the 1960s and 1990s, it is not a site to be associated with detention and the war on terror, but is rather "a quintessential American city that we just enjoy" (Kay 1).

The *Gazette* fiercely defends the base's integrity, as a home and community, as the arrival there in January 2002 of the first detainees and

Guantanamo Bay Gazette

CHINFO 2000 Merit Award Winner

Vol. 59 No. 7 Friday, February 15, 2002

Home Sweet Home

Photo by JOC Ric Evans

She's back! The familiar sight of YFB 93 was absent from Guantanamo Bay for several months while she underwent scheduled overhaul back in the states, but beginning last Friday, she began her familiar route from Windward to Leeward and back again, even sharing the duties with her sister ferry, YFB 92, on her first day back. Long-time residents of GTMO, if they were near the bay that afternoon, witnessed a sight that hadn't happened for some time, the two ferries passing each other at mid bay. That hadn't happened since the base population fell to a point where simultaneous departures from Leeward and Windward landings were no longer required.

OCSC Plans Cheese Gala, Casino Night

The OCSC is hosting a Wine, Cheese and Fondue Gala at the Sailing Center Feb. 22 at 6 pm. A variety of special cheeses and fondues will be served. Bring your favorite wine to sip and share. Tickets for the event are $5 and will be on sale at the NEX atrium Saturday, Feb. 9 from 10 am to noon. For more details, call Kathy at 2376.

Coming in March, OCSC's Casino Night. If you would like to learn how to be a dealer for the event, practice begins Thursday, Feb. 21 from 6 to 8 pm. Call Randi at 5444 for details.

BRIEFS

Black History Month at ES Media Center

Help your children learn about customs and traditions of the African-American culture. Visit the displays of traditional African-American ethnic objects and art work at the Elementary School Media Center.

The Black History children's book collection features African-American authors and biographies.

Media Center hours are 8 am to 4 pm, Monday-Friday. For more details, call 2207.

"Military Spouse" Apron Sale

The HSSO is accepting orders for "Military Spouse" aprons until Feb. 22. Aprons are royal blue and have a "recipe for military spouses" printed on front. Cost is $10 and is due at the time order is placed. All proceeds are used to make Welcome Baskets.

Orders can be placed at the NEX on Saturday, Feb 16 and at the hospital on Wednesday, Feb 20 from 11 am to 12:30 pm. Or, contact Mrs. Schmitz at 5355 and place your order. Aprons will be avaiable at the end of March.

Continued on page 3

FIGURE 3.1. *GUANTÁNAMO BAY GAZETTE*, FEBRUARY 15, 2002

Joint Task Force (JTF) personnel to oversee detention operations draws global attention to a place that has prided itself on its uneventfulness, while bringing it a much larger and more varied military population. The genteel hospitality of which base residents boast is amped up by several degrees of magnitude, in an explicit attempt to preserve the character and idiosyncrasies of life before 2002. "Something obvious to anyone who has lived in GTMO for more than a few weeks," states an article in the January 11, 2002, edition, "is that there are hundreds of Sailors, Soldiers and Marines who arrived less than a week ago in Guantanamo Bay. These new residents are settling in for varying lengths of stay, but they're being welcomed by permanent residents to their new home" ("JTF 160 Makes GTMO Home" 3). This home, however, accommodates discriminately, as the same article acknowledges: "It's probably safe to say the detainees will not receive the same hearty 'welcome aboard' afforded members of JTF-160" (3). The considerable challenge that arriving JTF personnel pose to the base's housing stock is similarly conceived in terms of integration and welcome, as discussion groups are hosted and holiday meals shared in an effort to make the new troops settle in. In its year-end review of 2002, certainly one of the most disrupted years in the base's history, the *Gazette* reports, "One month into the arrival of JTF, GTMO residents showed their determination to keep life in our little corner of Cuba as normal as possible . . . Operation Enduring Freedom and the detainee operations had begun here, but we were still GTMO" ("Year in Review" 3). Four years later, when abuses at the detention centers had caused worldwide outrage, the *Gazette* continued to cling to its normalcy and set its own standard for what is out of the ordinary, this being resolutely distant from the legal and humanitarian anomalies for which the base is now notorious. Its review of the year 2006 acknowledges that "sometimes things are unusual in Guantánamo," the captions accompanying its photo display being that "Weather is Strange" (post-hurricane), "Activities are Strange" (a bread-baking event), and some people have worn "Strange Outfits" (for Halloween) ("Sometimes Things Were Unusual" 12).

In the context of Guantánamo framed as home, ideas of safety and security are conscripted for the mundanely domestic, largely without reference to the detention centers. Although an initial fear of military family members when the detention centers are opened is that "they will be forced to leave for security reasons" (Gorenflo 6), the base is known among its current and former navy residents as a safe place for families, and the *Gazette*'s warnings and reminders are generally removed from the supposed national and global security threat posed by the detainees at the camps.[7] Home security advice largely consists of measures to prevent intrusion, although reports of crime are few and far between: a burglary in 2004 occasioned a WANTED notice for a suspect ("Wanted by the Naval Criminal Investigative Service" 11), and in 2008 a civilian employee was accused of stealing a truck and driving it into the sea (Williams, "Navy Divers" 1).[8] Hurricane safety is an annual concern, with an issue of the *Gazette* devoted to the topic in most years, and traffic safety is a perennial preoccupation—for example, a March 2004 cover story, with a photo of a gun and the headline "Security's Watching," introduces the speed guns of a traffic monitoring system ("Slow Down, GTMO" 1). Otherwise, community safety frequently takes the form of preventative public health measures, with articles on mental and physical health, particularly in relation to the base's tropical environment: base residents are put on alert when dengue fever is reported in Cuba, and it is often local wildlife that poses a significant threat to base residents. "Biting Iguana Finally Captured" is the headline of a 2005 issue about an aggressive iguana who had bitten people who refused to feed it (Cruse and Cole 1); a year later, the paper announces "Scorpion Stings Sailor's Sole" (Lamb 1) and recounts how a sailor required emergency treatment at the base's hospital.

There are, however, unnerving signs throughout the pages of the *Gazette* that not only is all not well at the home that is the base, but that this home is itself a fragile concept held together only tenuously by the efforts of its current residents, and their newspaper reporters, to make it cohere. New arrivals include not only new military families but also journalists and members of humanitarian organizations—the International Committee of the Red Cross, a human rights expert from the Organization for Security and Co-operation in Europe—whose engagement with base residents draws on ideas of security, comfort, and care from a very different lexicon to the one that permeates the *Gazette*'s pages. And as frequent as the birth announcements of new arrivals to the community are the goodbyes from military families leaving for new postings. That this is a transient community, which few identify as a primary home, is nowhere clearer than in features on the graduating senior class of the W. T. Sampson High School, part of the base's only school complex and operated by the Department of Defense. In the post–9/11 years, the graduating class rarely exceeded twelve students and the *Gazette* annually devoted one or two pages to headshots and biographical accounts of each one, listing their hometowns along with other personal details. Of the class of 2003, only one student lists "Guantánamo Bay, Cuba" as his hometown; others list cities in the United States and, in one case, "the Entire East Coast" ("W. T. Sampson's Class of 2003" 6). Members of the class of 2004 name their hometowns as Puerto Rico; Texas; Michigan; Springfield, New York; Miami, Monroe, Washington; Montgomery, New York; and Brooklyn; no one calls Guantánamo "home" ("W. T. Sampson's Class of 2004" 6–7). Hometowns are not listed for the class of 2005 but some students say where they were born and have lived, giving a sense of the mobility of the lives that have brought them to Guantánamo, however briefly: one was born in the Philippines and relocated to Guantánamo in his sophomore year; another was born in Hawaii and spent five years in Germany before joining W. T. Sampson High School a year before graduation; one, who "has been in GTMO for the past 13 years," has the distinction of being the longest established resident in his class ("W. T. Sampson High School Salutes Class of 2005" 3). Despite the concerted efforts of the *Gazette*'s editors to shape the naval base as a home community, "home" for most of its high school students, as for many of the military children in Queair's study, is not at the base, but in an elsewhere to which they feel a stronger attachment.

THE BASE'S SPECIAL CATEGORY RESIDENTS

The base, nevertheless, accommodates certain residents who have lived there for considerably longer than the families of many graduating seniors. As is evident from the *Guantanamo Bay Gazette*'s weekly list of religious services and its annual features on such celebrations as Jamaican Independence Day and Filipino Day, the military family experience that dominates the newspaper's framing of home and community is lived in tandem with experiences of civilian employees, many of whom spend longer at the base than do those associated with the US Navy. An April 2011 issue of the *Gazette*, for example, celebrates Jamaican Winston Lawrence for forty years of service as manager of the base's navy lodge (Mesta 8). Lawrence is one of many Jamaicans living on the base for whom a return home to Jamaica appears to be a principal goal, with years of labor at Guantánamo representing a well-planned stepping stone. An earlier issue of the *Gazette* features an interview with George Johnson, also from Jamaica, portrayed in the newspaper's relentlessly jocular tone as an embodiment of the conscientious migrant worker adapting the American Dream to the circumstances of his own life. George, it is reported, "Goes to a hot and difficult job seven days a week with a smile on his face and an infectious laugh. However, don't let his jovial nature fool you. He is a hard worker and serious about his job" ("Meet George Johnson" 9). His purpose in undertaking this work is well defined: "He hopes to open a pastry shop some day when he returns to Jamaica. He came to GTMO to make a better life for his family. He and his wife of 13 years have three children" (9).

There is a further group of residents at the base whose claim to it as home is longer established than any other, and is in many ways more complex and more definitive. These are the "Special Category Residents," Cubans employed at the base in the early 1960s who chose to stay there, rather than in Cuba, when US-Cuba relations soured. Initially numbering over four hundred, by 2002, when the base's population grew exponentially and diversified as dictated by the war on terror, seventy-five Cubans lived there, and their frequent obituaries punctuate issues of the *Gazette* over its subsequent fifteen years. Their role in life on the base, as well as their choice to "seek refuge" there "from the Marxist government of Fidel Castro" (Byington, "Cuban-American Friendship" 7), is celebrated in the annual Cuban American Friendship Day, the oldest such celebration on the base calendar and an occasion for *Gazette* reports on Cuban music, dance, and food, as well as on the reflective essay competition, generally on Cuba-US relations, for schoolchildren.

The Cuban Special Category Residents' long lives have often been lived across multiple borders: like a considerable number of eastern Cubans, as Andrea Queeley has traced, they are often migrants or children of migrants from Jamaica and elsewhere in the Caribbean. Most have been there since 1964 when Fidel Castro cut off the water supply to the base in response to perceived aggressions and the Lyndon B. Johnson administration retaliated with massive layoffs of Cuban workers, who were obliged to choose between Cuba and the base. As Jana K. Lipman recounts, "If workers chose 'Cuba,' they sacrificed their jobs, U.S. salaries, and government pensions. If they chose 'the base,' they had to cut all ties with Cuba and their families for the foreseeable future" (*Guantána-*

mo 183). The Special Category Residents of the twenty-first century are among the 448 who chose "the base," working and eventually retiring there with pensions and US Navy–funded housing and medical care. Many of them raised children who then relocated to the United States, frequently close to the large Cuban exile communities of South Florida, even as their extended families remained across the fence line in Cuba. Special Category Residents are extended a particular set of accommodations, set out in the National Defense Authorization Act of 2006 as allowing the secretary of the navy to provide for their "general welfare, including subsistence, housing, and health care" (United States, Congress, House and Senate, Armed Services, section 377).

The January 6, 2006, issue of the *Guantanamo Bay Gazette* celebrates the life of Claude McPherson, "considered a local authority on Cuban and base history" ("In Memory" 1), who lived on the base from the 1960s but whose remains were returned to his family "in mainland Cuba" (1). The July 28, 2006, issue includes the obituary of Eunice Alexander, a resident who was born in Grenada, migrated to Cuba, and then sought asylum on the base in the 1960s and spent the remainder of her life there; its front-page photograph is of her relatives, who live in the United States, but have come to pay their respects at the base's Cuzco Cemetery (Wordu 1). The life of Rafael Maura, whose obituary appears in the April 10, 2009, issue, was spent within a much smaller geographic area but, given its location, it involved multiple crossings of borders. Born in La Cidra, in eastern Cuba, he worked at the base before and after the Cuban Revolution; his son continued to work there after Maura's death, although the elder Maura's siblings remained in Caimanera and Guantánamo ("Eternal Love" 3). The funeral for longtime base resident Ernesto González was held at the base, where his wife still lived and worked; González had died in Virginia, near his daughter, and the base commander secured permission for González's brothers to visit from Cuba for the funeral and meet their widowed sister-in-law for the first time (Baker 1).

The ninety-seventh birthday celebrations for Cuban Special Resident Eldica Moore, featured in the July 13, 2007, issue of the *Gazette* as the base's oldest resident, are indicative of the demographic peculiarities of this particular group (Nixon 6). Having been of adult working age since 1959 or before, they live out their elderly years on the base, representing a lifestyle and set of medical needs quite different to those of military employees, who retire elsewhere; indeed, the navy inspector general's 2016 report on the base notes the magnitude of these needs and the likely eventual inadequacy of base facilities to fulfill them: "The exact nature of the U.S. Government's duties, rights, and obligations towards the SCRs is not settled. With the vast majority of SCRs advanced in age, providing for their general welfare will require accommodation of potentially complex health, legal, and personal needs typical of an advanced age population" (Department of the Navy 5). Chillingly, it has been frequently noted that the medical needs of some detainees, who are approaching old age in indefinite detention, are not dissimilar (K. B. Williams; Rosenberg, "Guantánamo Bay as Nursing Home").[9] An April 5, 2002, *Gazette* article tells of the distribution of Easter baskets to Special Category Residents who, as part of the base's Home Care Program, are "homebound" and "do not generally have visitors" (Allen 4): they are isolated in the ever-more constrained space that is a house in a demarcated section of fenced-off base on an embargoed island. When in January 2004 a Cuban Community Center is opened, where these residents "can cook, play cards, dominos or bingo or simply sit in the library area and read while enjoying the quiet," they finally, the *Gazette* reports, "have a special place to call their own" ("Cuban Community Center Opens" 5). The Cuban residents' historical experiences and cultural practices are celebrated in the *Gazette*, which is at pains to construct its readership as "a community of Cuban and American friends working together to make GTMO the truly unique family that it is" ("Cuban Community Center Opens" 5). A June 26, 2009, article by Cuban Community Assistance program manager Madhya Husta introduces the Special Category Residents through a few "did ya knows," that dwell on the singular flavor this group brings to base life. Among these are "did ya know . . . they brought their traditions and culture with them?" (Husta 5), an example being the two shrines at the base to Cuban patron saint Virgen de la Caridad del Cobre. Husta's response to "did you know that there is a small quintessentially Cuban village aboard the Station?" (5) is mired in the sensory delights of this local treasure: "It is easy to spot where the SCRs live, you just have to walk through Center Bargo, the colorful and well-tended gardens are a dead giveaway. If you stop for a minute and listen carefully, you will be able to hear their Caribbean music. And if you are lucky enough, you may even be invited to dance and enjoy a Cuban snack with them" (5).

As other exiles from Cuba and elsewhere have documented, transplanting the religious, culinary, and musical traditions of an old home to a new one does not replicate one as the other.[10] Unsurprisingly, the Special Category Residents' physical and affective links to Cuba are varied and complex. The retirement in 2012 of the last of the commuter workers, the base's other celebrated Cuban population, marked a new rupture for the Special Category Residents, for whom the commuters had represented a last lifeline to Cuba. The December 21, 2012, *Gazette* article "End of an Era for Naval Station Guantánamo Bay" reminds readers that the two last commuters, Harry Henry and Luis de la Rosa, "have served as an important conduit for the Special Category Residents, often know as Cuban Exiles," and that many Special Category Residents "communicate with their family members who remained in Cuba by passing photos and messages via Mr. Henry and Mr. La Rosa, who then deliver it to their family members" (Wirfel 6). Other connections with Cuba are more sporadic and sometimes newsworthy beyond the *Gazette*: two Cubans who had been housed at Guantánamo during the refugee crisis of 1994–1995 returned to the base as members of the US military, forming a tangential and largely symbolic part of its existing Cuban community, and in 2012 Cuban American Senator Marco Rubio of Florida spent part of his visit to the base, most of which was focused on detention operations, conversing in Spanish with Special Category Residents.[11] As has long been the case for Cubans in the towns bordering the base, the impossibility of physical passage from one side of the fence line to the other is subverted by the transmission of nonphysical signals: just as Cubans in Guantánamo Province were once able to watch the same television programs as base residents, and residents of Caimanera can now sometimes take advantage of the base's cell network for their phone and internet connections, so Special Category Residents listen to radio programs broadcast from Cuba.[12]

The affective relationships with Cuba expressed by many Special Category Residents share much with such relationships in the larger exile community. A nostalgic attachment to material reminders of Cuba looms large in their self-presentation, as does a vehement dislike for the country's governing political regime. When interviewed for the *Miami Herald* in 2002, for example, Special Category Resident Gloria Martínez shuns present-day Miami and Cuba, afraid of one and politically distanced from the other. Her preference is for the slowness of the Cuba she left behind: "'I'm afraid to live in the States alone,' she says. 'It's too crazy driving in Miami. If Cuba opens up, I'll go back and take the buses'" (Rosenberg, *Guantánamo Bay* 164). The November 14, 2008, *Guantánamo Bay Gazette* obituary for Mr. Valmar Burch, who had lived on the base since 1962 and was survived by two sons in Caimanera as well as a sister in New York, states, "At the time of his passing, he was holding a cigar that reminded him of his beloved Cuba" ("Mr. Valmar Burch" 3). Interviewed years later in the December 2, 2016, issue of the *Gazette*, after the funeral of her husband, Harry Sharpe's widow claims to be "content" to have him buried on the base: "I would not," she states, "take him back to the other side for anything" (Waener 5). Just one Cuban resident interviewed by the *Gazette* in the fifteen-year period from 2002 to 2017 is unambivalent in his embrace of the base as home: Ramón Romero, who has lived there since his grandparents left him there, with another family, when he was a child in the late 1950s. The base, Romero claims, "Is my home . . . I love this place" (Wirfel, "GTMO Resident" 3). For many Special Category Residents, Cuba and the base offer competing versions of home just as Cuba and Miami, or Cuba and Hialeah, do for exiles in the United States. The difference, in the strangely charged context that is Guantánamo, is that they in some ways have more claim to being at home, in this place that is environmentally if not politically continuous with Cuba, than do most others living there.

MAKING HOME IN THE SHADOW OF THE BASE

Not far from the home that the Special Category Residents have made at the base, but separated by the ideological and physical divider that is the base's fence line, for Cubans in the province of Guantánamo and particularly in the border town of Caimanera, the base and the idea of home relate uncertainly and unevenly to one another. This is a borderland region for which *home* has been overdetermined in its iteration as *homeland*, or *patria*, but whose more intimate domesticities and local interactions take shape with and despite the language of revolutionary struggle. Home in the sense that Yi-Fu Tuan gives it, as the familiar, secure, and incomparable, is overlaid in the Cuban context—as Benedict Anderson has shown it to be in most modern contexts—by an ostensibly unifying articulation of home as homeland, in this case rehearsed to and by the populace as *la patria*, the fatherland. The Cuban Revolution's version of la patria draws from Fidel Castro's tracing of a direct genealogy from the heroes of nineteenth-century independence wars to those of the 1959 revolution, cloaked in a gendered noun that aptly reflects the strongly masculinist, and indeed paternalist, biases of revolutionary leaders. Castro's 1953 address to a court of law as he faced charges for attacking the Moncada army barracks in eastern Cuba, almost six years before his rebel movement seized power, insists on this lineage, and it would remain central to revolutionary thinking thereafter ("History Will Absolve Me"). Home as the *patria* envisaged by the heroes of Cuba's nineteenth-century independence wars, however, was deeply embedded in the national imaginary before Castro's time. In her analysis of political martyrdom in the late 1940s in Cuba, for example, Lillian Guerra notes that "Cubans took seriously a past that unites the generations," such that "morir por la patria es vivir" (to die for the fatherland is to live) was not simply a line from the national anthem taught to schoolchildren, it was the central thesis of Cuba's national existence" (*Heroes, Martyrs* 29). Elsewhere, Guerra has commented on the transmutation of this line from the national anthem into a rigid expectation under Castro's rule, a "'Patria o Muerte [Fatherland or Death]' philosophy enforced by the increasingly authoritarian revolutionary government under Fidel Castro in Cuba after 1959," wherein the revolution "mandated that one's support for the Castro regime be all or nothing" ("Elián González" 8). Indeed, the most significant popular uprisings in twenty-first-century Cuba gained momentum around a music video titled *Patria y vida* (Fatherland and Life) performed by various well-known Cuban music artists as a reframing of the "Patria o Muerte" imperative of six decades of revolution. Released in early 2021 in support of artists and writers connected to the San Isidro Movement against government repression, the song's lyrics, as Robin Moore reports, "Call urgently for change, and they dismiss the current government as a relic of the past."

The Cuban areas bordering Guantánamo function as a peculiarly intense synecdoche for the *patria*. The US base, as Fidel Castro claimed in 1962, stands as "a dagger thrust in the side of the fatherland" ("Discurso pronunciado... el 26 de julio de 1962"). Following this metaphor, Guantánamo, and the border town of Caimanera in particular, is the anatomical rib of Cuba, the site where the base has been implanted. As such, the town has been calculatedly shaped as the *patria*'s first line of defense against imperialism, charged with defending the homeland against intrusion; opposition to this charge, and to the dominance of the Cuban Revolution's rhetoric and policy more generally, have been particularly salient in recent years.[13] Caimanera has been designated a military zone, for which special permission is required for entry by nonresidents, while residents must show a pass on arrival. Caimanera, and the small village of Boquerón that lies on the opposite side of Guantánamo Bay, are the only towns in Cuba subject to such restrictions on access, and as such they occupy a sui generis status as an enclave-like zone bordering, but closed off from, what Peter Hulme has called "the most perfect colonial enclave that ever existed" (377); namely, the base.

It is Caimanera's exceptional, vanguard role with regard to the defense of Cuba, and the similar, but less rigidly defined role of the city and province of Guantánamo, that shapes the testimonial qualities of two films made in Cuba across the span of a half century about the area's relationship to the base: José Massip's *Guantánamo* (1965) and Hernando Calvo Ospina's *All Guantánamo Is Ours* (2015). Massip was one of a group of cineastes whose work and vision were formative to the early years of Cuba's Institute for Cinematographic Art and Industries (ICAIC), founded in 1959 as a laboratory for revolutionary cinema. As Michael Chanan writes, "The Revolution . . . unleashed among a new generation of filmmakers a furious creative energy as they turned the cameras on the process they were living, and told the Cuban people—and anyone else who was interested—who they were and what they were doing" (4). Unimpressed by the socialist realism imposed on Soviet cinema, they "paid homage to both Eisenstein and Fellini, as well as the French New Wave and Brazilian Cinema Novo" (4). Writing about *Guantánamo* a year after its release, Massip recalls being inspired by Antonin Artaud's claim that "reality is superior to all history, to all fable, to all divinity, to all surreality" ("Guantánamo, Twice") to recognize that "the best film that I could make about Guantánamo was one that would start with the contemporary elements that constituted the city's daily life." He then wrote a script that "rejected the conventional treatment of narrative cinema" and was structured instead around interviews, archival footage, still photographs and re-enactments of "important and complex events" and "re-enactments that are more simple." The latter category includes what Massip calls "the last stare, filled with tragic premonitions, of a woman to her husband, worker Rubén López Sabariego, before his assassination at the Base"—a reenactment the widow herself performed, in one of the film's many intensely politically symbolic, and at the same time deeply personal, scenes with people who live near the base.

Indeed, the interviews with local residents with which Massip's *Guantánamo* is assembled coalesce around the collective portrayal of a particular kind of home: a usurped, unjustly occupied one that it is the duty of the rightful inhabitants of the Guantánamo region, as the vanguard of the Cuban *patria*, to defend and reclaim. The interviews are offered in brief fragments, their testimonial quality enhanced by the erasure of prompts; punctuating them is a series of short, typed sentences, appearing on-screen to loud bursts of music. The series begins by approaching the idea of *home* through Guantánamo's capacity to be just like any other city: the question "A city like any other?" (00:00:06 and 00:01:23) flashes across the screen twice, followed first by "the story of a boy who was sold for four pesos" (00:00:14)—cut to a young man, followed by a jeering crowd, who claims to have been sold to Americans as a child—and then to "the story of a philosopher" (00:01:17) with whom neighbors in the neighborhood of San Justo joined together to produce "a moral tale" (2:15). Further scenes of community life follow, to be disrupted around the fifth minute by footage of fighter planes and a soundtrack of gunshots around the base. The surprising question that then comes up on screen is "The Base: a city like any other?" (00:06:16), as though there might be a symmetry between the lives, the communities, or the normalcies of the two spaces. Such a speculation is systematically debunked, however, by the curation of speakers and footage in the remainder of the film: former workers at the base abused, ignored, and underpaid; residents of Caimanera whose lives were dominated by US Marines on leave in search of prostitutes; finally, long cameos recounting the lives, deaths, funerals and graves of each of three Cuban men allegedly killed by US soldiers stationed at the base. At the end of the film's sixty-two minutes, it is no longer plausible to consider either Guantánamo or the base a city like any other; rather, the two are adversaries, pitted against one another as representatives of the Cuban Revolution and US imperialism, with the former's victory simultaneously complete and continuous, in a composite temporality characteristic of what Antonio José Ponte has understood as a revolutionary time whose investment in the future leads to "its own immurement" ("What Am I Doing Here?" 15). "The city knows that it has triumphed" (1:01:27) but, nevertheless, "the city knows that the struggle continues" (1:01:49).

Calvo Ospina's *All Guantánamo Is Ours* (2016) draws on clips from Massip's film and other archival footage from the 1960s, most notably Che Guevara's 1964 speech to the United Nations denouncing provocations from the base, but its aesthetic ambitions are far more modest and it is primarily structured around interviews with current residents of Guantánamo, Caimanera, and Boquerón. Many of these are trained spokespeople on the history of the area and its relations to the base, while others—schoolchildren, college students, fishermen—speak on behalf of what is presented as a broader populace. As in Massip's film, their perspectives on the damage wrought by the base, and Cuba's rightful ownership of it, are so unified as to make of them a collective subject of defense against American imperialism. The soundtrack to the film draws heavily on Joseíto Fernández's song "Guantanamera," contrasting the outrage of speakers to the simplicity of the tune and the rural setting of the lyrics; even though one speaker insists that "Guantánamo is more than the base," when others refer to *home*, they do so in terms of usurpation. A soldier in the opening scene, for example, comments that "it is as if someone is in the backyard of your home stealing it" (0:49), while a young boy, interrupted as he plays in the streets of Caimanera, tells his interviewer, "That base . . . they should just give it back to us now" (34:06). A narrative of incompleteness, of the impossibility of Caimanera, Guantánamo, and Cuba being whole without the return of the base, permeates these interviews.

Ofelia García Campuzano, director of Caimanera's Museum of Municipal History and a frequent commentator in *All Guantánamo Is Ours* on the abuses inflicted on the area by the United States, deliberately deflects attention from the base in her 2009 book on the town, *Caimanera: Una mirada diferente* (Caimanera: A Different Viewpoint). García Campuzano, as she states in her introduction, is especially focused on the microhistory of Caimanera, and her interests in "the idiosyncrasy of a people" (10) take her from the town's development in the early nineteenth century to the architecture, foods, culture, and religious practices of the present day. It is these detailed accounts and the affective gesture with which they are presented—the invitation extended to the author's fellow citizens to "consider their own daily lives" (11), and a recognition of the pain and love from which the book was born—that shape García Campuzano's portrayal of Caimanera as a home steeped in tradition.

Caimanera is one of the two principal sources Pedro Gutiérrez and

Alexander Beatón acknowledge as a referent for their multimedia art project, *El camino de la estrategia* (*The Way of Strategy*); the second of these sources, the Samurai swordsman Miyamoto Musashi's "The Fire Scroll" from *The Book of Five Rings* (c.1645), originates in a vastly different time and tradition. Together, these two texts—one hewing close to intimate detail on life in the singular town of Caimanera, the other a meditation on combat that, in becoming what recent Musashi translator Alexander Bennett has called "a deeper philosophical understanding on the art of war" (38) is also a treatise in harmony—contribute to the particularly measured and conceptually ambitious perspective on Caimanera as home that Gutiérrez and Beatón offer in their project. Their interest, as Gutiérrez tells an interviewer, is much less in Caimanera's symbolic value within Cuban revolutionary discourse than in the barely written and barely seen experience of home lived by the town's inhabitants, one that holds value in and of itself: "We were more interested in the subtext, in what was left behind, in history, whose value we don't always see because it is so evident and mundane" ("Caimanera: El camino").

Exhibited in the cities of Guantánamo, Havana, and Providence, Rhode Island, "The Way of Strategy" sets survival and resilience as imperatives for inhabitants of the exceptional space that is the border zone, as well as in the broader context of a Cuba whose anti-imperialist rhetoric against the United States has often adopted a lexicon of war. Mindful of the bellicose languages that have converged at Guantánamo, the textual and visual components of *The Way of Strategy* suggest, as do Massip and Calvo Opsina's two films, that to live near the base is to live in a permanent state of vigilance. Their focus, though, is on marshalling the arts of war into a collective psychology that admits the uneasy togetherness that constitutes residence in a partially usurped, but nevertheless shared, portion of land and sea.

In an environment of hostility and restriction, the project has *convivencia*, roughly translatable as "living together" or "coexistence," as its guiding term (*Proyecto artístico*). Although *The Way of Strategy* does not explicitly acknowledge the resonance, convivencia is a term most closely associated with medieval Spain, and with the coexistence of Muslims, Jews, and Christians in the Muslim-ruled state of Al-Andalus between the late eighth century and 1492, the year in which the state fell to Spain's Catholic monarchs. Propagated by Spanish philologists Ramón Menéndez Pidal and Américo Castro, convivencia has become a much-contested theory for the history of Spanish culture as a meeting of three faiths. It was diluted in the post-Franco period, as Brian Catlos puts it, as a "near-synonym for tolerance" (x) that in fact "has no clear meaning and offers no explanatory dimension" (x); it remains, rather, a "troublesome, anachronistic concept" (x) that is neither fully reflective of interfaith relations in medieval Spain nor translatable to social and cultural relations in the late twentieth and twenty-first centuries. The Guantánamo for which Beatón and Gutiérrez posit convivencia is far removed from the medieval Spanish context for which the term was coined. The fragility and tenuousness of that context, rather than the harmony imputed to it in modern revivals of the term, nevertheless permeate the region that Beatón and Gutiérrez portray. In *The Way of Strategy*, convivencia is a mode and a process for seeking ways of being at home, in a space coopted by the anti-domestic forces of political hostility.

The Way of Strategy was shown in its most complete version at the Villa Manuela Gallery in Havana in March 2013, where it was composed of four separate pieces. The first of these, *The Circumstance*, invokes the surveillance to which people in the border zone are subjected daily in their labor and their domestic lives as well as the implications for individual lives and the local economy of Caimanera's proximity to the naval base. It is a replica of the watchtowers that line both sides of the base's border, from where the Cuban and US military watch out for suspicious activity. Two nine-foot-high towers face one another, each made of handwoven fishing nets, registering a local industry decimated by Caimanera's proximity to the base: one of the more frequent complaints of local residents is the restricted access to Guantánamo Bay afforded to local fishermen who, in being obliged to fish at the bay's northernmost end, have limited variety and supply.[14] Even as a large screen, one showing footage of an existing US watchtower and the other of a Cuban one, produces the effect of surveillance from all angles, the decking of replica watchtowers in nets that are suppler than the wood and metal with which the actual towers are constructed—and that, moreover, represent the shrouding of vantage points by the tools of a diminished local industry—suggests a softening of the vigilance that has opposed Cuban to American watchtowers at this site of enhanced hostility. No one lives in a watchtower: those around the base's border are for temporary occupancy and a forced, alert straining of the body and eyes, but they are nevertheless an extension of the homes that have been made at

FIGURE 3.2. ALEXANDER BEATÓN AND PEDRO GUTIÉRREZ, *WOUNDED BY HISTORY*. FROM *THE WAY OF STRATEGY* EXHIBIT. REPRINTED COURTESY OF THE ARTISTS.

and around Guantánamo, where, as the Samurai intertext of *The Way of Strategy* insists, strategy is a way of life.

In *Wounded by History*, the second piece in Gutiérrez and Beatón's exhibit, wooden rocking chairs belonging to Caimanera residents are hung from a wall (fig. 3.2). Their suspension severely curtails their natural movement, a concern raised in several of the oral testimonies playing on the small television screens balanced in the rockers' seats. While these testimonies reiterate some of the experiences of those in the films *Guantánamo* and *All Guantánamo Is Ours*, they cohere far less around the familiar anti-imperialist theme. Rather, speakers' objections to the base's presence are tempered by reflections on the day-to-day patterns of their lives and by speculation on how those lives might look in a different set of circumstances. Fishermen and former base workers are among those who speak to the peculiar experience of living in a town for which even visiting Cuban family members need entry permits and to the paradox of living close to Cuba's only land border but being prevented, mostly by economic constraints, from leaving even their own town. The fishermen imagine their livelihoods in the absence of restrictions on waters; a base worker recounts his divided loyalties and the need to self-censor any criticism of either the United States or Cuba; and García Campu-

FIGURE 3.3. ALEXANDER BEATÓN AND PEDRO GUTIÉRREZ, *IMAGINARY OF LOYALTY*. FROM *THE WAY OF STRATEGY* EXHIBIT. REPRINTED COURTESY OF THE ARTISTS.

zano, in her capacity as museum director, describes the deracination of Caimanera, cut off from the base as it is from the rest of Cuba. Longtime residents of the town explain how they were posted there in the early 1960s as ideological guards against US incursion, their commitment to the revolution having been proven through either military or Communist Party service. That the speakers in *Wounded by History* conceive of themselves as a community is evident in the insistence of several that everyone knows who belongs. "Strangers" who appear in Caimanera, they insist, are immediately identified as such, and are usually suspected of being aspiring migrants. An elderly fisherwoman tells of the many swimmers she has spotted over the years and reported to authorities for attempting to reach the base. Caimanera, one speaker says, is "a closed town": those enclosed there recognize the shared experience, and the circumscribed space, that constitute their anomalous home.

Imaginary of Loyalty, the third and most textual of the four pieces, moves overtly to disassemble the language and paradigms of hostility deployed around Guantánamo (fig. 3.3). Letters made with sea salt are pinned on a wall, spelling the words *primera trinchera contra el imperialismo* (first line of defense against imperialism), the slogan with which the Cuban Border Brigade enlists Caimanera residents in its defense of the border. Parts of the letters, however, have broken off, and have fallen to the floor to join a heap of broken, jumbled letters on a bed of salt. Salt extraction is key to Caimanera's local economy, and the decline of the industry is implied in the debris on the gallery floor. More powerfully, however, the fact that the letters, and hence the words, are crumbling, and that those on the floor form no words at all, is an indication that the slogan and the rhetoric that generated it are themselves obsolete, and are merely accumulating in an increasingly incoherent mass. In the context of the exhibit as a whole, the spoken words of interviewees in *Wounded by History* take on more life and relevance, despite their much more limited ambition, than the battle-drawn slogans with which the Cuban Revolution has attempted to define Caimanera.

The Way, the fourth and final work in the exhibit, is the most closely aligned with Musashi's "The Fire Scroll." It is also the work in which the inner experience and survival of individual laborers and their community is most clearly foregrounded. A rough-hewn trestle table extends the length of the exhibit space, suggesting one of the many quays that jut into the sea in Caimanera. Hooked along this table, forming a series of makeshift albums, are photographs of the town that span many decades. There are yellowing family portraits from the early twentieth century; photographs of entry permits to Caimanera and, for base workers only, to the naval base; and clear, serious images, photographed by Gutiérrez and Beatón, of the faces of today's residents and workers. The images bear captions from Musashi's text to establish oblique but intimately domestic relations between the text and a locale constituted by its proximity to a foreign military installation. The section of "The Fire Scroll" titled "The General Knows His Troops," for example, states that "you will come to think of the enemy troops as your own and be able to command them to move as you see fit" (125), while Gutiérrez and Beatón's images under this heading show close-ups of state-issued identity cards and worn faces. "Arresting the shadow," in Musashi's strategy, "is applied when you are unable to fathom the enemy's mind" and elicit a revelation (118); images under this heading in *The Way of Strategy* show the empty chairs of Caimanera patios and living rooms, some in shadows and others in full light. In its interweavings and visual renderings of Musashi's text, this final work articulates the importance of understanding the other despite that other's disproportionate power, and of being at home in that understanding. Here, just as in *The Way of Strategy* as a full project, the testimonies, artifacts, and representations of the lives of Caimanera's residents suggest that, even as they live in the inescapable shadow of the unwelcome naval base, they have nevertheless learned, as individuals and as a community, to incorporate that shadow into their selves and their own understanding of home.

DWELLING TOGETHER

In their initial proposal for *The Way of Strategy*, Beatón and Gutiérrez look to the project's visual and textual codes to undermine rigidly organized enmities and co-opt the strategies of war in the service of art. The artists' statement proposes a strategy of "invading cultural territories with the viewpoint of art," and offers art as a mediator for difference (*Proyecto artístico*). The co-optation of war as a metaphor for art leads to fusions that would destabilize the foundation of military power: in its description, the project itself is termed an "installation" but so too is the naval base, both presented in inverted commas that suggest fissures in the base's structural and political permanence. At the same time, however, Beatón and Gutiérrez draw art and war into a triad with home, through their project's conceptual grounding in their own version of the term *convivencia*: living together, cohabiting, or coinhabiting, as a form of living that includes but is not limited to resisting. As a guiding term, their convivencia opens to the human dimensions of a border zone that has long existed as what they term "a semantic territory, a geography that is half real and half suspected" (*Proyecto artístico*): an area whose physical and human manifestation must compete with the weight that Guantánamo, as a word and idea, has been made to bear.

Beatón and Gutiérrez's convivencia captures how the people of Caimanera have learned to live together: with one another and, albeit uncomfortably, with their close neighbor. Indeed, for all who live at and around Guantánamo Bay Naval Base, across the temporal spectrum from short-term to indefinite to permanent, convivencia is key to the making of home despite the many constraints on what a home can be in this place and time. For detainees more than others at Guantánamo, *home* is a tenuous, fragile, derisible, and barely possible ideal: it is built, as Ahmed Errachidi recounts, on distant memory or in the conjured present of the imagination. Military personnel and their families, posted to the US naval base for periods of months or years, vigorously manufacture the trappings and rehearse the life of a small-town community even as few consider it their home. Cubans, both the few dozen living out their old age on the base and the thousands more who live within sight of its fence line, stake the clearest affective and legal claim to home at Guantánamo in its broadest, territorially continuous sense, but they do so with a sense of incompletion, whose other and inevitable face is that of convivencia. Living together in awareness that others inhabit and share the same space, in a spectrum of sharing that runs from Errachidi's hospitality in his cell to the intensely constructed community of the naval station to the simultaneously mundane and exceptional experience of life in Caimanera, emerges as one of the few viable ways to begin making oneself at home in the otherwise hostile space of Guantánamo.

CHAPTER 4
THE FUTURE

More than twenty years into the establishment of the detention camps, and more than sixty into the Cuban Revolution, "What comes next?" has become an unmoored question for Guantánamo. For many who live on the base and across its fence line, as well as for those men released from the detention centers into a wider world onto which Guantánamo casts a long shadow, the constraining space and density of the present temper engagements with the future and trust of the past. Many of these individuals, inhabitants of and in a sense inhabited by Guantánamo, experience a present of little mobility, varyingly scarce material comforts, limited access to information, and routines predictable less in their detail than in their likelihood of causing distress. At the same time, the future of the detention camps themselves, of the naval base as territory leased by fiat, and of the long-standing Cuban revolutionary regime, has remained stubbornly if not always prominently on the agenda of those who direct American and Cuban foreign policies, and of primary concern for advocates, activists, and observers in the Caribbean region and across the globe.

This chapter addresses articulations of the future by and on behalf of Guantánamo's occupants, as it relates to their experience in a present of detention camps, on the one hand, and of the Cuban Revolution, on the other. In their memoirs, testimonies, and small-circulation journals, Guantánamo's former and current inhabitants contemplate different versions of deeply uncertain futures. At the same time, artists, activists, and scholars not resident at the base have offered speculations, visions, and plans for the base's next episodes, purveying what I will call "future perfect fictions" that are situated in a displaced post-present of conciliation. These articulations together push at the urgent question of how to imagine—or, better still, inhabit—a future while acknowledging and coming to terms with what will then be the past. They ask, in resonance with a much broader field of post-conflict contexts, what a repaired, restorative future might look like.

GUANTÁNAMO'S TEMPORALITIES

The governing temporality of Guantánamo's detention centers has long been the "indefinite": an orientation toward the future that is effectively a continuation of the constraints of the present for what may be a lifetime. The indefinite cast a broad reach at the birth of the war on terror, the useful lack of categorical rigor ascribed to "terror" as an enemy spilling over into, and justifying, a war that itself could have no end. "The war," Marc Redfield has written, "having no object except the abstraction 'terrorism' or 'terror,' is limitless and endless" (56); although the war on terror has itself approached a slow if equivocal end in the intervening years, its legacy of indefinite detentions has endured, both for the detainees who remain to enter old age at Guantánamo and for many of those who, although released, find that the complex and stultifying weight of the past extends into, and arrests, the experience of a future. Elizabeth Swanson and Alexandra Moore, reading the first and second editions of Mohamedou Ould Slahi's *Guantánamo Diary*, draw attention to "the simultaneously concrete and unfathomable future that is indefinite detention during the war on terror—even, paradoxically, after one's release" (35). "'Indefinite detention' and endless war," they claim, "are self-perpetuating because they have the capacity to produce the unfreedoms upon which they depend" (53). Once a detainee has been relegated to this temporal zone, there is little hope for an exit.

Swanson and Moore trace indefinite detention as it overlaps in the "simultaneously competing and complementary spatio-temporal frameworks" (33) of Slahi's text, one of these being his home in Mauritania where, restoring the first edition of his diary that had been published with heavy redaction, he was "confined and surveilled by both the Mauritanian and U.S. governments" (36), an experience only possible because of "the perhaps unavoidable deference of neocolonial Mauritania" to US empire (40). Indefinite detention and the imbalances of colonial power have long gone hand in hand, as Natsu Taylor Saito cites in her account of the internment of Indigenous peoples, slavery, and the indefinite detention of immigrants. In the United States, Taylor Saito writes, "Indefinite detentions may be exceptional in the sense that the formalities of legal process have been abandoned," but as centuries of example have shown, "they are not aberrational" (33).

The relationship between the indefinite and colonial power pertains to Cuba, too. Amy Kaplan's 2005 essay "Where Is Guantánamo?" attends closely to imperial precursors to the (mis)perceived anomaly that is the Guantánamo camp, finding these in the history of the Guantánamo base itself as well as in other territories tangentially within US purview. Among these is Puerto Rico, that the US Supreme Court, in the Insular Cases of 1902–1922, declared as "foreign to the United States in a domestic sense," "belonging to" but "not a part of the United States" (841). Kaplan insists that the "use of Guantánamo as a prison camp today demands to be understood in the context of its historical location," wherein a "logic grounded in imperialism" ensures that "coercive state power has been routinely mobilized beyond the sovereignty of national territory and beyond the rule of law" (832). Guantánamo's historical location, as a piece of land leased to the United States, was enshrined first in the Platt Amendment of 1903 and then further in the amendment's 1934 abrogation, the latter extending the lease in perpetuity or "so long as the United States of America shall not abandon said Naval Station" (Kaplan 836). "The language of the treaty," Kaplan writes, "places the United States in the active position of agent with the prerogative to stay or leave, and Cuba in the passive role of accepting either occupation or abandonment" (836). This indefinite lease, imposed on a Cuba that has no say in its termination and whose sixty years of calls for the United States' departure have been fruitless, is part of a ready-made context for the camps. Guantánamo is thus, as Kaplan states, "a chillingly appropriate place for the indefinite detention of unnamed enemies in what the administration calls a perpetual war against terror" (837).

Aside from the indefinite temporalities of detention and empire, other renderings of the present in its relation to past and future have overlaid Guantánamo. Among these we might include the time of the tour of duty for military personnel at Joint Task Force Guantánamo, ostensibly nine months long but often extended, producing at a smaller scale in guards the endlessness of detainees' experience. Other inclusions might be the longer but verifiably finite postings of US Navy servicepeople and their families and the civilian contractors who work with them at the base, and the likely life terms of the small number of Cubans exiled on the base in the 1960s and living out their last days within sight of their birthland. By far the most strident co-optation of the present and future on the Cuban side of the fence line—a co-optation that has intermittently extended its grip over the base itself—is the one that underpins the vision and public rhetoric of the Cuban Revolution. In this rhetoric the present is conceptualized as one of enduring struggle, bearing the torch of unfinished rebellions in the past. It is always conjugated in the future tense as the ubiquitous verb and slogan *venceremos* (we will overcome), moving toward the endlessly deferred fulfillment of a socialist society. As Emily A. Maguire has written, "The language of the Cuban Revolution itself evidences a contradictory sense of time, in that the Revolution is never referred to as a finished event but rather as an ongoing present, a process or struggle leading to a utopian future that never arrives" (326).

The Cuban Revolution achieved its founding moment of triumph, or its first fulfillment, on the first day of 1959 when, having ousted the reigning dictator Fulgencio Batista, a rebel movement led by the charismatic Fidel Castro assumed control of the Cuban government. María del Pilar Díaz Castañón has traced how this triumph represented what Cubans considered to be their *ahora sí*, or "now, finally" (91) moment, the culmination and justification of centuries of sensing that Cuba's political and economic potential had been frustrated by external forces and the consequent forging of a "myth of subjunctive possibility" (91). The subsequent six decades nevertheless generated a secondary revolutionary teleology, one that sent millions of Cubans into exile and mobilized those who remained into a collective project of epic scale—constructing a wholly new society whose reach extended into the public and private lives of all citizens, modifying theories of socialism to the immediate challenges at hand but, despite challenges, failures, compromises, and outright contradiciones, never renouncing the professed trajectory toward a future perfect. The history of this post–1959 revolution abounds with temporal warps: writing in 2003 of his life in Cuba, Antonio José Ponte describes every revolution as beginning in a condemnation of the past but ending with a continually looping celebration of its own founding moments, such that "what is proclaimed as an inexhaustible process of acceleration, an interminable series of metamorphoses, becomes the most hidden form of stagnation" ("What Am I Doing Here?" 15). Michael J. Bustamante's assessment, with reference to the post-Castro presidency of Miguel Díaz-Canel, is that "sixty years later, and despite all the water under the bridge, the myth of 'subjunctive possibility' for many Cubans—the 'now, finally' of the Cuban historical imagination—remains unfulfilled" (237). Indeed, one of the more widely circulated statements of the antigovernment movements that have emerged in Cuba is a music video that explicitly curtails the call of "Patria o Muerte" (Fatherland or Death) that has *venceremos* as its response. The song's artists call instead for an end of the false choice, and for "Patria y vida" (Fatherland and Life), privileging the personal present over the revolution's unfulfillable future.[1]

DETENTION AND THE FUTURE

Revolutionary temporality reaches detainee experience at some remove, but it does so through the conceptual overlap between the indefinite of detention and the deferred future of the Cuban Revolution, on the one hand, and, on the other, through Cuba's constitutive opposition to the United States, which has rendered the latter's government less concerned about local objections than it might have been had it held detainees at a facility in a "host" country where terms of engagement are less murky. Indefinite detention marks detainees' accounts of their time at Guantánamo more forcefully: as a present of extreme constraint marked by monotony and the predictability of unwarned change—a move to another cell, a new angle on interrogation, a new mind game—and as the foreclosing of agency over what the future may hold.

The proximity between the indefinite nature of the present and the inevitable deferral of the future resonates in one of the few live and unvetted statements by detainees to have been broadcast from Guantánamo. A 2017 episode of *PBS Frontline* about the life of Yemeni former detainee Mansoor Adayfi, who was released to Serbia in 2016, included an unauthorized exchange at Guantánamo Bay between journalist Arun Rath and Detainee 242, namely Yemeni citizen Khaled Qasim. Although the video recording of this exchange is cut off after Qasim calls out, "I need . . . go home" ("Out of Gitmo" 36:57) and identifies home as "Yemen" (37:06), Rath reports being told off-camera that Qasim expects to be at Guantánamo "forever" (37:29). Similarly, the open letter by Moroccan Abdul Latif Nasser, published in *Esquire Middle East* magazine in July 2020 following the broadcast of the Radiolab miniseries *The Other Latif*, by a journalist who shares his name, ends its account of ongoing detention with a reminder that after eighteen years of deprivation of his basic rights as a human being," he feels "trapped in a story I cannot read, hear or control, waiting for a happy ending that never comes" ("Exclusive: An Open Letter").[2]

Memoirs written after release register similar apprehension about the future as well as doubt that the indefinite detention of the Guantánamo experience will ever relax its grip. Swanson and Moore find in the prologue to the restored edition of Slahi's *Guantánamo Diary* an anticipation of the indefinite detention that even post-release life will hold (41). As Slahi contemplates his future, he identifies in it a continuation of the detained, or suspended, sense of time that governed his years at Guantánamo. Other former detainees who have written accounts of Guantánamo approach the future with apprehension and mistrust. Their depictions of life during detention and after release accord the future a silence that contrasts markedly with the narrative weight and progression of their pre-Guantánamo lives, which in many detainees' accounts fill as much as half the book and detail a life of purpose: humanitarian work in Afghanistan, in the case of Moazzam Begg, or in Bosnia, for Lakhdar Boumediène and Mustafa Ait Idir; a modest job that nevertheless allowed for rising through the ranks, as recounted by Ahmed Errachidi and by Murat Kurnaz; an itinerant existence that itself constituted a process of self-discovery, as David Hicks depicts his pre-detention life. What detainees' accounts portray during and after their time at Guantánamo is a contamination of their conception of the future by the physical detention, psychological abuse, and warping of temporal progress that they experience there: a contamination that endures beyond release, despite the ostensible opposition between captivity and freedom.

For detainees writing retrospectively about their detention at Guantánamo, the relation between an imputed past—one that is sup-

THE FUTURE

posed to have involved terrorist activities wholly incompatible with their own accounts—and a present of enclosure, isolation, deprivation, and, in many cases, torture, is so intense that it precludes the accommodation of a future. Their legal status corroborates this preclusion: there are no charges against them, little in the way of due process, and no formal sentence. Former detainees recount progressively losing trust in any future that might hold change, as a result of both the bait-and-switch of reneged promises that formed part of the military's strategy to make them talk and the stasis of their lived experience. Begg writes that "after eight months in Guantánamo I knew that the early promises by the Americans that I would get a lawyer were hollow . . . it seemed as though my Guantánamo life could go on forever, as I sat in my steel cell and saw young guards and interrogators come to the end of their term and be replaced by new faces" (*Enemy Combatant* 224). Hicks, having been tricked into thinking he might be released, resigns himself to an experience that stretches out endlessly: he observes new arrivals among his military guards, "knowing that I had been in here longer than they had been in the military" (250).

Narrating their release, even with several years of hindsight in many cases, former detainees are often reluctant to move too far from the close quarters of the present to a more promising time. Of his return to Bosnia and his first reencounter with his young son, Ait Idir writes, "I was not thinking about the future that stretched out before me or the past from which I will never be fully unshackled. For the first time in seven years, I could see my son" (211). For Kurnaz, returning home to Bremen was "like traveling through time" (224). "I knew," he writes, "that the life I had left behind in Germany was no longer going to be as I had imagined it all those years in Guantánamo" (225). Hicks finds himself able to contemplate a future, but at the very slow pace that his experience of detention has made necessary: "As time passes," he writes, "I am slowly able to put the negatives of the past behind me and replace them with the positives of the present and hopes for the future" (414). Hicks's impulse to focus on "the little, simple things in life that really matter" (415) is echoed by other released detainees, for whom a reduction in the scale and temporal scope of their expectations is a way of asserting agency over the present and the very near-term future. Back at his mother's home, Kurnaz writes, "I have a new appreciation for the value of simple things like sleeping and eating" (236). Boumediène, in admitting that he is "hopeful for the future" (232), is careful to limit the scale of his aspirations: he would like to start a "small business" and buy a "small house" (232).

Detainees' memoirs tend to close with a slow-moving present, extending toward the future with extreme caution. In the aftermath of an experience in which their agency has been severely curtailed, they express little great ambition to effect change or claim justice, even when this was in fact the course their post-Guantánamo lives took. Begg, for example, became a spokesperson for the advocacy group Cage Prisoners, Adayfi was awarded the Richard J. Margolis Award for social-justice journalism, and Slahi gained significant notoriety and a public platform with the release of *The Mauritanian*, a 2021 film based on his detention and torture at Guantánamo. Rather, the narratives themselves function as the primary vehicle for lending coherence to the Guantánamo experience, and for registering at a personal and institutional level the harm caused by detention. It is in this sense that Josephine Metcalf has read Guantánamo detainees' memoirs as a form of memorialization: "A lack of government apology forces (former) detainees to memorialize themselves and their own stories" (75). Bearing witness is an important further step, even as detainees rarely name nor know of a system of justice that will carry their accounts, whether literary or legal, through due process. As individual actors committed to the large-scale project of bearing witness for which an organization such as Witness to Guantánamo presents a public face, Kurnaz, for example, insists that "It's important that our stories are told" (236) while Errachidi writes of his memoir as a means to "bear testimony" (136).

The legacy of Guantánamo and its suspension of the future overshadow the post-detention lives of former detainees who have not published memoirs, as reported by a number of journalists who have found in these lives various manifestations of instability, economic and psychological insecurity, itinerance, and disappearance. French journalist Jerome Tubiana and graphic novelist Alexandre Franc, who together produced *Guantánamo Kid: The True Story of Mohammed El-Gharani* (2019), devote a fifth of the book—more than most former detainees' memoirs—to life after Guantánamo. In Mohammed el-Gharani's first-person voice and with his image, they trace a forced repatriation to Chad, the birthplace that el-Gharani, having grown up in Saudi Arabia, barely knew; an escape to Sudan; an arrest and further escape; and a

THE FUTURE

closing resolve to "make life better where I am" (149). The essay Tubiana has authored as a postscript catalogs the frustration of this resolve, as el-Gharani and his family move without documents through Cameroon, Benin, Ghana, and Nigeria, always in fear of the surveillance they know has followed them and that constantly threatens to destabilize their lives once again. The postscript is punctuated with el-Gharani's messages to Tubiana: "They're going to deport us" (159), "I have to run like a fugitive" (160). As of the book's publication, Tubiana writes, el-Gharani "was still waiting for a 'safe country' to grant him asylum" (161).

El-Gharani's fugitive itinerance traces just one branch of an expansive geographic network to which former detainees have been released, extending Guantánamo's reach and aftermath beyond, even, the various countries of origin of the almost 780 men who have been detained there. The geography of this network is itself closely bound to former detainees' contemplation of a future given that many, particularly those transferred to countries other than those they would consider to be home, have faced insurmountable obstacles in their attempts to rebuild their lives. Polly Rossdale and Katie Taylor, both of whom have worked with the British charity Reprieve's "Life After Guantánamo" project, which offers social care, health care, and legal intervention for former detainees, estimated in 2017 that of the 741 men who had then been transferred to 59 countries, 142 had been sent to countries with which they were entirely unfamiliar, a result of undisclosed agreements between these governments and the United States (51). Of the former detainees sent to third countries, Reprieve in 2022 estimated that one third had not been granted legal status, thus leaving them "vulnerable to deportation and restricting their ability to rebuild their lives" (Yachot). Among these was Lotfi bin Ali, a Tunisian held without charge at Guantánamo for twelve years and resettled in Kazakhstan in 2014; six years later he was once again transferred, to Mauritania, where he died due to complications of a heart condition for which he had been persistently denied adequate care (Hilal). In 2015 bin Ali was the subject of *Life after Guantánamo: Exiled in Kazakhstan*, a documentary made for *VICE News*. Directed and narrated by Simon Ostrovsky, the documentary follows bin Ali's attempts to communicate with the generally intransigent Kazakh Red Crescent about his urgent medical needs, uncertain legal status, lack of community, and concerns about surveillance, despite his inability to speak either Kazakh or Russian and the absence of any translation services before the arrival of Russian-speaking Ostrovsky and his Arabic-speaking assistant. Unable to work, get married, or start a family—all steps toward the future that bin Ali would have liked to take—he finds himself asking, "How long can I live like this?" He experiences his life in Kazakhstan as sometimes comparable to Guantánamo and sometimes even worse: he comments that "I feel like I'm in a second Guantánamo" but also that "In Guantánamo I might have had opportunities," such as leaning to paint. In an assessment that curtails any possibility of a future beyond Guantánamo, bin Ali acknowledges that "I want to get out of this country or go back to Guantánamo." This is a desire that similarly haunts the present of former detainee Younous Chekkouri, who, like bin Ali, was interviewed for a 2016 *New York Times* article on widespread post-traumatic stress disorder among former Guantánamo detainees (Apuzzo et al.). Chekkouri describes feeling that "your brain is playing games . . . You're still living in Gitmo. It's fear." Rossdale and Taylor's conclusions from their work with many detainees entering lives after Guantánamo describe a broader sense of a future co-opted by the experience of the detention centers. One former detainee told Rossdale and Taylor that if they intended to name their project "Life after Guantánamo," then they would have to "give life" (54); he was, they say, "expressing the sense that the Guantánamo regime destroys the feeling of being alive" (54). From other former detainees they heard "My future is black. I won't live longer than 10 years" (54) and "I'm going back to Gtmo where I just eat and sleep and wait for the end of my life" (55).

The unknowability, and feared impossibility, of a post-Guantánamo future is one of the dimensions of former detainees' lives at the forefront of artist Debi Cornwall's *Beyond Gitmo* series, part of her *Welcome to Camp America* project, a project that stands as a tribute to these men, and as a small-scale gesture in the direction of repair. Published in book form in 2017, *Welcome to Camp America* offers a disquieting assemblage of photographs taken by Cornwall at the Guantánamo Bay detention camps and naval station, and in the globally far-flung locations to which detainees have been transferred. It also offers fragments of personal and official text, some in English and some in Arabic, relating in direct or less evident ways to the detention camps. Alexandra Moore has read *Welcome to Camp America* through the lens of "forensic aesthetics" and "counterforensics," as proposed by Eyal Weizman and Thomas Keenan, respectively, finding in the project a commentary on

FIGURE 4.1. DEBI CORNWALL, *ANONYMOUS, UZBEK (ALBANIA)*. © DEBI CORNWALL, REPRINTED BY PERMISSION.

FIGURE 4.2. DEBI CORNWALL, *ANONYMOUS, CHINESE UIGHUR (ALBANIA)*. © DEBI CORNWALL, REPRINTED BY PERMISSION.

"the ways in the which the architectural and other material elements of detention, incarceration, and even postcarceral life are integral to the violence within those spaces" ("Across the Threshold of Detectability" 218). In Moore's reading, the violence of postcarceral life is at once manifest and challenged by the series of former detainees, photographed in the countries to which they have been transferred, facing away from the camera. Moore draws attention to the collaborative process with which these photographs are created, one that "invites the men to help stage their own portraits" (226), including, following the publication of the book, a collaboration in which a former detainee was invited to graphically alter images of Guantánamo cell blocks, inscribing a corrective and personal perspective on what the photograph seemed to show (227). The fact that detainees' faces are kept from view in Cornwall's photographs, Moore writes, need not necessarily be read as limiting their subjectivity, as portraiture itself can obscure the struggle behind the image (226).

In my own reading of *Welcome to Camp America*, it is the symmetrical harmony of each full, 8 x 10 frame and the format in which photographs of former detainees are inserted into the book that offers the most powerful ways of thinking about the future for these men. In most of the photographs, the subject occupies the center of the frame, surrounded by a scene that, in its palette and shape, complements rather than overwhelms him. Two of the subjects named as "Anonymous," for example, are photographed facing the seats of an empty stadium, one made of stone (fig 4.1) and the other painted blue (fig 4.2), mirroring in each case the color of the subject's clothing; they, like many of the other photographed subjects, stand with a stillness that suggests contemplation and self-possession rather than restraint. Most strikingly, each of the plates portraying a former detainee is a loose-leaf insertion in the otherwise bound book that is *Welcome to Camp America*. The plates thus lack fixity—a lack that in one sense, as Moore comments, invokes "the often arbitrary locations where detainees have been transferred" (227), but that also allows these detainees, via their unbound images, to disrupt the otherwise rigidly guarded history that *Welcome to Camp America* documents. In the most utopian of futures, it allows, even, for a conceptual freeing from that history altogether, or an alternative dissemination of the images of, and supposed intelligence on, these men. Not altogether uncoincidentally, this freeing is achieved through a means of transmission akin to the one that enabled the capture of many detainees: the scattering over Afghanistan of flyers offering significant financial rewards for identifying "terrorists," a practice that, as Mark P. Denbeaux and Jonathan Hafetz have observed, enticed Afghan bounty hunters to turn innocent men over to US authorities (307). While the former detainees' post-Guantánamo future is in almost all cases precarious, Cornwall's free-floating images, telling new versions of their subjects' stories, suggest tentative alternatives.

CUBAN FUTURES AND THE GUANTÁNAMO BAY NAVAL BASE

For Cubans in the vicinity of Guantánamo Bay Naval Base, the future has been co-opted at a national and rhetorical level by the teleology of the Cuban Revolution, as an ongoing and, indeed, indefinite process of building a socialist society whose future completion is both assured and deferred. Cuban citizens have, nevertheless and inevitably, envisioned other futures in their daily lives and plans, some coexisting in manageable contradiction of the future of revolution, as is the case, for example, of the "celebratory temporality" (802) that Hanna Garth has studied with regard to carnival and Cuban socialism, while others mount a direct and politically untenable challenge to this version of a collective future, positing radical change to the Cuban system of government or departure from the island as the only viable options.

While demands for change and migration from Cuba have continued relatively unabated from 1959 to the present day—Movimiento San Isidro and the ongoing stream of documented and undocumented departures being recent examples—two projects aimed at redefining Cuba's future have taken shape in the Guantánamo region, one unfolding at the base and the other in the dissident communities and prisons of Guantánamo Province, in an eerie if asynchronous symmetry with one another and with experiences of detainees at the base. Each project is named explicitly for a future other than that offered by the Cuban Revolution and its temporal rhetoric. The first, *El futuro*, is a handwritten journal produced by Cuban refugees held in camps at the Guantánamo naval base from 1994 to 1996 having been intercepted at sea while attempting to reach the United States during what has become known as the Balsero Crisis, or the Cuban Rafter Crisis. The second journal, titled *Porvenir* and published intermittently beginning in 2008, is a little-known publication of Alianza Democrática Oriental, the principal dissident organization in eastern Cuba, many of whose members have been political prisoners.

The Cuban Rafter Crisis reached a peak on August 5, 1994, when riots broke out in Havana in response partly to the severe economic decline that Cuba had faced since the collapse of the Soviet Bloc and, more specifically, to the sinking of a ferry by means of which citizens were attempting to leave the country and to what Susan Eckstein and Lorena Barberia describe as "the short-lived occupation of diplomatic premises by some 150 would-be emigrants" (806). Faced with a potential regime-ending revolt, Fidel Castro announced that Cuban border guards would not enforce laws against leaving the island. Between August and mid-September some thirty-six thousand Cubans took to the sea hoping to reach the United States where, in accordance with the then-prevailing Cuban Adjustment Act of 1966, they would be permitted an accelerated path to residency. Two weeks later, fearing a potentially overwhelming influx of new Cuban immigrants, President Bill Clinton ordered the US Coast Guard to intercept rafters and redirect them to the Guantánamo naval base where they would be held in temporary shelter, alongside ten thousand Haitians fleeing the continuing violence in their country, while Cuba and the United States negotiated new migration accords. These negotiations led to a revision of the Cuban Adjustment Act and, by early 1996, most of the Cubans held at Guantánamo had been paroled into the United States (Henken 394).

First-person accounts of Cuban rafters' time at Guantánamo are more abundant than those of post–9/11 detainees and have been subject to significantly less restriction, in production as well as dissemination. Among these are the interviews that make up the unlikely 2002 Catalan documentary *Balseros*, codirected by Carles Bosch and Josep Maria Domènech, who filmed seven Cubans from different backgrounds through their decisions to attempt a perilous departure from Cuba, their detention and long wait at Guantánamo, and their attempts to build new lives in the United States. Two prominent online archives, the University of Miami's *Between Despair and Hope: Cuban Rafters at the U.S. Naval Base Guantánamo Bay, 1994–1996*, and the Guantánamo Public Memory Project, bring together stories and visual materials from this episode. Elizabeth Campisi's *Escape to Miami: An Oral History of the Cuban Rafter Crisis* (2016) draws on observations and numerous conversations with *balseros* during the author's time working at the field office of the

US Justice Department's Community Relations Service at Guantánamo Bay to present the personal stories and political histories of the balseros and the "distinctive camp culture" (1) they developed.

The conditions under which balseros were held at camps at Guantánamo bear some similarities to those created for war on terror detainees. As Campisi records, balseros were held among "barbed wire, guard posts, high-intensity light, guards who sometimes patrolled with dogs, severe limitations on movement, poor sanitation, scarce potable water, regimented food distribution" (66). Although the situation improved with time, "at first, there was not enough clothing, medicine or doctors, and although there was enough food, it was poorly distributed" (66). One of the more chilling pre-figurations of the post-9/11 years is the use, during the balseros' time at Guantánamo, of Camp X-Ray as a castigation area for men who had misbehaved: like the first prisoners in the following decade, these men were kept at the mercy of the elements "in long, narrow, chain-link stalls that resembled large dog kennels, only worse, since they were topped with razor wire" (64). Nevertheless, there are significant differences between the US military's approach toward aspiring Cuban refugees at Guantánamo in the 1990s and its treatment of so-called enemy combatants rendered to the base after 9/11. Balseros were held at what Campisi terms "a low- to moderate-security extraterritorial immigration detention center" (66) rather than the prisons of years later, and they were treated with varying but increasing regard by members of the military, to the extent that they were eventually permitted to use different spaces around the base as art galleries and recreational facilities. The Cuban refugees were allowed to make phone calls to family members and lawyers (18), a privilege denied the Haitians whose detention at Guantánamo overlapped with theirs, and unavailable to war on terror detainees for the first years of the camps' existence.[3]

Isolation, interrogation, and torture—three of the most brutal aspects of the treatment of war on terror detainees—were not features of balseros' detention at Guantánamo. Rather, as Campisi reports, they quickly formed well-organized and efficient community structures, re-creating "social institutions such as churches and schools" (3) and, in the case of the somewhat anomalous Camp Alpha, developing a "high level of internal organization" (111) with "numbered blocks, rows and tents" to facilitate food distribution (111). Inhabitants of the camps would choose leaders from among their communities, designating these to act on their behalf with military authorities. "Their capacity for community organizing," Campisi observes, "reflected their experience in Cuba, as the majority of Cubans had participated in mass organizations in one way or another" (96). Cuba's Committees for the Defense of the Revolution established neighborhood block groups whose primary function, under the guise of defending the revolution, was vigilance and discipline, but which was organized to be inclusive yet hierarchical.[4] Balseros were also drawn into a broader community of Cubans who had sought refuge in the United States, and the by then well-established and politically influential Cuban American community sent visitors to the camps to report on the living conditions of the refugees, as well as legal and medical personnel to assist them, and performers—among them jazz musician Arturo Sandoval, singers Gloria and Emilio Estefan, and actor Andy García—for their entertainment (18).

Balseros briefly had in common with post–9/11 detainees, however, the indefinite temporality of their time there, in that their departure was uncertain; consequently, theirs was a forced stasis in a present that promised no different future. Taken to Guantánamo by the US Coast Guard beginning in August 1994, it was not until May 1995 that balseros learned that most of them would be admitted to the United States, according to a lottery system that was seemingly designed to produce uncertainty, even though by early 1996 the last numbers had been called (Campisi 15–19). Their creative work at the camps, however, engages with two distinct conceptualizations of the future: the ever-deferred fulfillment of collective utopia that underpinned Cuban revolutionary temporality, on the one hand, and on the other a future more clearly crafted by an individual's actions, decisions, and industry, understood by balseros (as by generations of aspiring immigrants before them) to be a tenet of US democratic society. As former balsero and artist Conrado Basulto claims in his oral history for the Guantánamo Public Memory Project, "Your decisions are what make your future. It was worth jumping in the ocean, it was worth the risk of leaving a place that has no future and finding yourself in a place that welcomes you and gives you a chance to develop yourself as a person."

The balseros became known for their creative artwork, the production of which was bolstered by the lack of structured time at the camps, the limited alternative opportunities for self-representation, and the training many had received through either Cuba's profession-

FIGURE 4.3. *EL FUTURO*, ISSUE 1, MARCH 26, 1995. REPRINTED BY PERMISSION OF JORGE DEL RÍO.

al art schools or its network of community workshops (Campisi 124). Although art materials were initially in short supply, balseros drew on "another skill that developed under the conditions of scarcity of the Cuban Revolution"—namely, "modifying an object for a new use" (123). It is through this process that "army cots became armchairs and rockers, caps from miniature Tabasco sauce bottles became chandeliers, and plastic spoon collections became 'beaded' curtains" (3), creations that are arguably what Guillermina De Ferrari has called "arts of repair" (547), "objects and performance art pieces that, either via their functionality or aesthetic merits (or a combination of both), reflect on the social and moral aspects of adaptive creativity" (547). Campisi has noted that once their eventual passage to the United States was assured, balseros tended to create art without political content, while their earlier work had been more critical in its approach. An early painting, for example, showed the Statue of Liberty blindfolded (131), suggesting apprehension toward the ambiguous promise of an American future, while Campisi's reading of Reynaldo González's paintings, depicting scenes in Cuba, emphasizes material scarcity and personal frustration in Cuba—consequences, in the present, of endlessly deferring the revolution's future.

El futuro (The Future) is the title of one of several journals produced by Cubans at Guantánamo. Written by hand, it began with the very small print run of the four to six copies that the US military would make of the original, but it eventually reached up to two thousand weekly copies. Like other balsero newspapers and *¿Qué pasa?*, the more official publication produced in collaboration with the US military, it is lavishly illustrated in color, in its masthead—a machete pointing away from the Cuban flag and toward a flaming torch—the incidental drawings in its sidebars, and the abundant cartoons that Tania Pérez-Cano has read as an archive of graphic testimony (fig. 4.3). In a transitional gesture not unlike the one that Campisi identifies in the balseros' Cuban-trained social organizing, Pérez-Cano traces in *El futuro* an aesthetic debt to a Cuban culture of graphic testimonies that are primarily "critical of the living conditions in Cuba and of Fidel Castro and the Cuban government" (Pérez-Cano 84–85). The lines and characters of *El futuro*'s graphic testimonies, she observes, "resemble the aesthetics of the kind of 'revolutionary' graphic art that was created in Cuba mainly as a form of propaganda, with a didactic purpose" (85).

Much of the graphic art of *El futuro* alludes in some way to the uncertain situation of the balseros at Guantánamo, caught in between Cuba and the United States and at the mercy of each government. The journal's editorials, however, are especially focused in their attempts to not only anticipate but also to shape what lies ahead despite the fact that, particularly in the early days of the journal before their eventual admission to the United States was assured, some balseros had been in the makeshift camps for eight months. A prevailing mood at that time is expressed in a contribution to the "Reflection" section of the first issue by Humberto Pérez, who writes, "When will we leave? Some of the more pessimistic among us say, will we leave? But will they leave? Will they leave what's oppressed them, what deprives them of any decent way of living?" (Pérez, "Carta a Osvaldo" 1).[5] The Editorial Committee's statement in the first issue asserts more definitively, declaring this new publication "an open tribune for FAITH IN THE FUTURE" ("Editorial" 1). The faith in the future that *El futuro*'s editorial committee proposes turns out to be a particularly activist one, grounded in marshalling the voices of balseros so that even in their powerlessness, their importance in the geopolitical arena is recognized. To define the newspaper as "an open tribune" (1) is, primarily, to take advantage of the heterogeneity of its format (in genre as in authorship) to articulate the future collaboratively and to stake a forum from which to claim rights from those who make decisions about refugees.

The editorial that opens *El futuro*'s second issue, dated April 2, 1995, asks that three camps (Hunt, Kilo, and India) not be relocated, as their occupants have formed a close, disciplined community that they value. Unlike the publication's earlier editorial statement, this one is written in Spanish and English; directed at readers in general as an open letter, it asks in particular that the community-designated leaders from each camp "intervene on our behalf before the General" ("Editorial: Nuestra Opinión" 1). This letter advocates for the status quo in the present, but with a view to a future in which rights will have a broader linguistic and political reach. The editorial of *El futuro*'s fourth issue, published in May 1995, is audaciously titled "Cuba's Destiny." In calling for both Cuba and the United States to move on from Cold War politics, it insists on the centrality of the balseros to Cuba's future and to Cuba-US relations: "Cuba's destinies are in play, and we the *balseros* of '94 are the key piece" ("El destino de Cuba" 1). The lack of voice that balseros themselves have in state-level confrontations and negotiations does not fully eclipse their right, and responsibility, to advocate for a more certain future, specifically, in this instance, for a clear plan from the United States for ending the crisis that is keeping them at Guantánamo. "In this 'major league' game," the editors write, "we have neither voice nor vote, but it is our ardent wish to express an opinion and we will do so" (1). That they consider themselves on solid ground in their claims, despite the legal and temporal limbo in which they find themselves, is indicated by the postscript to the editorial, a quote from Cuban independence hero José Martí. Overall, *El futuro* launches a projection of community that allows the editors and the diverse contributors to intervene and claim rights in the present, as a means to envisage and solidify a post-camp future.

A FUTURE IN GUANTÁNAMO'S SHADOWS

No more than thirty miles from the camps in which balseros have imagined their future, and during the first decade of so-called enemy combatants' detention at Guantánamo, other men held against their will called for a reorienting of the future, this time through the Spanish word *porvenir*, an almost-synonym of *el futuro* that translates more portentously as "that which is to come." Cuban political prisoners held at Guantánamo's provincial prison, known as el Combinado de Guantánamo, are a major focus of, and significant contributors to, the journal *Porvenir: La voz independiente de Guantánamo*, a monthly publication initiated in 2008 and continuing sporadically into the following decade. *Porvenir* was one of five regional publications of the dissident group Alianza Democrática Oriental, devoted to promoting independent, nonstate journalism in Cuba, under the sponsorship of the Directorio Democrático Cubano, a US-based organization of exiled Cubans calling for democracy and human rights.

Porvenir's founding editorial statement purports to offer a provincial and global purview, insisting on giving voice to Guantánamo in its cultural and historical dimensions. It begins by stating that "the works presented here are written by people from Guantánamo, and only Guantánamo ... It will address the municipalities, their syncretism, origin and roots, as well as the base of its development" (Editorial Committee of *Porvenir* 2).[6] In claiming a regular place in its pages for lists of prisoners, however, the journal extends the locality of Guantánamo to a broader context of human rights that includes the naval base as a migration route, and, hence, a pretext for incarceration in Cuba of would-be migrants, and a neighboring site of human rights abuses. The editorial statement commits to publishing "permanently . . . the list of political prisoners from Guantánamo held at the Combined Provincial Prison of Guantánamo, as well as those incarcerated for attempting to leave the country illegally" (2).

Each issue of *Porvenir* includes a section by journalist Jorge Corrales Ceballos on a municipality of Guantánamo, summarizing its history and, in some cases, its archaeology, and offering a number of color photographs. There are also short articles on the quality of life in the province—on public transportation, the state of repair of certain housing units, Cuba's precarious infrastructure—that, while adversarial in their tone, are standard fare for local newspapers in other contexts. Many issues, quite improbably, have a section titled "Consejos útiles/mujeres" (Useful Advice for Women), devoted to advice on caring for women's hair in the harsh Guantánamo climate. The bulk of all issues of *Porvenir*, however, is devoted to political repression in Guantánamo Province, with open letters and editorials calling for systemic change as well as testimonies from political prisoners. The first issue, for example, has sections on "Critical Hygiene and Food Conditions in the Combinado de Guatánamo Prison"; "Solidarity," reporting on a protest by "peaceful protesters, defenders of human rights" ("Críticas condiciones" 10) to draw attention to the plight of political prisoners Rolando Rodríguez Lobaina and Yordis García Fournier; and, on its last page, the photograph of a house of a political prisoner, under constant surveillance and, in a present-day version of the "acts of repudiation" that have marked the treatment of dissidents since the 1960s, smeared with feces by defenders of the Cuban Revolution ("Víctimas de la represión en Cuba" 22).

The "Testimonio" sections of *Porvenir* are written by those committed to the dissident movement, some incarcerated at the time of writing and others appearing on later issues' lists of political prisoners, as is the case of Yordis García Fournier, an editor of the journal, imprisoned six months after his account was published in the first issue. These sections trace their authors' paths to opposition and the acts of repression experienced along the way or describe the geography and routines of life in prison. Editorials place political prisoners' plight in a national context and in broader ones of pacifist opposition and human rights advocacy. The November 2008 issue opens with a full-page editorial on the hunger strike of three young human rights activists at the Combinado de Guantánamo, insisting that they are bringing greater awareness to ordinary Cubans about human rights violations on the island; the same issue includes an open letter to President Raúl Castro from political prisoner Ernesto Durán Rodríguez, listing the ways in which Cuba has violated its obligations under UN protocols, *The Universal Declaration of Human Rights*, and its own constitution. Mahatma Gandhi and Tiananmen Square are named in the journal's pages, as global referents for the struggle that engages residents of Guantánamo.

In accordance with the commitment made in the first issue, the following three issues close with a list of prisoners held in Guantánamo Province. These are presented under the capitalized heading DERECHOS HUMANOS (HUMAN RIGHTS) and are divided into two sublists: the first of political prisoners and the second of those jailed for attempting to leave Cuba without permission and via improper channels. All prisoners are named, with additional information on the first list that varyingly includes the charge for which they are detained, the length of their jail sentence, and a home address. Charges include "Disrespect and Violence," "Social Danger," and "Disrespect of the Figure of Commander Fidel Castro"; sentences range from four to twenty years. Additional information on the second list, that of those imprisoned for "Illegal Departure," includes "Returned from the Naval Base," indicating that migrants successfully reached the base but were returned by US authorities and subsequently imprisoned.

The first three issues have the same eleven names on the list of political prisoners and twenty-four on the list of those jailed for attempting to leave Cuba illegally. By the eighth issue, dated September 2008, only political prisoners are listed, and they now number twenty. The seventh issue introduces a new section listing the prisons in Guantánamo Province, their addresses, the number of prisoners held in each, and the dimensions of a cell; there are twelve prisons on the list, with the Combinado de Guantánamo being by far the largest. Preceding these lists in every issue is a section of several pages that documents acts of repression and aggression perpetrated against political prisoners and dissident citizens.

The testimonies and meticulously documented lists and accounts in *Porvenir* publicize information for which there are extraordinarily few other sources within Cuba—other than those we must assume are guarded with a high level of secrecy—and even in the archives of international human rights organizations that attempt to monitor Cuba. It is information published at great risk, with limited circulation, little opportunity for corroboration and, therefore, with the anticipation that it will be called into question. In standing thus, it nevertheless sets a stake in the ground for internally generated change in Cuba, one that redirects the country's future toward democratic politics. The choice of a name for the journal—*Porvenir*, or "that which is to come"—directly references the party-line journalism that has long been a staple in Cuba as well as the bellicosity and revolutionary teleology this journalism is mired in. Justifying the name in response to the putative question "Why *Porvenir*?" the editors explain with reference to the future-conjugated title of Guantánamo's provincial newspaper, *Venceremos*: "Well, it's because we understand that, unlike the clichéd *Venceremos* (the only official, provincial channel to publish its editions weekly), *Porvenir* is the image of a future yet to be realized . . . *Porvenir* is not a war cry because we don't spend all our lives fighting" (Editorial Committee of *Porvenir* 2). Rather than a continually deferred struggle for an always-distant ideal, the editors offer "the image of a future yet to be realized," a rendering in the present of what the future can and should be. And rather than embed the future in a discourse of war on imperialism, they advocate a peaceful path.

SPECULATIVE FUTURES FOR GUANTÁNAMO

Injustice in the present animates the future articulated from detention centers, balsero refugee camps, and Cuban prisons. At the same time, Guantánamo's presence in a broader, global frame of reference has given rise to more speculative renderings, drawing on the many abuses layered upon the region to imagine a future that would make amends and repair. The three renderings considered here come from different disciplinary areas. The first, the Tea Project's speculative text "Reparations for Guantánamo Torture Survivors," included in Amber Ginsburg, Aaron Hughes, Aliya Hussein, and Audrey Petty's edited book *Remaking the Exceptional: Tea, Torture, and Reparations | Chicago to Guantánamo* (2022), mines the implicit relationship linking art, imagination and ideal worlds; as does the second, artist Ian Alan Paul's *Guantánamo Bay Museum of Art and History* virtual museum project. The third, a proposal to build a marine research facility and peace park at the site of the detention centers, is the work of conservation biologist Joe Roman, in collaboration with legal scholar James Kraska. I propose reading all three projects, however, as forms of symbolic reparation in the future—as gestures, that is, of both acknowledgement and commemoration of a present that in fact has yet to pass.

The future delineated in detainee memoirs, *El futuro* and *Porvenir* in each case gestures at, and in some explicitly demands, the possibility of conciliation and repair; although official, state-led repair (certainly in the form of reparation) has barely materialized for former detainees, balseros, or Cuban political prisoners. Helen Duffy has commented on "the refusal of many States to provide simple recognition to victims that they have had their rights violated" (86) in being rendered to Guantánamo, with the formal apology and $8 million compensation payment that the Canadian government offered to former child detainee and Canadian citizen Omar Khadr standing as both anomalous and controversial (86). Ex gratia payments and settlements have been offered by several governments, Duffy notes, but "often without explicit recognition of wrongdoing or apology" (86). While the question of reparation for balseros is not an active one, *El futuro*'s editors' expressed faith in the future was predicated on admission to the United States as conciliation with a wider Cuban community and as recompense in the form of economic opportunity, yet the interviewees in Bosch and Domenech's *Balseros*, as just one example, testify to the uneven distribution of both admission and recompense. Similarly, national reconciliation and repair are central to the advocacy of Alianza Democrática Oriental and *Porvenir*, as they have been to other pro-democracy projects steered by Cubans largely outside the United States, such as the Washington, DC-based Cuba Archive and the Task Force on Memory, Truth and Justice's report *Cuban National Reconciliation* (2003). Imagining a future for Cuba in *Porvenir*'s first issue, Rolando Tudela Iríbar appeals to "all Cubans on and off the island, to implore them to fight for their emancipation, to see the awakening of participatory democracy, to see ideas of freedom channeled toward justice and hope" (3).

In the absence of high-level reparation, either economic or in the form of apology and recognition, attempts to remember and repair have reached those held against their will at Guantánamo, both on and off the base, in largely piecemeal ways. As Rossdale and Taylor write of the work of Reprieve's "Life after Guantánamo" project, "In a context where there is no legal remedy or redress, such as Guantánamo, the importance of broadly conceived reparations is even greater for moral, strategic and for therapeutic reasons. In the absence of compensation or formal redress, the provision of rehabilitation support can itself be reframed as an aspect of reparation" (56). Other efforts to repair and commemorate have come more clearly from the domain of the arts, in which the founders of the Symbolic Reparation Research Project, self-defined as "a group of humanities and legal scholars specializing in human rights, art, and culture" (1), identify a particular capacity to imagine change. "Committed to fostering the arts, cultural practices, and humanities as a crucial means of developing the efficacy of symbolic reparations for victims of gross violations of human rights," the group insists that memorialization practices "necessarily draw on artistic and cultural forms, practices, and traditions to generate aesthetic experiences that are fundamental to engendering new perspectives and new modes of social interaction" (2). The balsero exodus—part discrete historical episode and part node in a phenomenon that preceded it and continues to the present day—has generated small-scale memorialization practices in the form of art exhibits and gatherings, especially in South Florida. Such tributes as Cornwall's *Welcome to Camp America*, and the engagements with the detention camps that Barbara Harlow includes in her account of "extraordinary renditions" literature, might be seen in this light with regard to post–9/11 detainees. Repair for Cuban political prisoners, however, is still elusive.

The practices of commemoration and memorialization that form a cornerstone of symbolic reparation have been most widely proposed in post-conflict societies committed to processes of national conciliation: this is yet to be the case for Guantánamo, an extra-national site of ongoing hostility and atrocity.[7] Liz Ševčenko draws attention to the atypical context in her discussion of the Guantánamo Public Memory Project, an online public history project that brings together interviews, written testimony, photographs, and historical analysis of people who have passed through the base since the 1950s. The project's founders initially wondered whether it was "too soon for a 'memory' project" (Ševčenko, *Public History for a Post-Truth Era* 158), with Guantánamo "not in the past" (158), but concluded that in fact "the absence of official investigations imposed both burdens and opportunities for creating an alternative space to confront the past" (159). Ševčenko's discussion situates the Guantánamo Public Memory Project firmly within the scope of the International Sites of Conscience Coalition, from which it was launched in 2009. Sites of Conscience are historic places that aim to "draw connections between past and present" (82) and "interpret history through site" (82); they are often museums curated to honor the experiences of victims, survivors and broader communities. While Guantánamo Bay as a site is currently unavailable for such use, the Guantánamo Public Memory Project nevertheless seeks to "raise public awareness of the century-long history of use and reuse of the U.S. Naval Base at Guantánamo Bay and to foster dialogue on the future of this place, its people, and its policies" (Ševčenko, "Public Histories" 141).

"Reparations for Guantánamo Torture Survivors," the *Guantánamo Bay Museum of Art and History* project, and Roman and Kraska's proposal perform an especially bold relationship to the future, eliding the unevenness and temporal lags in repair for the many layers of abuse at Guantánamo by standing as what we might think of as anticipatory commemoration. They implicitly locate Guantánamo as a Site of Conscience in a future in which apology, atonement, and repair have already been made. All three projects occupy—the first two in an imaginative leap, the second by inference—what we might think of as the narrative future perfect that has also marked engagements with Guantánamo by two of its more prominent stakeholders: former US president Barack Obama and Clive Stafford-Smith, the British lawyer who founded Reprieve and has represented numerous Guantánamo detainees. Obama's future perfect for Guantánamo is brief, tenuous, prescient, and clearly in the realm of speculation: "Imagine a future—," he asked an audience at the National Defense University in May 2013, "ten years from now, or twenty years from now—when the United States of America is still holding people who have been charged with no crime on a piece of land that is not a part of our country" (Obama). Stafford-Smith's is more sustained, in a piece labeled as a "fictional account" that *Al Jazeera* published in 2017 with the title "How Will Guantánamo Be Remembered?" and the subheading "It Is 2046 and Clive Stafford-Smith Has Returned to Guantánamo, Where His Clients Were Once Imprisoned and Tortured." In it an eighty-seven-year-old Stafford-Smith takes his grandson to Guantánamo and interweaves his memories of the Guantánamo of detention camps in 2016 with the subsequent version in which, for example, a Camp Echo cell is "preserved just as it would have been when Shaker [Amer] suffered there, albeit with the temperature set at a rather more comfortable level." The tone of Stafford-Smith's account is self-consciously instructive, both to the grandson—who has recently visited the Sachsenhausen concentration camp near Berlin and is invited to draw comparisons with what he learns of Guantánamo—and for readers thirty years before 2046 for whom the injustices of the US government's reaction to 9/11 are still in the present.

"Reparations for Guantánamo's Torture Survivors," part of the 2022 DePaul Art Museum exhibit and subsequent book *Remaking the Exceptional: Tea, Torture, and Reparations | Chicago to Guantánamo*, does not announce itself as fictional. Rather, it stands as a performative text in which the absence of acknowledgement, apology, and reparation for abuses at Guantánamo, on the part of the US government, is forcefully eclipsed by the present-tense proclamation of all three of these. Written by artists Aaron Hughes and Amber Ginsburg, in collaboration with advocacy groups HeaRT, CAGE, Witness Against Torture, and Chicago Torture Justice Memorials, it is modeled on the speculative reparations ordinance drawn by the latter for the city of Chicago, which was eventually incorporated into the Chicago Reparations Ordinance of 2015, providing financial and other compensation to victims tortured under the command of former Chicago police commander Jon Burge (Hughes and Ginsburg, 201). "Reparations for Guantánamo's Torture Survivors" aims to effect change in the law by enacting it in creative language. "Like poetry," Hughes and Ginsburg write in their introduction to the text, "the official language of apology and reparations begins in the imagination—words and ideas that can be shaped into legal language and concretized into legal documents" (200). The text itself conceals its imaginative status: its twelve clauses, beginning with the conspicuously legal "whereas," culminate in a forceful "BE IT ORDAINED THAT THE U.S. GOVERNMENT" that introduces twelve further clauses starting with "hereby." These latter command into being demands that detainees, their families, and a broader community of advocates and activists have been making for over two decades: a formal apology on behalf of the United States of America; the closure of the military prison at Guantánamo and the ending of military commissions, "which have served to launder evidence of torture" (Hughes and Ginsburg 207); safe release and compassionate resettlement for former detainees here referred to as "survivors"; financial assistance, counseling, health care, and reeducation services upon release; a fund that devotes to post-release support programs an amount equal to or greater than the $380 million it cost to run Guantánamo in 2021; and "a compensation equivalent to the international standard amount for recompense for torture" (207). The status quo announced in "Reparations for Guantánamo's Torture Survivors" was not in effect at the time of its writing, nor subsequently, and yet, within the imaginative parameters of the text, it comes into being.

Like "Reparations for Guantánamo's Torture Survivors," the *Guantánamo Bay Museum of Art and History* takes advantage of art's capacity to revise the real and assume a radically different relationship among past, present, and future. Rather than announcing immediate change to the present, it elides the "hereby" in favor of an unfiltered, present-tense immersion in a Guantánamo unrecognizable at the time of the project's creation. Kalyan Nadiminti has called the *Guantánamo Bay Museum of Art and History* "a conceptual reality but a spatial hoax" (343); it is this because it is also a temporal hoax, naturalizing for its visitors a present that exists only as aspiration. The project's landing page, the "Welcome," presents the museum's mission as "Collectively Remembering a Past Future," while its "Message from the Director" explains that it is "located at the site of the former site of the Guantánamo Bay Detention Facility in Guantánamo Bay, Cuba" and "dedicated to remembering the U.S. prison which was active between 2002 and 2012 before it was permanently closed" (*Guantánamo Bay Museum of Art and History*). Its administrators, unlike those of the site in its former use, claim to have made every effort to make the museum accessible to visitors: opening hours and contact numbers are posted clearly, and the "Plan Your Visit" link leads to a wealth of advice on travel to the base, including on direct flights "from several major airports around the world" and by "a limited boating service from several ports in the United States, Mexico, and Guatemala for those visitors who wish to experience an ocean voyage as part of their visit" (*Guantánamo Bay Museum of Art and History*).

Ian Alan Paul, the museum project's creator and curator since its opening in 2012, describes the project's form on his personal website as "Speculation, Website, Installation, Performance," and its operation as "a critical fiction and experimental documentary, asserting that the Guantanamo Bay detention facilities have been closed and replaced by a museum that critically reflects on the social and political significance of the prison" (Paul). Cathlin Goulding, in an article that addresses didactic dimensions of the *Guantánamo Bay Museum of Art and History* alongside those of a rendering of Guantánamo in the video platform Second Life, terms its narrative of the closure of Guantánamo "speculative history" (161), and draws attention to its upending of "phenomenological conceptions of place as concrete, material, or bound to human memory and histories" (145). Its creators, Goulding writes, "Envisioned and fabricated the place of exception *as it might be* to educate public audiences, promote civic engagement, and stimulate dialogue about the imprisonment of suspected terrorist at Guantánamo Bay Prison" (145). "In this fictive space," Goulding writes, "other kinds of truths are illuminated: Why isn't Guantánamo closed? When will it close? What kind of political conditions have kept it open for so many years?" (164).[8]

The four tabs reachable from the *Guantánamo Bay Museum of Art and History*'s "Welcome" page are for "Current Exhibitions," "Center for Critical Studies," "About the Museum" and "Contact Us," and while the fourth of these upholds the museum's fictive temporality, the first three border on a more familiar present, where the project's activist program becomes more visible and its display of what has been achieved fuses with an agenda of what must be done in the immediate present. Exhibitions include three by the collaborative team of Carling McManus and Jen Susman, introduced as Virginia-based artists whose three series in tribute to Guantánamo detainees are dated 2012, as are the works by Jenny Odell and Jon Kuzmich; *Exit Ticket*, by Fiamma Montezemolo, is dated 2015. The articles linked from the museum's Jumah al-Dossari Center for Critical Studies, several of which have been previously published elsewhere, are written from a time when the detention camps are still in operation. Harsha Walia's essay, "Omar Khadr: Race, Empire and Unexceptional Detention," addresses the case of Khadr—a Canadian citizen held at Guantánamo from the age of fifteen—and states that "at the time of writing, Khadr was still being held at Guantánamo Bay." (In a more recent present, albeit not that of the museum, Khadr has been released). Derek Gregory's article, "The Black Flag: Guantánamo Bay and the State of Exception," similarly marks its present as anticipating, but not witnessing, change: "To date, 267 prisoners have been released from Guantánamo and eighty more have been transferred to their own countries for continued detention." (The total of these numbers has since risen to over seven hundred). The remaining two essays in the museum's Center for Critical Studies—Judith Butler's "Precarious Life; Indefinite

Detention" and Martin Puchner's "Guantánamo Bay: A State of Exception"—are also written from a time in which the detention centers continue to operate. Critical discourse, the project implies, cannot afford to inhabit the virtual, future present, as easily as art can, yet the discrepant temporalities of the two are crucially interdependent in effecting the change that is, after all, the political agenda of the *Guantánamo Bay Museum of Art and History*. In reporting that "it took more than 3 years for a concert of international human rights campaigns, groups of artists and curators organized in opposition to the prison, and coalitional social movements to finally manifest the political strength to shutter all of the facilities and halt their operations," the timeline narrated in the "About the Museum" section credits artists and political actors—and, more importantly, artists as political actors, and vice versa—with an ability to overturn political decisions that has not yet manifested itself fully in the present day. Rather, the museum project demands of today's viewers and "visitors" a facility to move conceptually between different versions of the present.

The *Guantánamo Bay Museum of Art and History* posits a grammatical future perfect, a "this atrocity will have been eradicated," or a "these prisons will have been closed," bringing into being a moment and a scenario that are better than our current present. It is a moment in which the detention centers at the base become a Site of Conscience, a notorious prison and torture center reclaimed to honor the memory of its victims—like others around the world, such as the Espacio Memoria y Derechos Humanos in Buenos Aires, formerly a clandestine prison and torture center under the direction of the Navy Mechanics School (Ševčenko, *Public History* 95). The political, legal, and economic obstacles to such a repurposing are glossed over in the timeline proposed on the museum's site, in whose version it is initiated by President Obama signing an order to close the detention camps and followed by protest on the part of Congress and advocacy groups, but the museum project's dual status, as a work of art and advocacy in our present that poses as an already constructed site of memory in the future, invites its visitors to imagine not only that the camps are closed, but that a museum commemorating them may be possible. In this way the *Guantánamo Bay Museum of Art and History* simultaneously performs and anticipates symbolic reparation as the Symbolic Reparations Research Project outlines it, drawing on the "non-conclusive indeterminacy of the aesthetic experience" (4) to make amends for a yet-to-be terminated pain. It promotes compassionate commemoration of a historical moment that is, effectively, our own; in occupying a future that is considerably better than the present, it advocates action that will achieve that imagined state.

The *Guantánamo Bay Museum of Art and History* locates repair in a future perfect, a gesture facilitated by art's transformational potential but extending to, and sustained by, one of the most enduring forces for conciliation and community in the Guantánamo region: the natural environment. The museum project's "Plan your Visit" section offers a three-day ecological tour that "includes a variety of activities which all engage with the broader ecological and geological history of the area," the rationale of this offer being "to help reverse much of the damage done to the bay" during its years as a military base: to repair for harm inflicted not only on people held at the base but also on the area's plant and animal life. This is a rationale that resonates with the similarly conciliatory and imaginative proposal for the future of the base developed by Joe Roman and James Kraska. Although their proposal envisages the future from a more clearly identifiable present, and from the field of environmental studies rather than the creative arts, in anticipating future conciliation during a moment in which harm is still being done, it offers a similar vision of atonement, repair and collaboration.

Science magazine published Roman and Kraska's co-authored article "Reboot Gitmo for U.S.-Cuba Research Diplomacy" in March 2016, soon after Presidents Barack Obama and Raúl Castro had agreed to renew diplomatic relations between the United States and Cuba. Coming in the wake of several high-profile calls for a return of the base to Cuba, the article provides a road-map for a use of the naval station consistent with the new (and, as it turned out, short-lived) political climate of rapprochement. Without advocating for the return of the base to Cuba in the short-term, the article calls for a closure of the detention centers and a subsequent practice of cooperation between the two national powers sharing space in the Guantánamo region. Its central proposal reads: "The United States should deliver on President Obama's recent plan to close the military prison at U.S. Naval Station Guantánamo Bay and repurpose the facilities into a state-of-the-art marine research institution and peace park, a conservation zone to help resolve conflicts between the two countries" (1258).

Roman's fuller version of the proposal, "Guantánamo 2:0: Transforming Gitmo into a Peace Park and Research Center," is included in a 2019 volume of essays on the natural capital created by landscapes of war whose editors, Todd R. Lookingbill and Peter D. Smallwood, state as the book's central premise "that sites of past warfare and related military activity represent potential opportunities for future ecosystem services and warrant environmental conservation" (5). It is in this broader international postwar context that Roman develops the proposal for a research center and a peace park, with discussion of the endangered reptiles, mammals, corals, and other marine life at and in the waters of the naval base, and in comparison with other borderland peace parks established in the aftermath of conflict, along the corridor of the former Iron Curtain, between Israel and Jordan, and at the Cordillera del Condor Corridor between Ecuador and Peru ("Guantánamo 2.0" 255). Roman's article includes a photograph of the naval base's historic Northeast Gate, through which passage has been severely restricted since the 1960s, in juxtaposition with an artist's rendering of this gate in the future as an opening, welcoming area signaling continuity rather than rupture between the Cuba and the United States. It is marked by "an installation of photos of species native to the Guantánamo Bay region, with freestanding panels extending from the base checkpoint through the Cuban and U.S. borders" (253).

Although the conceptualization of this proposal draws less directly from the arts than does the *Guantánamo Bay Museum of Art and History* project, its vision of conciliation includes collaborative artistic work. Roman envisages that "laboratories for molecular genetics and geographic information systems could be built alongside videoconference rooms, and even art music and design studios, hosting scientists, scholars, and artists from Cuba, the United States, and around the world" (254). Like that of the *Guantánamo Bay Museum of Art and History*, this proposal's future is one that recalibrates Guantánamo's openness—geopolitically and in terms of local, natural borders. Rather than the hostilities that have gridlocked Cuba, the United States, and the so-called enemy whom detainees at Guantánamo are made to represent, Roman and Kraska's proposal offers "a third path that would benefit Cuba, the U.S. and beyond" ("Reboot Gitmo" 1259). Moreover, in claiming that "the name Guantánamo could become associated with redemption and efforts to preserve and repair the planet" (1260), it acknowledges a relationship between global and very local ecologies and the imperviousness of both to man-made dividing lines.

The futures occupied by "Reparations for Guantánamo Torture Survivors" and the *Guantánamo Bay Museum of Art and History*, and envisaged by Roman and Kraska, are invoked speculatively, from locations and disciplinary practices that grant freedoms incommensurable with the experience of detainees, balseros, and Cuban political prisoners. For Guantánamo's involuntary residents, the space is closed and guarded, and the future—both immediate and distant—is subject to myriad constraints. Nevertheless, these artistic and environmental projects offer hope of repair to come, through their distinctive articulations of possible futures where all forms of human life are respected, and where those who suffer in the currently lived present are honored and commemorated.

AFTERWORD

"Did you know we were there? I used to climb up to a tiny hole at the top of my cell; when I looked through and saw a palm tree, I reminded myself that we were in Cuba, and wondered if anyone there was thinking about us."

Ahmed Errachidi's conversation with José Ramón Sánchez was impromptu and unprecedented: it came at the end of a rainy day in an art gallery in Graz, Austria, in May 2022, during a conference to mark the twentieth anniversary of the detention camps at Guantánamo. Fifteen years earlier, Errachidi had been released without charge from five and half years of mostly solitary confinement at the Guantánamo detention camps. Sánchez has spent most of his life in Guantánamo Province, Cuba, close to the naval base but prohibited from entering it.

Sánchez's public reading of his "secondhand poetry," where he imagines the experience of detainees at Guantánamo, prompted Errachidi to approach him. It was my privilege to translate their exchange, back and forth between Sánchez's Cuban Spanish and the English that Errachidi had perfected during the pre-Guantánamo years he spent as a chef in London. Errachidi asked Sánchez to make a hole with his fist, look through it and think of himself as a detainee catching a hopeful glimpse of Cuba, and thus to move a step closer to inhabiting the subject position that his poetry re-creates. He asked if, given the chance, Sánchez would have exchanged places with him for a moment, in turn allowing Errachidi to know what it is to live in Cuban Guantánamo. Sánchez said that he would have, to which Errachidi responded that, had he known that just beyond the palm tree he saw from his cell a Cuban poet was imagining, and wanting to share, his suffering, then that suffering would have diminished and his horizons of hope would have expanded. He said that, even in retrospect, this knowledge cast a newly comforting light on his memory of the darkest years of his life.

I invoke this encounter in closing because, even as it was singular and likely unprecedented, given not only the separation of the Guantánamo Bay Naval Base from Cuba but also the barriers to international travel that both Cuban citizens and former Guantánamo detainees face, it is a powerful expression of the alternative Guantánamo that has taken shape in the shadow of the relentless hostilities of the past two decades and more. This alternative Guantánamo—one where Sánchez and Errachidi can be so invested in understanding one another's experience that they can envisage exchanging a cell at the detention camps for a home in Guantánamo City—is constituted by curiosity, empathy, and care. It is a Guantánamo whose scale is local, embedded in the geography of a fenced-off base in eastern Cuba, even as its significance extends across the globe, and whose temporalities are complex and overlapping, as a brutal past lingers stubbornly into the present, and imagination, hope, and activism attempt to map a still uncharted future. It is, finally, a Guantánamo that has persisted—quietly, defiantly, and against the odds—laying the ground for the large-scale change that has to come.

NOTES

INTRODUCTION: BORDERLANDS

Epigraph: This is my translation of a line included in Sánchez's poem "Los quilos" as it was published in the Cuban journal *La noria* in 2014. Later version of the poem omit this line.

1. In *The Least Worst Place: Guantánamo's First 100 Days*, Karen J. Greenberg traces the US government's interest in the Guantánamo base as offering a potential legal limbo in which to hold detainees, noting that lawyers at the Department of Justice's Office of Legal counsel did their best "to accede to what was rumored to be Secretary Rumsfeld's request for 'the legal equivalent of outer space'" (7).

2. The unevenness and asymmetry of comparative work underpins the proposal, for example, for a "Comparative Global Humanities," made by Lisa Lowe and Kris Manjapra, which, "rather than adopting the comparative method that has structured modern humanities and social science fields," advances "an *analytic of relation*, or a mode of study that attends to the contradictory and tensile entanglements that are the con-

dition for different modes of social organization in the longer time of the global" (26).

3. Admiral Harris's comments were reported by James Risen and Tim Golden in the *New York Times* ("3 Prisoners Commit Suicide").

4. In *Frames of War: When is Life Grievable?*, Butler reads in detainees' poetry a "precarious status" that "can become the condition of suffering," but can also serve as "the condition of responsiveness, of a formulation of affect, understood as a radical act of interpretation in the face of unwilled subjugation" (61).

5. Former detainee David Hicks describes guards as bored, hopeless and feeling "traumatised" (297). Jason Leopold, in an article for *VICE* magazine in 2016, cites an Army Institute of Public Health study in which high levels of behavioral health conditions were found among army and navy troops whose work required them to have "routine detainee exposure." The *Guantánamo Bay Gazette*, the naval community's newspaper that is a focus of chapter 4, frequently advertises support and counseling groups for service people. Several poems by José Ramón Sánchez, as I discuss in chapter 1, elaborate forms of close identification between poet and detainee.

6. Reporting on the events that subsequently became known as Cuba's Black Spring, Amnesty International noted that beginning on March 18, 2003, the Cuban government made targeted arrests of a large number of dissidents, releasing some but subjecting seventy-five to "hasty and manifestly unfair trials" and long prison sentences ("Document—Cuba"). Amnesty International's report on the one year anniversary of the July 11, 2021, protests states that, despite Cuban authorities' insistence that their response was appropriate, they in fact used crimes "inconsistent with international law," including "public disorder," "contempt," and "instigation to commit a crime," to criminalize protesters. ("Five Things You Should Know").

7. In *Planet Cuba*, her study of twenty-first-century Cuban writing and art, Rachel Price observes that "the everyday, the planetary, and the digital increasingly replace national, regional and analog narratives and counter-narratives" (1).

8. Castro's speech in Havana on July 26, 1961, for example, includes the word *guerra* six times and *imperialismo* or its derivatives forty-one ("Discurso Pronunciado . . . el 26 de julio de 1961").

9. This argument underpins Ponte's book of essays *La fiesta vigilada*

and is expressed succinctly in a series of on-camera interviews he gives in Florian Borchmeyer's documentary *Havana: A New Art of Making Ruins* (2005).

10. The Revolutionary Offensive, restricting ownership of small businesses in Cuba, was announced by Fidel Castro on March 13, 1968. The Cuban sociologist Haroldo Dilla reassess its effects in a 2012 article in *Encuentro con la cultura cubana*. As Kapcia notes, the launch of the Battle of Ideas coincided with Cuba's attempts to reclaim Elián González from his relatives in Miami, after the child had been found alone on a raft off the Florida coast.

11. Fidel Castro's "Reflections," published periodically in the Cuban state newspaper *Granma*, have such titles as "The Empire's Illegal Wars" (October 1, 2007), "Empire and Lies" (September 11, 2007), and "Submission to Imperial Power" (August 27, 2007). Raúl Castro's "Battle against crime and corruption" was announced in 2011 (Efe News Service). Díaz-Canel's reference to imperial aggression was reported in the state newspaper *Granma* in December 2021 (Perera Robbio et al.).

12. The billboard is oriented toward people entering Havana from the airport and it reads "El bloqueo: El genocidio más largo de la historia" (The embargo: the longest genocide in history). In September 1999 the Cuban National Assembly issued a proclamation declaring the US embargo an act of genocide, drawing on the United Nations' 1948 Convention on the Prevention and Punishment of the Crime of Genocide, wherein genocide can be constituted by "deliberately inflicting on the group conditions of life calculated to bring about its physical destruction in whole or in part" ("Proclamation by the National Assembly"). A September 2010 article on the website Cubadebate revisits this claim, in terms of economic losses to Cuba and their effects on malnutrition ("El bloqueo sigue").

13. It is Fidel Castro's straightforward coupling of human rights abuses at the base's detention centers with the occupation of the base as itself an abuse of rights that, for Iván de la Nuez, explains the Cuban government's relative "containment" (269) with regard to the post-9/11 use of the base. In this logic, de la Nuez writes, the US presence at the base is ample proof for Cubans that "in democracies, too, human rights are abused" (269).

14. Marc Redfield regards as crucial to this "exceptional" (59) declaration of war a "mingling of reactive and proactive rhetoric" (53) wherein

the declaration of war must originate elsewhere, in order for the sovereign United States to declare its own war. He posits that at the heart of sovereignty is terror—"in a sense a terror *of* itself" (54)—and, more broadly, that the phantasmic idea of war on terror refers back to "the French Revolution and the opening of the era of human rights, mass politics, and biopolitical power" (86).

15. Linda A. Malone traces the evolution of the first three of these terms through the courts and the administrations of Bush and Obama.

CHAPTER 1: TRANSLATION

1. Following the publication of *Poems from Guantánamo*, Mohamedou Ould Slahi's *Guantánamo Diary* was published, in its first and heavily redacted version, while Slahi was still detained. Slahi was released from Guantánamo to his native Mauritania in October 2016 and, a year later, published a "restored version" of the diary, in which redactions appear in lighter ink and text is visible underneath them.

2. The *Camp Delta Standard Operating Procedures*, effective March 1, 2004, list "writing on cups," alongside "drawings" and "modified items of linen" as evidence of possible suicide attempts (6.2) and mandates that cups with writing on them be confiscated and given to an evidence custodian (12).

3. Martin Mubanga's "Terrorist 2003" poses an exception to the absence of place names in *Poems from Guantánamo*, in that it names Nablus, Jenin, and Guantánamo Bay. It was, however, reconstructed from memory after Mubanga's release, as Falkoff has explained to Andy Worthington (Falkoff, "Poetry and Politics").

4. Goldman discusses Lezama and Piñera's writings on insularity, as do José Quiroga and, more recently, Juan Carlos Quintero Herencia. Enrique del Risco addresses the heated struggles over intellectual terrain, including claims to *insularismo*, among members of the Orígenes literary group, particularly Piñera, Lezama, and Cintier Vitier.

5. José Ramón Sánchez's will to describe, occupy, and empathize with subjects whose suffering he imagines, and in some poems invokes as akin to his own, raises many of the questions of "speaking for others," and the perils of empathy, that long-established critical work such as that of Linda Alcoff and Doris Sommer has signaled. The extent to which an also peripheral, and far from hegemonic, subject such as Sánchez can be taken to task for engaging in the appropriative gestures that both Alcoff

and Sommer problematize is, to my mind, ambiguous, although there is without question room for further nuance in several of his poems.

6. The assessment is based on the risk a detainee poses to the United States, its allies, and interests; his risk to fellow prisoners; and his continuing intelligence value. The criteria are enumerated in the introduction to the Detainee Assessment Briefs published by the University of California at Davis's Guantánamo Testimonials Project.

7. An example is the statement that "detainee is on a list of high-risk detainees from a health perspective" immediately followed by the statement that "detainee is in overall good health." To the extent that these two statements are compatible, it is because the detainee has "a history of Antisocial Personality Disorder diagnosis." The *New York Times* prefaces each document in its "Guantánamo Docket" with the statement "These documents include some assertions that cannot be independently verified. Many allegations have been contested by detainees and their lawyers, and some have been undercut by other evidence."

8. All translations of Boti's *El mar y la montaña* are my own.

9. All translations of Rodríguez Lobaina's poetry are my own.

10. Sierra Madero's analysis of labor camps in the 1960s argues that they were key to various forms of social control. In recent years, the question of state-sanctioned forced labor in Cuba has focused primarily on the international medical missions into which numerous Cuban doctors claim to have been conscripted. See the US Department of State's *2021 Trafficking in Persons Report*, and also Kirk, *Healthcare without Borders*.

CHAPTER 2: GUARDS

1. Citing primarily a 2004 *New York Times* investigation and accounts of military officials' complaints that they were not receiving enough "high value" prisoners at Guantánamo, Anne McClintock notes "the consensus that of nearly seven hundred men held at Guantánamo, 'only a relative handful,' could yield any information at all" (65). "Only 5 percent," she continues, "were 'scooped up' on anything that could be called a battlefield. In a majority of cases they were not even picked up by the US military but by such dubious forces as the Northern Alliance, the Pakistani military and intelligence, and frequently handed over for considerable bounties (US$5,000 to $10,000), sometimes betrayed by neighbors or by people simply seeking remuneration" (65).

2. In June 2018 the *Miami Herald* published a detailed description,

based on information then available, of the thirteen different structures, including ten "camps," in service at the base since 2002 ("Guantánamo Prison").

3. David Hicks describes the fear instilled in guards that detainees would "talk them into opening our cage doors so we could kill them" (218); Murat Kurnaz remembers being pinned to the ground "like an animal about to be drawn and quartered" (101); and Moazzam Begg recalls overhearing, as he attempted to exercise in one of the orange jumpsuits issued to all detainees, a guard comment that "it's just like watching a mouse run around in a cage" and joke that he would ask a police dog, "Hey, do you want to chase some orange meat?" (206).

4. Drawing on the work of Julia Reinhardt Lupton and Eric Santner, Terri Tomksy proposes a notion of rights based in "creaturely cosmopolitanism," as a way to include both animals and detainees within the sphere of rights. Andreja Zevnik, reading with Giorgio Agamben and Hanna Arendt, makes a related claim that "inmates—not only of Guantanamo but also of concentration camps, prisons, etc.—are always constructed as less human, non-human or barbarian" (156).

5. Guards in the early years of the detention centers often had experience as military police officers in Iraq or Afghanistan and, subsequently, many military police units rotated through Guantánamo on short-term assignments. In an interview preceding the deployment to Guantánamo of the Wisconsin Army National Guard's 32nd Military Police Company in June 2016, for example, the commander, Captain Brian Schwalbach, observed that "there are many differences between the unit's current mission and the mission it conducted in Iraq in 2009–10 at a theater internment facility" ("Military Police Unit Ready for Guantánamo Bay Mission").

6. A 2011 report by the Army Institute of Public Health found high rates of post-traumatic stress and severe depression among troops given "routine detainee exposure" and documented the secret evacuation of at least nineteen troops who had had such exposure, due to severe behavioral health reasons. Experiences like those of the detainees, although not perceived as either common or shared, were cited as primary reasons for guards' stress: they reported feeling ill-prepared to deal with verbal and physical abuse from detainees, and to adapt to poor living conditions (Leopold).

7. Moazzam Begg speaks further of his shared experiences with

nonwhite guards in an interview with Claire Chambers, commenting on the complexity of his own personal identifications, as an "Asian, British Muslim, Pakistani/Indian" (4) Urdu-speaker in 1970s and 1980s Britain. In response to a question from Chambers about his memoir's representation of the relative segregation of Hispanic, white, and Black soldiers, he says that "when people feel marginalized, they tend to come together" (6).

8. The minimum requirement to enlist in the US Army is a high school diploma or GED; former Guantánamo guards Terry Holdbrooks and Chris Arendt have both described enlisting because of a lack of other economically viable options and as a path to, rather than a result of, higher education. The level of education among detainees varies greatly, some being well-traveled, multilingual, and highly educated. Moazzam Begg, for example, is a former law student, while Mohamedou Ould Slahi is a German-trained engineer. "The Guantánamo Docket," published by the *New York Times*, contains detailed biographical information on all current and former detainees.

9. The 2005 Schmidt-Furlow Report was commissioned from within the US Armed Forces, by the commander of US Southern Command. It acknowledges what became known as the "magic marker" incident—"the use of faux 'menstrual blood' during an interrogation" (*Army Regulation 15-6: Final Report* 2)—and another incident in which a female military interrogator performs a "lap dance" (2) on a detainee, but it finds no evidence of "torture or inhumane treatment" (1). The higher-profile and more comprehensive Feinstein Report, in the unclassified but heavily redacted version released to the public, does not mention these instances specifically, although it refers to a group of CIA officers assigned to the Detention and Interrogation Program who "had reportedly admitted to sexual assault" (Senate Select Committee on Intelligence 59).

10. Hal Klepak offers an account of high-level cooperation between Cubans and Americans in Guantánamo. Jana K. Lipman has traced the history of Cuban workers at the base both before and after the Cuban Revolution, including the commuters who faced suspicion both in Cuba and on the base as they continued their employment there (Lipman, *Guantánamo*). The last commuter retired in 2012, as reported by Kelly Wirfel ("End of an Era").

11. Ernesto "Che" Guevara nevertheless proceeded to give 1,323 as the number of provocations in the year 1964, including "minor provo-

cations such as violation of the boundary line, launching of objects from the territory controlled by the United States, the commission of acts of sexual exhibitionism by US personnel of both sexes, and verbal insults" and "extremely serious provocations including those of crossing the boundary line and starting fires in installations on the Cuban side, as well as rifle fire" ("Create Two, Three, Many Vietnams" 335).

12. Amy Kaplan situates the current use of Guantánamo Bay Naval Base in terms of over a century of imperialist designs on Cuba, Puerto Rico, and other territories. Nicole Waller reads poetry by former detainees Mohammed el-Gharani and Ibrahim al-Rubaish, included in Marc Falkoff's *Poems from Guantánamo: The Detainees Speak* (2007), as mapping Guantánamo and Cuba "into global space as a site of both static imprisonment and dynamic resistance and connection" (367).

13. Speaking on November 13, 1960, to Cubans who still commuted daily from Caimanera to their civilian jobs on the base, for example, Fidel Castro assured them that "imperialism becomes each day more powerless as it faces the revolutionary government . . . We are winning this struggle and we are going to go on winning it and the other side could not possibly ever prevent us from going on victoriously" ("Discurso pronunciado . . . 1960").

14. Susan Eckstein and Lorena Barberia have long been among the foremost scholars of Cuban transnational ties. Albert Sergio Laguna's *Diversión: Play and Popular Culture in Cuban America* (2017) addresses the changing character of these ties as manifest in the expression and dissemination of popular culture.

15. On March 28, 1980, a group of Cubans stole a bus and crashed through the gates of the Peruvian embassy in Havana, demanding asylum. The Peruvian ambassador refused to return them to the Cuban government for prosecution and, eventually, over ten thousand Cubans made their way into the embassy grounds. Castro subsequently authorized the Mariel boatlift, permitting Cubans residents in the United States to evacuate family members and others he deemed undesirable via the port of Mariel (García, *Havana, USA* 54–74). María Cristina García describes the acts of repudiation of this period thus: "The Cuban government encouraged *actos de repudio* (acts of repudiation) against those who applied to leave the country via Mariel, and gangs of thugs accosted them on the street and at work or school, or pelted their homes with rocks, bottles and spoiled food during nightly rampages" (63).

16. Law No.151 of Cuba's Penal Code forbids departure from the country without completing the requisite legal formalities. In September 2022 the Cuban government approved raising the prison sentence for illegal departure to a maximum of eight years, from a previous maximum of three (Ministerio de Justicia 2643).

17. Susan Eckstein's *Cuban Privilege: The Making of Immigrant Inequality in America* (2022) analyzes what she terms "the ongoing privileging of Cubans for more than half a century" (xxi) within the US immigration system. This includes measures such as the Cuban Adjustment Act of 1966, which facilitated Cubans' entry to the United States without visas and granted them eligibility for permanent resident status after one year, and the "Wet Foot, Dry Foot" migration policy put in place during the Clinton presidency that offered a path to residency to those Cubans who reached US soil (Cubans intercepted at sea were to be returned to Cuba). As Eckstein writes, during President Barack Obama's last full week in office, in January 2017, he revoked key entitlements that Cubans had been afforded since the 1960s, aligning their path to entry more closely with that available to immigrants from other countries (xiv).

18. The Cuban Rafter Crisis of 1994–1995 saw over thirty thousand Cubans held at Guantánamo Bay Naval Base while new migration accords were negotiated between the United States and Cuba. Most eventually emigrated to the United States.

19. The story was carried by the *Cibercuba* website (Redacción de Cibercuba), the online news outlet *Diario de Cuba* (Tur Valladares) and the Miami-based *Martí* ("14 Cubanos encarcelados"), the latter of which reported that a large number of Cubans were drawn to Guantánamo Province in February 2019 by a false rumor that President Donald Trump had sent a ship to the base to pick up Cuban refugees.

20. Issues of *Porvenir* are available on the blog of the journal's former editor in chief, Jorge Corrales, https://jorgecorralesblog.wordpress.com/acerca-de/.

21. Amnesty International's 2003 report names Claro Sánchez Altarriba as one of the known detainees of the Black Spring ("Cuba: Massive Crackdown on Dissent" 7).

22. Maria C. Werlau's article, "Cuba Refuses to Tear Down its Wall," states that the Cuba Archive "has record of 80 people killed or missing in attempts to reach the base" and has received "anecdotal accounts of many more cases."

23. I address the short stories of this corpus in relation to contemporary Cuban literature more broadly, and to the Cuban government's varying statements on the holding of detainees at the base, in my article "Cuban Borderlands: Local Stories of the Guantánamo Naval Base."

24. For *Atrabilarios*, Doris Salcedo gathered the shoes of women who had disappeared in Colombia and preserved them in a coarsely-sewn layer of cow bladder. The Auschwitz-Birkenau Memorial and Museum's *Evidence of Crime* exhibit includes shoes and other personal belongings of people deported to Auschwitz; see https://www.auschwitz.org/en/gallery/exhibits/evidence-of-crimes,1.html.

25. I address the matchstick art in Geny Jarrosay's series *La maldita circunstancia del fuego por todas partes* (The Cursed Circumstance of Fire Everywhere, 2015) in my article "Guantánamo and Community." Daniel Ross claims in an interview with Jorge Suñol that every matchstick in *La espera* represents someone who has attempted to cross the border between Cuba and the base.

26. Roberto de Jesús Quiñones alludes to this incident in his 2015 article "Una base yanquí en las narices del comunismo."

27. Katie Taylor, coordinator of the *Life after Guantánamo* project for the British charity Reprieve, reports that "agreements between the US government and host governments are confidential. We never know what the trade-off is, if there is one. There have been rumors over the years that there have been trade deals, money involved. But we can only guess" (Mirk 162). In 2015 Supreme Court Justice John Paul Stevens called for the US government to offer reparations to some former Guantánamo detainees, but there has been no serious consideration of this proposal (Rosenberg, "Retired Justice Stevens").

28. In 2010, Fidel Castro assumed responsibility, although fell short of apologizing, for widespread persecution of gay men in Cuba in the 1960s and 1970s (Lira Saade).

CHAPTER 3: HOME

1. Debi Cornwall's observation is foundational to her work in *Welcome to Camp America*, and she has expressed it on several occasions. See, for example, Izabela Radwanska Zhang, "In Paris: Debi Cornwall's *Welcome to Camp America—Inside Guantánamo Bay*."

2. These dimensions and description of contents are drawn from the

2008 Human Rights Watch report "Locked up Alone: Detention Conditions at Guantánamo."

3. See, particularly, the "Gitmo, It's a Base, Too" section of Rosenberg's *Guantánamo Bay: The Pentagon's Alcatraz in the Caribbean.*

4. The Department of Defense's Military OneSource community support website, for example, lists "free or inexpensive recreation like scuba diving, snorkeling, fishing, bowling, boating and beach activities" among benefits of living at the base, although cautions that "living and working at NSGB is not, however, for everyone" (US Department of Defense, "Naval Station Guantánamo Bay").

5. Issues of the *Guantánamo Bay Gazette* from 1991 to 2017 have been digitized by the Florida Digital Newspaper Library of the University of Florida.

6. Christina Linhardt and Michael L. Rose directed the film *Guantánamo Circus*, released in 2013. My book chapter "Guantánamo and Community: Visual Approaches to the Naval Base" addresses this engagement with the paradoxes of Guantánamo as a site (165–66).

7. As Alexander Nazaryan puts it in "Guantánamo Bay Is the Most Ridiculous Place on Earth," his deeply ironic 2014 article for *Newsweek*, "A refrain you often hear from the Americans on base is that it is incredibly safe at Guantánamo Bay, especially for children, who can roam here as they presumably no longer can in the United States, which is awash in the depredations of sexual predators and drug fiends and Justin Bieber's posse. Life's ironic rhythms are apparently not threatened by the 154 men imprisoned at the detention camp just over the hill from the W.T. Sampson Elementary School, a few of whom stand legitimately accused of trying to kill Americans through various acts of terror."

8. The navy community incident most widely reported in the US press in recent years, the 2020 obstruction of justice conviction of former base commander Captain John R. Nettleton, in regard to the death of a base employee with whose wife he was romantically involved, played out after the *Gazette*'s closure in 2017 (Rosenberg, "Former Guantánamo Bay Commander").

9. The National Defense Authorization Act of 2020–2021, even as it prohibited the use of funds to close or transfer detainees from Guantánamo, as it had repeatedly over the years, stipulated that the chief medical officer of the naval station was to provide a report on medical facilities

there, specifically in the light of "the likely effects of aging" on detainees' medical conditions (S.1605, Section 1036b 5).

10. Gustavo Pérez Firmat's *Life on the Hyphen: The Cuban-American Way* is a key scholarly work on the relationship of first-generation exiles to place. Scholarship on more recent Cuban migration to the United States, such as that of Albert Sergio Laguna, prioritizes mobility and improvisation over the static attempt to recreate the old in the new.

11. Carol Rosenberg reported on the "round trip" of Petty Officer Virgilio Franqui, a former refugee at Guantánamo, in 2006 ("From Raft to U.S. Navy"); the return of Petty Officer Second Class Ramón Núñez, also a former refugee at the base, is reported in the February 6, 2009, issue of the *Guantánamo Bay Gazette*. Photographs from Senator Marco Rubio's trip are archived on his official web page ("Rubio Visits Guantánamo Bay Naval Base").

12. On a rarely permitted visit to Caimanera in 2018, CNN reporter Patrick Oppmann met residents who "showed off how the base's T-Mobile cell phone service reaches their town" (Oppmann, "In This Isolated Cuban Town").

13. Caimanera was the site of anti-government protests in May 2023, for example (Oppmann, "Cuban Police Crack Down").

14. Reporting from Caimanera in 2014, the BBC's Sarah Rainsford interviewed fisherman not permitted to pass through US-controlled waters to the open sea, and restricted to the inner zone of Guantánamo Bay. One insists, referring to the Americans, that "the best catch is in their zone," adding that "we're just waiting, praying for the Americans to leave" (Rainsford).

CHAPTER 4: THE FUTURE

1. Released on YouTube in February 2021 by well-known performers Yotuel Romero, Descemer Bueno, Maykel Osorbo, El Funky, and the duo Gente de Zona, the video gained enormous popularity. Robin Moore situates it in a genealogy of protest music in Cuba, this time directed against, rather than in favor of, the revolution.

2. Abdul Latif Nasser was released from Guantánamo and repatriated to Morocco in July 2021, a year after the publication of his open letter.

3. Joint Task Force Guantánamo authorized occasional phone calls home for prisoners who met certain conditions in 2008, followed in 2010

by the authorization of video-link conferences, facilitated by the International Red Cross (Rosenberg, "Prison Camps Mum").

4. As Ann Halbert-Brooks comments, "In the early 1960s CDRs worked to inculcate the populace in revolutionary culture, then selectively empowering individuals to enforce revolutionary norms by monitoring their neighbors. CDRs played an integral role in reshaping Cuban society in the early 1960s" (26).

5. I am grateful to Jorge del Río, part of the editorial team of *El futuro* during his time as a *balsero* at Guantánamo, for providing me with scanned copies of most issues of *El futuro*. The original journals are held at the Cuban Heritage Collection of the University of Miami Libraries, in the Guantánamo Naval Base Collection (Manuscript Collections CHC0503).

6. All translations from *Porvenir* are my own.

7. Writing about symbolic reparation in post-conflict Northern Ireland, for example, Kevin Hearty includes "official apologies, truth-telling, commemoration and memorialization" (338) among its most frequent forms and, drawing on the work of Martha Minnow, signals the "moral importance" of such reparations in comparison to economic ones, as they are better placed to address the causes and consequences of, rather than resultant material needs arising from, past harms (337).

8. Rebecca Adelman situates *The Guantánamo Bay Museum of Art and History* project in relation to liberal imaginaries that, paradoxically, obscure or overlay detainees' experience. "If the fetishization of detainee creativity enacts one kind of erasure," Adelman writes with reference to the publication of detainee poetry and art, then the exclusion of detainee creativity from the archive of the museum project (only one detainee, she notes, being mentioned by name), "reflects another kind of violence" (*Figuring Violence* 211).

WORKS CITED

"14 Cubanos encarcelados tras rumor infundado sobre éxodo por la Base Naval." *Martí*, 28 Mar. 2019, https://www.radiotelevisionmarti.com/a/cubanos-encarcelados-tras-rumor-infundado-sobre-%C3%A9xodo-por-la-base-naval/233213.html.

Ackerman, Holly. "The Cuban Rafter Phenomenon: A Unique Exodus." *Latino Studies*, vol. 3, no. 3, 2005, pp. 417–20.

Adayfi, Mansoor. *Don't Forget Us Here: Lost and Found at Guantánamo*. In collaboration with Antonio Aiello. Hachette Books, 2021.

Adayfi, Mansoor. "In Our Prison on the Sea." *The New York Times*, 15 Sept. 2017, https://www.nytimes.com/2017/09/15/opinion/sunday/guantanamo-early-years-sea.html.

Adelman, Rebecca A. "'Safe, Humane, Legal, Transparent': State Visions of Guantánamo Bay." *Reconstruction: Studies in Contemporary Culture*, vol. 12, no. 4, 2013, http://reconstruction.digitalodu.com/Issues/124/Adelman_Rebecca.shtml.

Adelman, Rebecca A. *Figuring Violence: Affective Investments in Perpetual War*. Fordham UP, 2018.

WORKS CITED

Alcoff, Linda. "The Problem of Speaking for Others." *Cultural Critique*, Winter 1991–1992, pp. 5–32.

al-Rubaish, Ibrahim. "Ode to the Sea." *Poems from Guantánamo: The Detainees Speak*, edited by Marc Falkoff, U of Iowa P, 2007, pp. 65–66.

Allen, Ron. "'A Group of Friends' Spread Easter Joy." *Guantanamo Bay Gazette*, 5 Apr. 2002, p. 4, https://dloc.com/UF00098616/01014/images/3.

Amnesty International. "Amnesty International Annual Report 1998." 16 June 1998, https://www.amnesty.org/en/documents/pol10/0001/1998/en/.

Amnesty International. "Cuba: Massive Crackdown on Dissent." 2 Apr. 2003, https://www.amnesty.org/en/documents/amr25/008/2003/en/.

Amnesty International. "Cuba: One Year Too Many: Prisoners of Conscience from the March 2003 Crackdown." 16 Mar. 2004, https://www.amnesty.org/en/documents/amr25/005/2004/en/.

Amnesty International. "Five Things You Should Know a Year on from Cuba's 11 July Protests." 11 July 2022, https://www.amnesty.org/en/latest/news/2022/07/five-things-you-should-know-cubas-11-july-protests/.

Anderson, Benedict. *Imagined Communities: Reflections on the Origin and Spread of Nationalism*. Verso, 2016.

Anderson, Laurie. *Habeas Corpus*. 2–4 Oct. 2015, Park Avenue Armory, New York.

Anzaldúa, Gloria. *Borderlands/La Frontera: The New Mestiza*. Aunt Lute, 1987.

Apuzzo, Matt, Sheri Fink, and James Risen. "How U.S. Torture Left a Legacy of Damaged Minds." *The New York Times*, 8 Oct. 2016, https://www.nytimes.com/2016/10/09/world/cia-torture-guantanamo-bay.html.

Arenas, Reinaldo. *Before Night Falls*. Translated by Dolores M. Koch, Penguin Books, 1993.

Arendt, Christopher. "What It Feels Like . . . to Be a Prison Guard at Guantánamo Bay." *Esquire*, 30 July 2008, https://www.esquire.com/lifestyle/a4821/guantanamo-guard-0808/.

Army Regulation 15–6: Final Report: Investigation into FBI Allegations of Detainee Abuse at Guantanamo Bay, Cuba Detention Facility. 1 Apr. 2005 (Amended 9 June 2005), https://www.thetorturedatabase.org/files/foia_subsite/pdfs/schmidt_furlow_report.pdf.

WORKS CITED

Art from Guantánamo. 16 Oct. 2017–26 Jan. 2018, President's Gallery, John Jay College of Criminal Justice, New York.

"Art from Guantánamo." *Postprint Magazine,* Oct. 2017, https://static1.squarespace.com/static/5909e8a26a4963e281825c2d/t/623df7d67ef80e5d6873024e/1648228317960/Art_from_Guantanamo_Postprint_Magazine_reduced.pdf.

Avilés-Santiago. *Puerto Rican Soldiers and Second-Class Citizenship.* Palgrave Macmillan, 2014.

Baker, Rusty. "GTMO Resident Returns Home to Final Resting Place." *Guantanamo Bay Gazette,* 7 Sept. 2012, pp. 1, 6, https://dloc.com/UF00098616/00271/pdf.

Basulto, Conrado. "Transcription of Conrado Basulto Oral History." Interview by Guantánamo Public Memory Project, https://gitmomemory.org/wp-content/uploads/2012/12/transcript.-Conrado-Basulto.pdf.

Beatón, Alexander. *Susurros.* 22–25 June 2021. Consejo Provincial de las Artes Plásticas Guantánamo, Guantánamo, Cuba.

Beatón, Alexander, and Pedro Gutiérrez. "Caimanera: El camino de la estrategia." Interview by Yisel Reyes Laffita, 4 Mar. 2013, https://cadaminutocuenta.wordpress.com/2013/03/04/caimanera-el-camino-de-la-estrategia/#more-659.

Beatón, Alexander, and Pedro Gutiérrez. *El camino de la estrategia.* Mar. 2013, Galería Villa Manuela, Havana, Cuba. Exhibited as *The Way of Strategy,* Sept. 2014, Perry and Marty Granoff Center for the Creative Arts, Brown University.

Beatón, Alexander, and Pedro Gutiérrez. *Proyecto artístico: El camino de la estrategia.* UNEAC Guantánamo, 2009.

Begg, Moazzam, with Victoria Brittain. *Enemy Combatant: My Imprisonment at Guantánamo, Bagram, and Kandahar.* New Press, 2006.

Begg, Moazzam. "'Guantánamo Boy': An Interview with Moazzam Begg." Interview by Claire Chambers, *Postcolonial Text,* vol. 6, no. 2, 2011, pp. 1–12.

Ben Jelloun, Tahar. *French Hospitality: Racism and North African Immigrants.* Translated by Barbara Bray. Columbia UP, 1999.

Booth, William. "Growing Number of Cubans Take the Direct Route." *The Washington Post,* 31 Aug. 1994, https://www.washingtonpost.com/archive/politics/1994/08/31/growing-number-of-cubans-take-the-direct-route/2300a73b-28e7-4954-803a-92a139b62205/.

WORKS CITED

Borchmeyer, Florian. *Havana: The New Art of Making Ruins*. Raros Media, 2007.

Bosch, Carles, and Josep María Domènech, directors. *Balseros*. Lauren Films, 2002.

Boti y Barreiro, Regino Eladio. *Arabescos mentales: (Poemas)*. Tobella Impresor, 1913.

Boti y Barreiro, Regino Eladio. *El mar y la montaña*. Ediciones Unión, 2002.

Boumediène, Lakhdar, and Mustafa Ait Idir. *Witnesses of the Unseen: Seven Years in Guantánamo*. With Daniel Hartnett Norland, Jeffrey Rose, and Kathleen List. Stanford UP, 2017.

Bustamante, Michael J. *Cuban Memory Wars: Retrospective Politics in Revolution and Exile*. U of North Carolina P, 2021.

Butler, Judith. *Precarious Life: The Powers of Mourning and Violence*. Verso, 2004.

Butler, Judith. *Frames of War: When Is Life Grievable?* Verso, 2009.

Butler, Judith. "Precarious Life; Indefinite Detention." *Guantánamo Bay Museum of Art and History*, https://www.guantanamobaymuseum.org/?url=butlertext. Previously published in *Precarious Life: The Power of Mourning and Violence*, Verso, 2004, pp. 90–100.

Buzzanco, Robert. "Fidel Castro (1926–2016) and Global Solidarity." *The Sixties: A Journal of History, Politics and Culture*, vol. 10, no. 2, 2017, pp. 274–80.

Byington, Stacey. "Housing Town Hall Meeting Addresses Residents' Concerns, Ongoing Projects." *Guantanamo Bay Gazette*, 16 Sept. 2005, p. 1, https://dloc.com/UF00098616/01158/images.

Byington, Stacey. "Basel to Receive 'Humanitarian of the Year' Award." *Guantánamo Bay Gazette*, 19 Aug. 2005, p. 3, https://dloc.com/UF00098616/01155/images/0.

Byington, Stacey. "Cuban-American Friendship Spans Many Years." *Guantanamo Bay Gazette*, 3 Feb. 2006, pp. 1, 7, https://dloc.com/UF00098616/00019/pdf.

Calvo Ospina, Hernando. *Todo Guantánamo es nuestro/All Guantánamo Is Ours*. Resumen Latinoamericano, 2016.

Camp Delta Standard Operating Procedures (SOP).1 Mar. 2004, http://hrlibrary.umn.edu/OathBetrayed/sop_2004.pdf.

Campisi, Elizabeth. *Escape to Miami: An Oral History of the Cuban Rafter Crisis*. Oxford UP, 2016.

WORKS CITED

Case, Mary Ann. "Gender Performance Requirements of the U.S. Military in the War on Islamic Terrorism." *Confronting Torture: Essays on the Ethics, Legality, History, and Psychology of Torture Today*, edited by Scott A. Anderson and Martha C. Nussbaum, U of Chicago P, 2018.

Castro, Fidel. "At the United Nations General Assembly." *The Fidel Castro Reader*, edited by David Deutschmann and Deborah Shnookal, Ocean Press, 2007, pp. 133–84.

Castro, Fidel. "Discurso pronunciado por el Comandante en Jefe Fidel Castro Ruz ante los pbreros de la Base Naval de Caimanera, en el local del Instituto de Segunda Enseñanza de dicha ciudad, en Guantánamo, el 13 de noviembre de 1960." *Fidel, Soldado de las Ideas*, http://www.fidelcastro.cu/es/discursos/discurso-ante-los-obreros-de-la-base-naval-de-caimanera-en-el-local-del-instituto-de.

Castro, Fidel. "Discurso pronunciado por el Comandante Fidel Castro Ruz, en la Plaza de la Ciudad de Camagüey, el 4 de Enero de 1959." *Cuba Gobierno Discursos*, http://www.cuba.cu/gobierno/discursos/1959/esp/f040159e.html.

Castro, Fidel. "Discurso pronunciado por el Comandante Fidel Castro Ruz, Primer Ministro del Gobierno Revolucionario, en la conmemoración del viii aniversario del ataque al cuartel Moncada, en la Plaza de la Revolución "José Martí,' en la Habana, el 26 de Julio de 1961." *Cuba Gobierno Discursos*, http://www.cuba.cu/gobierno/discursos/1961/esp/f260761e.html.

Castro, Fidel. "Discurso pronunciado por el Comandante Fidel Castro Ruz, Primer Secretario General de las ORI y Primer Ministro del Gobierno Revolucionario de Cuba, en la concentración celebrada con motivo de conmemorarse el noveno aniversario del 26 de julio en Santiago de Cuba, el 26 de julio de 1962." *Cuba Gobierno Discursos*, http://www.cuba.cu/gobierno/discursos/1962/esp/f260762e.html.

Castro, Fidel. "El Imperio y la mentira." *Diario Granma*, 11 Sept. 2007, https://www.granma.cu/granmad/secciones/reflexiones/esp-048.html.

Castro, Fidel. *Guantánamo: Why the Illegal US Base Should Be Returned to Cuba*. Ocean Press, 2011.

Castro, Fidel. "History Will Absolve Me (Santiago de Cuba, October 16, 1953)." *Fidel Castro Reader*, edited by David Deutschmann and Deborah Shnookal, Ocean Press, 2007, pp. 41–101.

WORKS CITED

Castro, Fidel. "Las guerras ilegales del Imperio." *Diario Granma*, 1 Oct. 2007, https://www.granma.cu/granmad/secciones/reflexiones/esp-053.html.

Castro, Fidel. "La sumisión a la política imperial." *Diario Granma*, 27 Aug. 2007, https://www.granma.cu/granmad/secciones/reflexiones/esp-045.html.

Castro, Fidel. "Words to Intellectuals (Havana, June 30, 1961)." *Fidel Castro Reader*, edited by David Deutschmann and Deborah Shnookal, Ocean Press, 2007, pp. 213–40.

Castro, Raúl. "Discurso pronunciado por el General del Ejército Raúl Castro Ruz, Presidente de los Consejos de Estado y de Ministros, en las conclusiones de la Primera Sesión Ordinaria de la VII Legislatura de la Asamblea Nacional del Poder Popular. Palacio de las Convenciones, La Habana, 11 July 2008, 'Año 50 de la Revolución.'" *Cuba Gobierno Discursos*, http://www.cuba.cu/gobierno/rauldiscursos/2008/esp/r110708e.html.

Catlos, Brian. "Foreword: Thomas F. Glick and *Convivencia*." *Convivencia and Medieval Spain: Essays in Honor of Thomas F. Glick*, edited by Mark T. Abate, Palgrave Macmillan, 2019, pp. vii–xiii.

Cavarero, Adriana. *Horrorism: Naming Contemporary Violence*. Columbia UP, 2009.

Center for the Study of Human Rights in the Americas. *The Guantánamo Testimonials Project*, https://humanrights.ucdavis.edu/projects/the-guantanamo-testimonials-project.

Center for the Study of Human Rights in the Americas. "Testimony of Spc. Brandon Neely." 29 Oct. 2009, http://humanrights.ucdavis.edu/projects/the-guantanamo-testimonials-project/testimonies/testimonies-of-military-guards/testimony-of-brandon-neely.

Chanan, Michael. *Cuban Cinema*. U of Minnesota P, 2003.

Cibercuba, Redacción de. "Bajo arresto y a la espera de juicio 14 jóvenes que intentaron entrar a la Base Naval de Guantánamo." *Cibercuba*, 28 Mar. 2019, https://www.cibercuba.com/noticias/2019-03-28-u1-e129488-s27061-bajo-arresto-espera-juicio-14-jovenes-intentaron-entrar-base.

Clark, Edmund. *Guantánamo: If the Light Goes Out*. Dewi Lewis Publishing, 2011.

Congressional Research Service. *Diversity, Inclusion, and Equal Opportunity in the Armed Services: Background and Issues for Congress*.

Updated 5 June 2019, https://crsreports.congress.gov/product/pdf/R/R44321.

Cornwall, Debi. *Welcome to Camp America: Inside Guantánamo Bay.* Radius Books, 2017.

Crabapple, Molly. "The Art of Molly Crabapple: Guantánamo Images and Imaginaries." https://mollycrabapple.com/guantanamo-images-and-imaginaries-engaging-with-the-prison-through-art-by-ecchr/.

Crewe, Ben, Susie Hulley, and Serena Wright. "Swimming with the Tide: Adapting to Long-Term Imprisonment." *Justice Quarterly*, vol. 34, no. 3, 2017, pp. 517–41.

"Críticas condiciones de higiene y alimentación en el Combinado de Guantánamo." *Porvenir: La voz independiente de Guantánamo*, vol. 1, Feb. 2008, p. 10.

Cruse, Fifi, and Sheldon Cole. "Biting Iguana Finally Captured." *Guantanamo Bay Gazette*, 15 Apr. 2005, p. 1, https://dloc.com/UF00098616/01138/images.

Cuba Archive. "Truth and Memory Project." https://cubaarchive.org/truth-and-memory/the-project/.

"Cuban Community Center Opens." *Guantanamo Bay Gazette*, 30 Jan. 2004, p. 5, https://dloc.com/UF00098616/01078/images/4.

De Ferrari, Guillermina. "Net, Module, Chance: Repairing Cuba." *Interventions: International Journal of Postcolonial Studies*, vol. 23, no. 4, 2021, pp. 544–69.

de Jesús Quiñónes, Roberto. "La fuga." *El mar y la montaña (Guantánamo)*, vol. 2, 2012, pp. 24–29.

de Jesús Quiñónes, Roberto. "Una base yanqui en las narices del comunismo." 14 Jan. 2015, https://www.cubanet.org/destacados/una-base-yanqui-en-las-narices-del-comunismo/?print=print.

de la Nuez, Iván. *Inundaciones. Del Muro a Guantánamo: invasiones artísticas en las fronteras políticas.* Random House Mondadori, 2010.

del Risco, Enrique. "Piñera y profecía." *La Habana Elegante*, vol. 52, Autumn-Winter 2012, http://www.habanaelegante.com/Fall_Winter_2012/Dossier_Pinera_DelRisco.html.

Denbeaux, Mark P., and Jonathan Hafetz, editors. *The Guantánamo Lawyers: Inside a Prison Outside the Law.* New York UP, 2009.

Department of the Navy, Naval Inspector General. "Area Visit of Naval Station Guantanamo Bay, Cuba." 28 Jan. 2016, pp. 1–104, https://www

.secnav.navy.mil/ig/FOIA%20Reading%20Room/NAVINSGEN%20 Area%20Visit%20of%20GTMO%2028%20Jan%202016.pdf.

Derrida, Jacques, and Anne Dufourmantelle. *Of Hospitality: Anne Dufourmantelle Invites Jacques Derrida to Respond*. Stanford UP, 2000.

"Desde la base naval de Guantánamo hablamos con uno de los balseros del 11J interceptados por la Guardia Costera." *AméricaTeve*, 26 July 2022, https://www.americateve.com/guardia-costera/desde-la-base-naval -guantanamo-hablamos-uno-los-balseros-del-11j-interceptados -la-guardia-costera-n1145135.

Díaz Castañón, María del Pilar. "'We Demand, We Demand . . .' Cuba, 1959: The Paradoxes of Year 1." *The Revolution from Within: Cuba, 1959–1980*, edited by Michael J. Bustamante and Jennifer L. Lambe, Duke UP, 2019, pp. 95–116.

@DiazCanelB. "Ya Son 20 Años De Escandalosos Abusos En Territorio Cubano Ilegalmente Ocupado En La Bahía De #Guantánamo Por Parte De Los Mayores Violadores De Los #Ddhh En El Mundo." *Twitter*, 11 Jan. 2022, 6:14 a.m., https://twitter.com/diazcanelb/ status/1480875710105407488.

Dilla, Haroldo. "¿Recuerdan la Ofensiva Revolucionaria de 1968?" *Cubaencuentro*, 9 July 2012, https://www.cubaencuentro.com/opinion/ articulos/recuerdan-la-ofensiva-revolucionaria-de-1968-278323.

Dost, Shaikh Abdurraheem Muslim. "Two Fragments." *Poems from Guantánamo: The Detainees Speak*, edited by Marc Falkoff, U of Iowa P, 2007, p. 36.

Duffy, Helen. "Dignity Denied: A Case Study." *Human Dignity and Human Security in Times of Terrorism*, edited by Christophe Paulussen and Martin Scheinin, T. M. C. Asser Press, 2020, pp. 67–96.

Eckstein, Susan. *Cuban Privilege: The Making of Immigrant Inequality in America*. Cambridge UP, 2022.

Eckstein, Susan, and Lorena Barberia. "Grounding Immigrant Generations in History: Cuban Americans and their Transnational Ties." *The International Migration Review*, vol. 36 no. 3, 2002, pp. 799–837.

Editorial Committee of *El futuro*. "Editorial." *El futuro* (Guantánamo Bay, Cuba), vol. 1, 1995, p. 1.

Editorial Committee of *El futuro*. "El destino de Cuba." *El futuro* (Guantánamo Bay, Cuba), vol. 4, 1995, p. 1.

Editorial Committee of *El futuro*. "Editorial: Nuestra Opinión." *El futuro* (Guantánamo Bay, Cuba), vol. 2, 1995, p. 1.

Editorial Committee of *Porvenir*. "Editorial." *Porvenir: La voz independiente de Guantánamo*, vol. 1, February 2008, p. 2.

"El Bloqueo sigue siendo un acto de genocidio y de guerra económica." *CubaDebate*, 15 Sept. 2010, http://www.cubadebate.cu/especiales/2010/09/15/el-bloqueo-sigue-siendo-un-acto-de-genocidio-y-de-guerra-economica-infografias/.

El, Islam. "Ex-Guantánamo Guard and Former Prisoner Moazzam Begg Reunite." *Middle East Eye*, 19 Aug. 2016, https://www.middleeasteye.net/news/watch-ex-guantanamo-bay-guard-and-former-prisoner-moazzam-begg-reunite.

el-Gharani, Mohammed. "First Poem of My Life." *Poems from Guantánamo: The Detainees Speak*, edited by Marc Falkoff, U of Iowa P, 2007, pp. 37–40.

Errachidi, Ahmed, with Gillian Slovo. *The General: The Ordinary Man Who Challenged Guantanamo*. Random House, 2013.

Estupiñán Zaldívar, Leandro. "Abducción." *Como raíles de punta: Jóven narrativa cubana*, edited by Caridad Tamayo Fernández, Ediciones Sed de Belleza, 2013, pp. 41–46.

"Eternal Love." *Guantanamo Bay Gazette*, 10 Apr. 2009 p. 3, https://dloc.com/UF00098616/00071/images/2.

Evans, Ric. "Gitmo 'Mayor' Ends Tour." *Guantanamo Bay Gazette*, 28 Mar. 2003, pp. 1–3, https://dloc.com/UF00098616/01035/images.

Fagen, Richard R. *The Transformation of Political Culture in Cuba*. Stanford UP, 1969.

Falkoff, Marc. *Poems from Guantánamo: The Detainees Speak*. U of Iowa P, 2007.

Falkoff, Marc. "Poetry and Politics at Guantánamo: An Interview with Marc Falkoff, Editor of *Poems from Guantánamo: The Detainees Speak*." Interview by Andy Worthington, 3 Oct. 2007, *Andy Worthington*, https://www.andyworthington.co.uk/2007/10/03/poetry-and-politics-at-guantanamo-an-interview-with-marc-falkoff-editor-of-poems-from-guantanamo-the-detainees-speak/.

"Ferry Landing Beach Open." *Guantanamo Bay Gazette*, 23 Apr. 2004, p. 3, https://dloc.com/UF00098616/01090/images/2.

"First Video of Author Mohamedou Slahi after Release from Gitmo."

YouTube, uploaded by ACLU, 28 Oct. 2016, https://www.youtube.com/watch?v=R_KkkwlLBWY.

Fischer, Sibylle. *Modernity Disavowed: Haiti and the Cultures of Slavery in the Age of Revolution*. Duke UP, 2004.

Funk, Marcus. "Imagined Commodities? Analyzing Local Identity and Place in American Community Newspaper Website Banners." *New Media and Society*, vol. 15, no. 4, 2012, pp. 574–95.

Fusco, Coco. *A Field Guide for Female Interrogators*. Seven Stories Press, 2008.

Gandhi, Leela. *Affective Communities: Anticolonial Thought, Fin-de-siècle Radicalism, and the Politics of Friendship*. Duke UP, 2006.

García, María Cristina. *Havana, USA: Cuban Exiles and Cuban Americans in South Florida, 1959–1994*. U of California P, 1996.

García Calzada, Ana Luz. *Heavy Rock*. Ediciones Oriente, 1995.

García Calzada, Ana Luz. "'Kites' and 'Breathing Room,' with an Introduction by the Author." *Guantánamo and American Empire: The Humanities Respond*, edited by Don E. Walicek and Jessica Adams, translated by Jessica Adams, Palgrave Macmillan, 2017, pp. 173–82.

García Campuzano, Ofelia. *Caimanera: Una mirada diferente*. Editorial el mar y la montaña, 2009.

"A Garden Party." *Guantánamo Bay Gazette*, 30 May 2003, p. 8, https://dloc.com/UF00098616/01044/images/0.

Garth, Hannah. "Consumption, Temporality, and Celebration in Contemporary Santiago de Cuba." *American Anthropologist*, vol. 121, no. 4, 2019, pp. 801–14.

Geary, James. *I Is an Other: The Secret Life of Metaphor and How It Shapes the Way We See the World*. HarperCollins, 2011.

Ginsburg, Amber, Aaron Hughes, Aliya Hussein, and Audrey Petty, editors. *Remaking the Exceptional: Tea, Torture, and Reparations | Chicago to Guantánamo*. DePaul Art Museum, 2022.

Goetz, John. *Guantánamo Diary Revisited*. Cinema Libre, 2022.

Goldman, Dara E. *Out of Bounds: Islands and the Demarcation of Identity in the Hispanic Caribbean*. Bucknell UP, 2008.

Goldman, Dara E. "There's (Always) Something about Cuba: Security and States of Exception in a Fundamentally Unsafe World." *South Atlantic Quarterly*, vol. 107, no. 2, 2008, pp. 339–54.

Gorenflo, April. "Residents Air Concerns at Town Hall Meeting."

Guantanamo Bay Gazette, 8 Feb. 2002, p. 6, https://dloc.com/UF00098616/01007/images/5.

Goulding, Cathlin. "Teaching and Learning in Virtual Places of Exception: 'Gone Gitmo' and the Guantánamo Bay Museum of Art and History." *Mass Violence and Memory in the Digital Age*, edited by Eve Monique and David J. Simon Zucker, Palgrave Macmillan, 2020, pp. 141–73.

Goyal, Yogita. "The Genres of *Guantánamo Diary*: Postcolonial Reading and the War on Terror." *The Cambridge Journal of Postcolonial Inquiry*, vol. 4, no. 1, Jan. 2017, pp. 69–87.

Greenberg, Karen J. *The Least Worst Place: Guantanamo's First 100 Days*. Oxford UP, 2009.

Greenberg, Karen J. *Subtle Tools: The Dismantling of American Democracy from the War on Terror to Donald Trump*. Princeton UP, 2021.

Gregory, Derek. "The Black Flag: Guantánamo Bay and the State of Exception." *Guantánamo Bay Museum of Art and History*, https://www.guantanamobaymuseum.org/?url=gregorytext. Previously published in *Geografiska Annaler: Series B, Human Geography*, vol. 88, no. 4, 2006, pp. 405–27.

Guantánamo Bay Museum of Art and History. https://www.guantanamobaymuseum.org/?url=welcome.

Guantánamo Public Memory Project. https://gitmomemory.org/.

"The Guantánamo Docket." *The New York Times*, n.d., https://www.nytimes.com/interactive/2021/us/guantanamo-bay-detainees.html.

"Guantánamo Prison: A Primer." *The Miami Herald*, 9 June 2018, https://www.miamiherald.com/news/nation-world/world/americas/guantanamo/article1939250.html.

Guerra, Lillian. "Elián González and the 'Real Cuba' of Miami: Visions of Identity, Exceptionality, and Divinity." *Cuban Studies*, vol. 38, 2007, pp. 1–15.

Guerra, Lillian. "Feeling like Fidel: Scholarly Meditations on History, Memory, and the Legacies of Fidel Castro." *Cuban Studies*, vol. 47, 2019, pp. 111–42.

Guerra, Lillian. *Heroes, Martyrs, and Political Messiahs in Revolutionary Cuba, 1946–1958*. Yale UP, 2018.

Guerra, Lillian. *Visions of Power in Cuba: Revolution, Redemption and Resistance, 1959–1971*. U of North Carolina P, 2012.

Guevara, Ernesto "Che." "At the United Nations (December 11, 1964)."

Che Guevara Reader, edited by David Deutschmann, Ocean Press, 2003, pp. 325–39.

Guevara, Ernesto "Che." "Create Two, Three, Many Vietnams (Message to the Tricontinental, April 1967)." *Che Guevara Reader*, edited by David Deutschmann, Ocean Press, 2003, pp. 350–62.

Gutiérrez Alea, Tomás, and Juan Carlos Tabío. *Guantanamera*. Instituto Cubano de Arte e Industrias Cinematográficas (ICAIC), 1995.

Halbert-Brooks, Ann. "Cederistas: Women's Education and Vigilance in Cuban Comités de Defensa de la Revolución, 1960–1970." *The Latin Americanist*, vol. 62, no. 1, Mar. 2018, pp. 26–45.

Hamlin, Janet. *Sketching Guantanamo: Court Sketches of the Military Tribunals, 2006–2013*. Fantagraphics, 2013.

Hansen, Jonathan M. *Guantánamo: An American History*. Hill & Wang, 2011.

Harlow, Barbara. "'Extraordinary Renditions': Tales of Guantánamo, a Review Article." *Race & Class*, vol. 52, no. 4, 2011, pp. 1–29.

Hartmann-Mahmud, Lori. "War as Metaphor." *Peace Review*, vol. 14, no. 4, 2002, pp. 427–32.

Hatuqa, Dalia. "Fidel Castro: The Palestinian Connection." *Al Jazeera*, 26 Nov. 2016, https://www.aljazeera.com/news/2016/11/26/fidel-castro-the-palestinian-connection/.

Hearty, Kevin. "Problematising Symbolic Reparation: 'Complex Political Victims,' 'Dead Body Politics' and the Right to Remember." *Social & Legal Studies*, vol. 29, no. 3, 2020, pp. 334–54.

Henken, Ted. "*Balseros, Boteros* and *El Bombo*: Post-1994 Cuban Immigration to the United States and the Persistence of Special Treatment." *Latino Studies*, vol. 3, 2005, pp. 393–416.

Hernández-Reguant, Ariana. "Multicubanidad." *Cuba and the Special Period: Culture and Ideology in the 1990s*, edited by Ariana Hernández-Reguant, Palgrave Macmillan, 2009, pp. 69–88.

Hicks, David. *Guantanamo: My Journey*. Random House Australia, 2010.

Hilal, Maha. "The Death of a Former Guantánamo Prisoner Exposes How the U.S. Controls the Life and Death of Its Captives." *Business Insider*, 3 Apr. 2021, https://www.businessinsider.com/former-guantanamo-bay-prisoners-us-terrorism-release-lufti-bin-ali-2021-3.

Holdbrooks, Terry C. "My Time as a Guard at Guantánamo Bay." *VICE News*, 11 Nov. 2014, https://www.vice.com/en/article/av4bwk/my-time-as-a-guard-at-guantanamo-bay-terry-holdbrooks-475.

Holdbrooks, Terry C. *Traitor?* Create Space Independent Publishing Platform, 2013.

Hughes, Aaron, and Amber Ginsburg. *Invitation to Tea: A Tea Project Archive and Recipe Book*. StepSister Press, 2022.

Hulme, Peter. *Cuba's Wild East: A Literary Geography of Oriente*. Liverpool UP, 2011.

Human Rights Watch. "Locked up Alone: Detention Conditions and Mental Health at Guantánamo." 9 June 2008, https://www.hrw.org/report/2008/06/09/locked-alone/detention-conditions-and-mental-health-guantanamo.

Husta, Madya. "Who Are the Special Category Residents?" *Guantanamo Bay Gazette*, 26 June 2009, p. 5, https://dloc.com/UF00098616/01245/images/4.

"In Memory." *Guantanamo Bay Gazette*, 6 Jan. 2006, p. 1, https://dloc.com/UF00098616/00015/pdf.

Inter-American Commission on Human Rights. "Resolution 24/2021 Precautionary Measure No. 374–20: Roberto De Jesús Quiñones Haces Regarding Cuba." 9 Mar. 2021, https://www.oas.org/en/iachr/decisions/mc/2021/res_24-2021_mc%20374-20_cb_en.pdf.

"JTF 160 Makes GTMO Home." *Guantanamo Bay Gazette*, 11 Jan. 2002, p. 3, https://dloc.com/UF00098616/01004/images/2.

Kapcia, Antoni. "*Batalla de Ideas*: Old Ideology in New Clothes?" *A Changing Cuba in a Changing World*, Bildner Center for Western Hemisphere Studies, 2008, pp. 73–88.

Kaplan, Amy. "Where Is Guantánamo?" *American Quarterly*, vol. 57, no. 3, 2005, pp. 831–58.

Kay, Keegan. "Reunion Group Returns for 2016 Trip." *Guantanamo Bay Gazette*, 19 Feb. 2016, p. 1, https://dloc.com/UF00098616/01179/pdf.

Kell, Dara, and Veena Rao. *A Ship from Guantánamo*. The New York Times, 6 July 2021, https://www.nytimes.com/video/opinion/100000007783198/a-ship-from-guantanamo.html.

Kempster, Norman. "Cuba Kills 4 Swimming to Guantánamo; U.S. Protests." *Los Angeles Times*, 8 July 1993, https://www.latimes.com/archives/la-xpm-1993-07-08-mn-11175-story.html.

Kenney, Padraic. *Dance in Chains: Political Prisoners in the Modern World*. Oxford UP, 2017.

Khan, Mahvish Rukhsana. *My Guantánamo Diary: The Detainees and the Stories They Told Me*. Public Affairs, 2008.

Kirk, Amy. "Farewell from the Editor." *Guantanamo Bay Gazette*, 1 Oct. 2004, p. 10, https://dloc.com/UF00098616/01113/images/9.

Kirk, John M. *Healthcare without Borders: Understanding Cuban Medical Internationalism*. UP of Florida, 2015.

Klepak, Hal. "Reflections on U.S.-Cuba Military-to-Military Contacts." *Strategic Forum*, vol. 295, 2016, pp. 1–5.

Kumaraswami, Par. "Cultural Policy and Cultural Politics in Revolutionary Cuba: Re-Reading the *Palabras a los intelectuales* (Words to the Intellectuals)." *Bulletin of Latin American Research* vol. 28, no. 4, 2009, pp. 527–41.

Kurnaz, Murat. *Five Years of My Life: An Innocent Man in Guantanamo*. With Helmut Kuhn. Translated by Jefferson Chase. Palgrave Macmillan, 2008.

Laguna, Albert Sergio. *Diversión: Play and Popular Culture in Cuban America*. New York UP, 2017.

Lakoff, George, and Mark Johnson. *Metaphors We Live By*. U of Chicago P, 1980.

Lamb, Robert. "Scorpion Stings Sailor's Sole." *Guantanamo Bay Gazette*, 29 Sept. 2006, p. 1, https://dloc.com/UF00098616/00053/pdf.

Lastre, Reinaldo. "Ficciones de frontera: La base naval de Guantánamo como lugar afectivo." *El toque*, 5 June 2023, https://eltoque.com/la-base-naval-de-guantanamo-como-lugar-afectivo-cine-cubano.

Leopold, Jason. "Guantanamo Guards Have High Rates of Post-Traumatic Stress, Exclusive Documents Show." *VICE News*, 25 Oct. 2016, https://www.vice.com/en/article/9kn9p3/guantanamo-guards-have-high-rates-of-post-traumatic-stress-exclusive-documents-show.

Li, Darryl. "Captive Passages: Geographies of Blackness in Guantánamo Memoirs." *Transforming Anthropology*, vol. 30, no. 1, Apr. 2022, pp. 20–33.

Life after Guantánamo: Exiled in Kazakhstan. YouTube, uploaded by VICE News, 15 Oct. 2015, https://www.youtube.com/watch?v=dUBbxIoGNaw.

Linhardt, Christina, and Michael L. Rose. *Guantánamo Circus*. Amazon Prime Video, 2013.

Lipman, Jana K. *Guantánamo: A Working-Class History between Empire and Revolution*. U of California P, 2009.

Lipman, Jana K. "Where's Guantánamo in *Granma*? Competing Dis-

WORKS CITED

courses on Detention and Terrorism." *Guantánamo and American Empire: The Humanities Respond*, edited by Don E. Walicek and Jessica Adams, Palgrave Macmillan, 2017, pp. 215–42.

Lira Saade, Carmen. "Soy el responsable de la persecución a homosexuales que hubo en Cuba: Fidel Castro." *La jornada*, 31 Aug. 2010, https://www.jornada.com.mx/2010/08/31/mundo/026e1mun.

Lookingbill, Todd R., and Peter D. Smallwood. "Collateral Values: The Natural Capital Created by Landscapes of War." *Collateral Values: The Natural Capital Created by Landscapes of War*, edited by Todd R. Lookingbill and Peter D. Smallwood, Springer, 2019, pp. 3–14.

Lowe, Lisa. *The Intimacies of Four Continents*. Duke UP, 2015.

Lowe, Lisa, and Kris Manjapra. "Comparative Global Humanities after Man: Alternatives to the Coloniality of Knowledge." *Theory, Culture and Society*, vol. 36, no. 5, 2019, pp. 23–48.

Lubin, Alex. *Never-Ending War on Terror*. U of California P, 2021.

MacDonald, Kevin, director. *The Mauritanian*. Universal Pictures Home Entertainment, 2021.

Maguire, Emily A. "Temporal Palimpsests: Critical Irrealism in Generation Zero's *Cuba in Splinters*." *Revista de Estudios Hispánicos*, vol. 51, no. 2, 2017, pp. 325–48.

Malone, Linda A. "The Legal Dilemma of Guantánamo Detainees from Bush to Obama." *Criminal Law Forum*, vol. 23, no. 4, 2012, pp. 347–62.

Martí, Irene. "A 'Home' or 'a Place to Be, but Not to Live': Arranging the Prison Cell." *The Prison Cell: Embodied and Everyday Spaces of Incarceration*, edited by Jennifer Turner and Victoria Knight, Palgrave Macmillan, 2020, pp. 121–42.

Massip, José. *Guantánamo*. Instituto Cubano de Artes e Industrias Cinematográficas (ICAIC), 1965.

Massip, José. "Guantánamo, Twice." Translated by Susannah Rodríguez Drissi and Ariana Hernández Reguant, *Cuba Counterpoints*, 2017 (1966), https://cubacounterpoints.com/archives/4045.html.

May, Brian. "Cuban American Friendship Day: Celebration, Food and Fun for Everyone." *Guantanamo Bay Gazette*, 6 Feb. 2009, p. 4, https://dloc.com/UF00098616/00004/images/3.

McClintock, Anne. "Paranoid Empire: Specters from Guantánamo and Abu Ghraib." *Small Axe*, vol. 13, no. 1, 2009, pp. 50–74.

"Meet George Johnson of the GTMO Recycling Team." *Guantanamo*

Bay Gazette, 26 Mar. 2004, p. 9, https://dloc.com/UF00098616/01086/images/8.

Mesta, Bill. "Navy Lodge Manager Honored for 40 Years Service." *Guantanamo Bay Gazette*, 15 Apr. 2011, p. 8, https://dloc.com/UF00098616/00209/pdf.

Metcalf, Josephine. "'O Prison Darkness . . . Lions in the Cage': The 'Peculiar' Prison Memoirs of Guantánamo Bay." *The Palgrave Handbook of Incarceration in Popular Culture*, edited by Meredith A. Harmes, Barbara Harmes, and Marcus K. Harmes, Palgrave Macmillan, 2020, pp. 67–87.

Meyer, Jane. "The Memo: How an Internal Effort to Ban the Abuse and Torture of Detainees Was Thwarted." *The New Yorker*, 27 Feb. 2006, https://www.newyorker.com/magazine/2006/02/27/the-memo.

"Military Police Unit Ready for Guantánamo Bay Mission." *Wisconsin National Guard*, 22 June 2016, https://ng.wi.gov/news/16061.

Miller, Flagg. "Forms of Suffering in Muslim Prison Poetry." *Poems from Guantánamo*, edited by Marc Falkoff, U of Iowa P, 2007, pp. 7–16.

Ministerio de Justicia de Cuba. *Gaceta Oficial de la República de Cuba*, 1 Sept. 2022, https://www.tsp.gob.cu/sites/default/files/documentos/goc-2022-o93_0.pdf.

Mirk, Sarah. *Guantánamo Voices: True Accounts from the World's Most Infamous Prison*. Abrams Comicarts, 2020.

Moore, Alexandra S. "Exception as Alibi: Rhetorics of Emergency and Bare Life in the War on Terror." *Liberal Disorder, States of Exception, and Populist Politics*, edited by Valur Ingimundarson and Sveinn M. Jóhannesson, Routledge, 2021, pp. 71–89.

Moore, Alexandra S. "Across the Threshold of Detectability: Guantánamo in the Work of Debi Cornwall." *ASAP/Journal*, vol. 6, no. 1, Jan. 2021, pp. 211–34.

Moore, Robin D. "Cuba Sings Its Political Story." *The Wall Street Journal*, 5 Aug. 2021, https://www.wsj.com/articles/cuba-sings-its-political-story-11628175989.

Morales Blanco, Sandra. "Revelan infierno en Guantánamo." *Univisión*, 12 Sept. 2007, http://humanrights.ucdavis.edu/projects/the-guantanamo-testimonials-project/testimonies/testimonies-of-military-guards/revelan-infierno-en-guantanamo.

Morán, Francisco. "Modernismo e identidad en Julián del Casal y José Martí: Cuba en la encrucijada finisecular." *La Habana Elegante*, vol. 3, Fall 1998, http://www.habanaelegante.com/Fall98/Hojas.htm.

WORKS CITED

Morsi, Eman. "Cuba in Arabic and the Limits of Third World Solidarity." *The Global South*, vol. 13, no. 1, Spring 2019, pp. 145–77.

"Mr. Valmar Burch." *Guantanamo Bay Gazette*, 14 Nov. 2008, p. 3, https://dloc.com/UF00098616/01235/images/2.

Mubanga, Martin. "Terrorist 2003." *Poems from Guantánamo: The Detainees Speak*, edited by Marc Falkoff, U of Iowa P, 2007, pp. 55–57.

Musashi, Miyamoto. *The Complete Musashi: The Book of Five Rings and Other Works*. Translated and with an introduction by Alexander Bennett, foreword by Graham Sayer, Tuttle Publishing, 2021.

Nadiminti, Kalyan. "The Detainee's Two Bodies: Intellectual Property and Fugitivity at Guantánamo Bay." *Humanity: An International Journal of Human Rights, Humanitarianism, and Development*, vol. 13, no. 3, 2022, pp. 343–66.

Nasser, Abdul Latif. "Exclusive: An Open Letter from Guantánamo Bay." *EsquireMiddleEast*, 21 July 2020, https://www.esquireme.com/culture/features/46945-exclusive-an-open-letter-from-guantanamo-bay.

Nasser, Latif. *The Other Latif*. WNYC Studios, 2020.

Nazaryan, Alexander. "Guantánamo Bay Is the Most Ridiculous Place on Earth." *Newsweek*, 3 Apr. 2014, https://www.newsweek.com/2014/04/11/guantanamo-bay-most-ridiculous-place-earth-248095.html.

Nixon, Honey. "Eldica Moore Celebrates Her 97th Birthday." *Guantanamo Bay Gazette*, 13 July 2007, p. 6, https://dloc.com/UF00098616/00125/pdf.

Nussbaum, Martha. *Anger and Forgiveness: Resentment, Generosity, Justice*. Oxford UP, 2016.

Obama, Barack H. "Remarks by the President at the National Defense University." The White House, Office of the Press Secretary, 23 May 2013, https://obamawhitehouse.archives.gov/the-press-office/2013/05/23/remarks-president-national-defense-university.

Oppmann, Patrick. "Cuban Police Crack Down on Demonstrators Protesting Widespread Shortages." *CNN*, 8 May 2023, https://www.cnn.com/2023/05/08/americas/cuba-police-crackdown-protests-intl-hnk/index.html.

Oppmann, Patrick. "In This Isolated Cuban Town on Guantanamo Bay, They Still Call Americans 'the Enemy,'" *CNN*, 1 July 2018, https://www.cnn.com/2018/07/01/americas/caimanera-cuba-guantanamo-bay/index.html.

"Out of Gitmo." *PBS Frontline*, 21 Feb. 2017, https://www.pbs.org/wgbh/frontline/documentary/out-of-gitmo/.

WORKS CITED

Paik, A. Naomi. *Rightlessness: Testimony and Redress in U.S. Prison Camps since World War II*. U of North Carolina P, 2016.

Parmly, Michael. "The Guantánamo Bay Naval Base: The United States and Cuba—Dealing with a Historic Anomaly." *The Fletcher Forum of World Affairs* vol. 27, no. 3, 2013, pp. 57–83.

Paul, Ian Alan. *Guantánamo Bay Museum of Art and History*. https://www.ianalanpaul.com/guantanamo-bay-museum-of-art-and-history/.

Pedriali, Federica. "Bared and Grievable: Theory Impossible in No Man's Land." *Mobilizing Cultural Identities in the First World War*, edited by Federica G. Pedriali and Cristina Savettieri, Palgrave Macmillan, 2020, pp. 149–81.

Perera Robbio, Alina, René Tamayo León, and Yaima Puig Meneses. "Díaz-Canel: «Tenemos un digno y heroico pueblo»." *Granma*, 16 Dec. 2021, https://www.granma.cu/cuba/2021-12-16/diaz-canel-tenemos-un-digno-y-heroico-pueblo.

Pérez Firmat, Gustavo. *Life on the Hyphen: The Cuban-American Way*. U of Texas P, 1994.

Pérez, Humberto. "Carta a Osvaldo." *El futuro* (Guantánamo Bay, Cuba), vol. 1, 1995, p. 1.

Pérez-Cano, Tania. "Graphic Testimonies of the *Balsero* Crisis of 1994: Narratives of Cuban Detainees at the Guantánamo Naval Base." *International Journal of Comic Art (IJOCA)*, Spring/Summer 2019, pp. 79–104.

Piñera, Virgilio. *The Weight of the Island: Selected Poems of Virgilio Piñera*. Translated by Pablo Medina, Diálogos Books, 2014.

Pinter, Harold. "Art, Truth and Politics." Nobel Lecture, 2005, https://www.nobelprize.org/prizes/literature/2005/pinter/lecture/.

Ponte, Antonio José. "What Am I Doing Here?" *Cuba on the Verge: An Island in Transition*, edited by Terry McCoy, Bullfinch Press, 2003, pp. 14–16.

Ponte, Antonio José. *La fiesta vigilada*. Editorial Anagrama, 2007.

Pratt, Mary Louise. "Harm's Way: Language and the Contemporary Arts of War." *PMLA*, vol. 124, no. 5, 2009, pp. 1515–31.

Price, Rachel. *Planet/Cuba: Art, Culture, and the Future of the Island*. Verso, 2015.

"Proclamation by the National Assembly of People's Power of the Republic of Cuba." *Cuba Gobierno Discursos*, 13 Sept. 1999, http://www.cuba.cu/gobierno/documentos/1999/ing/a130999i.html.

Puchner, Martin. "Guantánamo Bay: A State of Exception." *Guantánamo Bay Museum of Art and History*, https://www.guantanamobaymuseum.org/?url=puchnertext. Previously published in *London Review of Books*, vol. 26, no. 24, 16 Dec. 2004, https://www.lrb.co.uk/the-paper/v26/n24/martin-puchner/guantanamo-bay.

Queair, Edward C. *Children of the U.S. Military and Identity: A Narrative Inquiry into the "Brat" Experience.* 2018. Antioch U, PhD dissertation.

Queeley, Andrea. *Rescuing Our Roots: The African Anglo-Caribbean Diaspora in Contemporary Cuba.* UP of Florida, 2015.

Quintero Herencia, Juan Carlos. *La Hoja De Mar (:) Efecto Archipiélago I.* Almenara, 2016.

Quiroga, José. "On the Weight of Insular Flesh." *Hispanisms and Homosexualities*, edited by Sylvia Molloy and Robert Irwin, Duke UP, 1998, pp. 269–86.

Rainsford, Sarah. "Guantánamo Bay a Thorn in Cuba's Side." *BBC*, 16 July 2014, https://www.bbc.com/news/world-latin-america-28309760.

"Raúl Castro declara la guerra a la corrupción, 'sin contemplaciones.'" *El Mundo*, 23 Dec. 2011, https://www.elmundo.es/america/2011/12/23/cuba/1324651081.html.

Redfield, Marc. *The Rhetoric of Terror: Reflections on 9/11 and the War on Terror.* Fordham UP, 2009.

Risen, James, and Tim Golden. "3 Prisoners Commit Suicide at Guantánamo." *The New York Times*, 11 June 2006, https://www.nytimes.com/2006/06/11/us/11gitmo.html.

Rivera, Ray. "Suspicion in the Ranks: Inside the Spy Investigation of Captain James Yee." *The Seattle Times*, 9–16 Jan. 2005, https://special.seattletimes.com/o/html/nationworld/2002142925_yeeabout.html.

Rochelle, Safiyah. "Encountering the 'Muslim': Guantánamo Bay, Detainees, and Apprehensions of Violence." *Canadian Journal of Law and Society/ Revue Canadienne de Droit et Société*, vol. 32, no. 2, 2019, pp. 209–25.

Rodríguez Lobaina, Néstor. *Con el alma cautiva.* Aduana Vieja Editorial, 2007.

Roman, Joe. "Guantánamo 2.0: Transforming Gitmo into a Peace Park and Ecological Research Center." *Collateral Values: The Natural Capital Created by Landscapes of War*, edited by Todd R. Lookingbill and Peter D. Smallwood, Springer, 2019, pp. 235–60.

WORKS CITED

Roman, Joe, and James Kraska. "Reboot Gitmo for U.S.-Cuba Research Diplomacy." *Science*, vol. 351, no. 6279, 2016, pp. 1258–60.

Rosenberg, Carol. "Former Guantánamo Bay Commander Sentenced to 2 Years in Prison." *The New York Times*, 8 Oct. 2020, https://www.nytimes.com/2020/10/08/us/politics/guantanamo-bay-commander-sentenced.html.

Rosenberg, Carol. "From Raft to U.S. Navy, Camp Tour Is Round Trip." *The Miami Herald*, 22 Oct. 2007, https://www.miamiherald.com/news/nation-world/world/americas/guantanamo/article1928416.html.

Rosenberg, Carol. "Guantánamo Bay as Nursing Home: Military Envisions Hospice Care as Terrorism Suspects Age." *The New York Times*, 27 Apr. 2019, https://www.nytimes.com/2019/04/27/us/politics/guantanamo-bay-aging-terrorism-suspects-medical-care.html.

Rosenberg, Carol. *Guantánamo Bay: The Pentagon's Alcatraz of the Caribbean*. Mango Media, 2016.

Rosenberg, Carol. "Pentagon Lifts Trump-Era Ban on Release of Guantánamo Prisoners' Art." *The New York Times*, 7 Feb. 2023, https://www.nytimes.com/2023/02/07/us/politics/guantanamo-art.html.

Rosenberg, Carol. "Prison Camps Mum: Red Cross Establishes Video Link for 90 Captives." *The Miami Herald*, 29 Dec. 2010.

Rosenberg, Carol. "Retired Justice Stevens Says Some Guantánamo Captives May Deserve Reparations." *The Miami Herald*, 6 May 2015, https://www.miamiherald.com/article20362164.html.

Ross, Daniel. "Daniel Ross: 'Cada fósforo de la película es un hombre que cruza la frontera.'" Interview with Jorge Suñol, 10 May 2023, https://www.cubanoticias360.com/daniel-ross-cada-fosforo-de-la-pelicula-es-un-hombre-que-cruza-la-frontera/.

Ross, Daniel. *La espera*. Studio DaRoDe Productions, 2022.

Rossdale, Polly, and Katie Taylor. "An Account of 'Life after Guantánamo': A Rehabilitation Project for Former Guantánamo Detainees across Continents." *Torture*, vol. 27, no. 2, 2017, pp. 47–61.

"Rubio Visits Guantánamo Bay Naval Base." https://www.rubio.senate.gov/public/index.cfm/guantanamo-bay-naval-base.

Saar, Erik, and Viveca Novak. *Inside the Wire: A Military Intelligence Soldier's Eyewitness Account of Life at Guantánamo*. Penguin, 2005.

Salcedo, Doris. *Atrabilarios*. Institute of Contemporary Art, Boston, 1996.

Sánchez Altarriba, Claro. "Cómo lo vieron las víctimas." *Porvenir: La voz independiente de Guantánamo*, vol. 3, May 2008, p. 7.

Sánchez Guerra, José. "Guantánamo in the Eye of the Hurricane." *Guantánamo and American Empire: The Humanities Respond*, edited by Don E. Walicek and Jessica Adams, Palgrave Macmillan, 2017, pp. 183–213.

Sánchez, José Ramón. *The Black Arrow*. Translated by Katerina Gonzalez Seligmann and Esther Whitfield, Linkgua Ediciones, 2023.

Sánchez, José Ramón. "Los Quilos." *La noria*, vol. 7, 2014, p. 61.

Sánchez, José Ramón. *Talibán*. Editorial Casa Vacía, 2018.

Scarry, Elaine. *The Body in Pain: The Making and Unmaking of the World*. Oxford UP, 1985.

Schoenfeld, Paul. "Painted Bunting." *Guantanamo Bay Gazette*, 22 Aug. 2003, p. 9, https://dloc.com/UF00098616/01056/images/8.

Senate Select Committee on Intelligence. *Committee Study of the Central Intelligence Agency's Detention and Interrogation Program*. 3 Dec. 2014, https://www.feinstein.senate.gov/public/_cache/files/7/c/7c85429a-ec38-4bb5-968f-289799bf6d0e/D87288C34A6D9FF736F9459ABCF83210.sscistudy1.pdf.

Serra, Ana. *The "New Man" in Cuba: Culture and Identity in the Revolution*. UP of Florida, 2007.

Ševčenko, Liz. *Public History for a Post-Truth Era: Fighting Denial through Memory Movements*. Routledge, 2022.

Ševčenko, Liz. "Public Histories for Human Rights: Sites of Conscience and the Guantánamo Public Memory Project." *The Oxford Handbook of Public History*, edited by James B. Gardner and Paula Hamilton, Oxford UP, 2017, pp. 141–62.

Shane, Scott. "U.S. Drone Kills a Top Figure in Al Queda's Yemen Branch." *The New York Times*, 14 Apr. 2015, https://www.nytimes.com/2015/04/15/world/middleeast/us-drone-kills-a-top-figure-in-al-qaedas-yemen-branch.html.

Sharrock, Justine. *Tortured: When Good Soldiers Do Bad Things*. John Wiley & Sons, 2010.

Sierra Madero, Abel. ""El trabajo os hará hombres": Masculinización nacional, trabajo forzado y control social en Cuba durante los años sesenta." *Cuban Studies*, vol. 44, no. 1, 2016, pp. 309–49.

Slahi, Mohamedou Ould. "Guard Duty." *Evergreen Review*, Spring/Summer 2021, https://evergreenreview.com/read/guard-duty/.

WORKS CITED

Slahi, Mohamedou Ould, with Larry Siems. *Guantánamo Diary*. Little, Brown and Company, 2015. Restored Edition, 2017.

Slaughter, Joseph R. "Life, Story, Violence: What Narrative Doesn't Say." *Humanity: An International Journal of Human Rights, Humanitarianism, and Development*, vol. 8, no. 3, 2017, pp. 467–83.

Slaughter, Joseph R. "Vanishing Points: When Narrative Is Not Simply There." *Journal of Human Rights*, vol. 9, no. 2, 2010, pp. 207–23.

"Slow Down, GTMO, Security's Watching." *Guantánamo Bay Gazette*, 5 Mar. 2004, p. 1, https://dloc.com/UF00098616/01083/images.

Smith, Steven D. "Introduction: An Archaeology of Asymmetric Warfare." *Partisans, Guerillas, and Irregulars: Historical Archaeology of Asymmetric Warfare*, edited by Steven D. Smith and Clarence R. Geier, U of Alabama P, 2019.

Solis Ybarra, Priscilla. "Borderlands as Bioregion: Jovita González, Gloria Anzaldúa, and the Twentieth-Century Ecological Revolution in the Río Grande Valley." *MELUS*, vol. 34, no. 2, 2009, pp. 175–89.

"Sometimes Things Were Unusual in GTMO." *Guantanamo Bay Gazette*, 29 Dec. 2006, p. 12 https://dloc.com/UF00098616/00066/pdf.

Sommer, Doris. *Proceed with Caution, When Engaged by Minority Writing in the Americas*. Harvard UP, 1999.

Stafford Smith, Clive. *Eight O'Clock Ferry to the Windward Side: Seeking Justice in Guantánamo Bay*. Nation Books, 2008.

Stafford Smith, Clive. "How Will Guantánamo Be Remembered?" *Al Jazeera*, 23 Jan. 2017, https://www.aljazeera.com/features/2017/1/23/how-will-guantanamo-be-remembered.

Stetler, Ryan. "Guantánamo Reunion, by Way of BBC." *The New York Times*, 10 Jan. 2010, https://www.nytimes.com/2010/01/11/business/media/11bbc.html.

Suárez, Felipa, and Pilar Quesada. *A escasos metros del enemigo: Historia de la Brigada de la Frontera*. Ediciones Verde Olivo, 1996.

Swanson, Elizabeth, and Alexandra S. Moore. "Indefinite Detention: Chronotopes of Unfreedom in Mohamedou Ould Slahi's *Guantánamo Diary*." *Ariel: A Review of International English Literature*, vol. 52, no. 1, Jan. 2021, pp. 33–60.

Sylvester, Christine. *War as Experience: Contributions from International Relations and Feminist Analysis*. Routledge, 2013.

Symbolic Reparations Research Project. "Guidelines on the Use of Art in Symbolic Reparations." https://issuu.com/symbolicreparations/docs/srrp-guidelines-on-the-use-of-art.

Szitanyi, Stephanie. *Gender Trouble in the U.S. Military: Challenges to Regimes of Male Privilege*. Palgrave Macmillan, 2020.

Task Force on Memory, Truth and Justice. *Cuban National Reconciliation*. Florida International University, Latin American and Caribbean Center, 2003.

Taub, Ben. "Guantánamo's Darkest Secret." *The New Yorker*, 15 Apr. 2019, https://www.newyorker.com/magazine/2019/04/22/guantanamos-darkest-secret.

Taylor Saito, Natsu. "Indefinite Detention, Colonialism and Settler Prerogative in the United States." *Social & Legal Studies*, vol. 30, no. 1, 2021, pp. 32–65.

"Teaching the Past to the Future." *Guantanamo Bay Gazette*, 13 Feb. 2004, p. 5, https://dloc.com/UF00098616/01080/images/1.

Thompson, Erin. "What We Can Learn from Art Painted inside Guantánamo." *The Nation*, 4 Dec. 2017, https://www.thenation.com/article/archive/what-we-can-learn-from-art-painted-inside-guantanamo/.

Tomsky, Terri. "Iguanas and Enemy Combatants: Reconsidering Cosmopolitanism through Guantánamo's Creaturely Lives." *Cosmopolitan Animals*, edited by Karen Jones Kaori et al., Palgrave Macmillan, 2015, pp. 201–15.

Topham, Laurence. *My Brother's Keeper*. The Guardian, Feb. 2021, https://www.theguardian.com/world/ng-interactive/2021/feb/23/my-brothers-keeper-a-former-guantanamo-detainee-his-guard-and-their-unlikely-friendship.

Trapp, Erin. "The Enemy Combatant as Poet: The Politics of Writing in Poems from Guantánamo." *Postmodern Culture*, vol. 21, no. 3, May 2011, doi:10.1353/pmc.2011.0023.

Trouillot, Michel-Rolph. *Silencing the Past: Power and the Production of History*. Beacon Press, 1995.

Tuan, Yi-Fu. *Space and Place: The Perspective of Experience*. U of Minnesota P, 1977.

Tubiana, Jérome, and Alexandre Franc. *Guantánamo Kid: The True Story of Mohammed El-Gharani*. Self-Made Hero, 2019.

Tudela Iríbar, Rolando. "Una declaración al Pueblo." *Porvenir: La voz independiente de Guantánamo*, vol. 1, Feb. 2008, p. 3.

WORKS CITED

Turner, Jennifer, and Victoria Knight, editors. *The Prison Cell: Embodied and Everyday Spaces of Incarceration*. Palgrave Macmillan, 2020.

Tur Valladares, Alejandro. "Ocho jóvenes cienfuegueros, procesados por acercarse a la Base Naval de Guantánamo." 23 Mar. 2019, https://diariodecuba.com/cuba/1553299585_45308.html.

United States, Congress, House and Senate, Armed Services. *National Defense Authorization Act for Fiscal Year 2006*. Government Printing Office, 2006. 109th Congress, House Report 1815, https://www.congress.gov/bill/109th-congress/house-bill/1815/text.

United States, Congress, Senate, Energy and Natural Resources. *National Defense Authorization Act for Fiscal Year 2022*. Government Printing Office, 2022. 117th Congress, Senate Report 1605, https://www.congress.gov/bill/117th-congress/senate-bill/1605/text.

United States, Department of Defense. "Naval Station Guantanamo Bay: In-Depth Overview." *Military Installations*, https://installations.militaryonesource.mil/in-depth-overview/naval-station-guantanamo-bay.

United States, Department of State, Office to Monitor and Combat Trafficking in Persons. *2021 Trafficking in Persons Report: Cuba*. https://www.state.gov/reports/2021-trafficking-in-persons-report/cuba/.

United States, Supreme Court. *Boumediène v. Bush*. 553 U.S. 723 (2008).

United States, Supreme Court. *Rasul v. Bush*, 542 U.S. 466 (2004).

University of Miami Libraries. *Between Despair and Hope: Cuban Rafters at the U.S. Naval Base Guantánamo Bay, 1994–1996*. https://scholar.library.miami.edu/digital/exhibits/show/guantanamo.

Valladares, Armando. *Against All Hope: The Prison Memoirs of Armando Valladares*. Knopf, 1986.

Valls, Jorge. *Twenty Years and Forty Days: Life in a Cuban Prison*. Americas Watch, 1986.

van Nieuwkerk, Karin. "'Conversion' to Islam and the Construction of a Pious Self." *The Oxford Handbook of Religious Conversion*, edited by Lewis R. Rambo and Charles E. Farhadian, Oxford UP, 2014.

"Víctimas de la represión en Cuba." *Porvenir: La voz independiente de Guantánamo*, vol. 1, Feb. 2008, p. 22.

Vine, David. *Base Nation: How U.S. Military Bases Abroad Harm America and the World*. Metropolitan Books, 2015.

Voyce, Steven. "Reading the Redacted." *Amodern*, vol. 6, July 2016, https://amodern.net/article/reading-the-redacted/.

WORKS CITED

Waener, John. "Hasta Luego, Señor Sharpe." *Guantanamo Bay Gazette*, 2 Dec. 2016, pp. 4–5, https://dloc.com/UF00098616/01322/pdf.

Waller, Nicole. "Terra Incognita: Mapping the Detention Center in Edwige Danticat's *Brother, I'm Dying* and the U.S. Supreme Court Ruling *Boumediène v. Bush*." *Atlantic Studies*, vol. 6, no. 3, 2009, pp. 357–69.

Walia, Harsha. "Omar Khadr: Race, Empire, and Unexceptional Detention." *Guantánamo Bay Museum of Art and History*, https://www.guantanamobaymuseum.org/?url=waliatext.

"Wanted by the Naval Criminal Investigative Service." *Guantanamo Bay Gazette*, 20 Feb. 2004, p. 11, https://dloc.com/UF00098616/01081/images/10.

Weber, Elisabeth. "Literary Justice? Poems from Guantánamo Bay Prison Camp." *Comparative Literature Studies*, vol. 48, no. 3, 2011, pp. 417–34.

Weber, Elisabeth. *Kill Boxes: Facing the Legacy of US-Sponsored Torture, Indefinite Detention, and Drone Warfare*. Punctum Books, 2017.

Werlau, Maria C. "Cuba Refuses to Tear Down Its Wall." *The Miami Herald*, 19 Nov. 2014, https://www.miamiherald.com/article4020570.html.

Whitfield, Esther. "Cuban Borderlands: Local Stories of the Guantánamo Naval Base." *Modern Language Notes*, vol. 130, no. 2, 2015, pp. 276–97.

Whitfield, Esther. "Guantánamo and Community: Visual Approaches to the Naval Base." *Guantánamo and American Empire: The Humanities Respond*, edited by Don E. Walicek and Jessica Adams, Palgrave Macmillan, 2017, pp. 149–72.

Wild, Tim. "The Restaurant at Guantánamo Bay." *Bon Appetit*, 21 Sept. 2020, https://www.bonappetit.com/story/ahmed-errachidi-restaurant-guantanamo-bay.

Williams, Katie Bo. "Guantánamo Is Becoming a Nursing Home for Its Aging Terror Suspects." *The Atlantic*, 28 Apr. 2019, https://www.theatlantic.com/politics/archive/2019/04/guantanamo-geriatric-terror-suspects/588202/.

Williams, Kim. "Navy Divers, Marines Pull Truck from GTMO Bay Inlet." *Guantanamo Bay Gazette*, 22 Feb. 2008, pp. 1, 8, https://dloc.com/UF00098616/00148/pdf.

Wirfel, Kelly. "End of an Era for Naval Station Guantanamo Bay."

Guantanamo Bay Gazette, 21 Dec. 2012, pp. 1, 6, https://dloc.com/UF00098616/00284/pdf.

Wirfel, Kelly. "GTMO Resident Reflects on Nearly Sixty Years at Naval Station." *Guantanamo Bay Gazette*, 31 Aug. 2012, p. 3, https://dloc.com/UF00098616/00270/pdf.

Witness to Guantánamo. https://witnesstoguantanamo.com/about_wtg/.

Wordu, Igo. "Eunice Alexander Laid to Rest." *Guantanamo Bay Gazette*, 28 July 2006, pp. 1–7, https://dloc.com/UF00098616/00044/pdf.

Worthington, Andy. *The Guantánamo Files: The Stories of the 774 Detainees in America's Illegal Prison.* https://www.andyworthington.co.uk/the-guantanamo-files/.

"W. T. Sampson High School Salutes Class of 2005." *Guantanamo Bay Gazette*, 17 June 2005, pp. 2–3, https://dloc.com/UF00098616/01147/images/1.

"W. T. Sampson's Class of 2003." *Guantanamo Bay Gazette*, 23 May 2003, p. 6, https://dloc.com/UF00098616/01044/images/5.

"W. T. Sampson's Class of 2004." *Guantanamo Bay Gazette*, 21 May 2004, pp. 6–7, https://dloc.com/UF00098616/01094/images/5.

Yachot, Noa. "Exclusive: Many Resettled Guantánamo Detainees in Legal Limbo, Analysis Shows." *The Guardian*, 9 Jan. 2022, https://www.theguardian.com/us-news/2022/jan/09/guantanamo-resettled-no-legal-status.

"Year in Review, 2002." *Guantanamo Bay Gazette*, 3 Jan. 2003, p. 3, https://dloc.com/UF00098616/01023/images/2.

Yee, James, and Aimee Molloy. *For God and Country: Faith and Patriotism under Fire.* 1st ed., Public Affairs, 2005.

Zevnik, Andreja. "Becoming-Animal, Becoming-Detainee: Encountering Human Rights Discourse in Guantánamo." *Law Critique*, vol. 22, no. 2, 2011, pp. 155–69.

Zhang, Izabela Radwanska. "In Paris: Debi Cornwall's *Welcome to Camp America—Inside Guantánamo Bay.*" *British Journal of Photography*, 6 Nov. 2017, https://www.1854.photography/2017/11/debi-cornwall-welcome-to-camp-america-inside-guantanamo-bay/.

INDEX

Note: Page references in *italics* refer to figures.

"Abducción" story (Estupiñán Zaldívar), 69–70, 96, 98
Abud, Abdulmalik, 54
Ackerman, Holly, 11
Adams, Jessica, 96
Adayfi, Mansoor, 3–4, 40, 50, 56, 68, 143; *Don't Forget Us Here: Lost and Found at Guantánamo*, 32, 41, 50–52; "In Our Prison on the Sea" essay, 52–53
Adelman, Rebecca A., 8, 44, 187n8
Agamben, Giorgio, 180n4
Ahmed, Ruhal, 102
Ait Idir, Mustafa, 35, 73
Al-Alwi, Moath, 30, 79
Al-Bihani, Ghaleb, 54–56, *55*

al-Halabi, Ahmad, 73
al-Rubaish, Ibrahim, 41, 56, 68, 182n12; "Ode to the Sea" poem, 31, 44, 45, 53, 57, 62; *Poems from Guantánamo: The Detainees Speak*, 40, 42–48
Alcoff, Linda, 178n5
Alexander, Eunice, 124
Alfonso Puerta, Yariel, 94
al Hikimi, Ahmed, 61–62, 64
Alianza Democrática Oriental, 95, 151, 162
Ali, Lotfi bin, 29, 147
Amnesty International, 12, 42, 65, 97, 176n6
Anderson, Benedict, 116–17, 127
Anderson, Laurie, 29

INDEX

The Andy Griffith Show, 115, 117
"Animal Planet" poem (Sánchez), 13
Ansi, Muhammad, 54
Anzaldúa, Gloria, 31
Arabescos mentales (Mental Arabesques) (Boti y Barreiro), 62
Arafat, Yasser, 46
Arenas, Reinaldo, 12, 94–95
Arendt, Chris, 27, 69, 101, 181n8
Arendt, Hannah, 180n4
Army Institute of Public Health study, 176n5
Art from Guantánamo exhibition, 26–27, 32, 41, 68
asymmetries of Guantánamo, 5–6, 13; anticolonial friendships, 6–7; asymmetrical scale of corpus, 7–8; disciplinary location, 10–11; legibility of textual and visual record, 9–10; suffering in detention centres, 11–12
Atrabilarios (Salcedo), 99, 184n24
Avilés-Santiago, Manuel, 77

Balsero Crisis. *See* Cuban Rafter Crisis
Balseros (Catalan documentary), 152, 162
Barberia, Lorena, 152, 182n14
Basulto, Conrado, 154
Batista, Fulgencio, 142
Bay of Pigs invasion (1961), 88, 92
Beatón, Alexander, 31, 35, 36; *El camino de la estrategia* project, 132–33; *Imaginary of Loyalty*, 135; *Susurros* photography exhibit, 36–38, *37*, 136–37; *Wounded by History*, 134
Before Night Falls (Arenas), 94–95
Begg, Moazzam, 33, 49, 75, 102, 180n3, 181n8; Begg's interactions with guards, 78; connection around religious faith, 83–84; experiences with nonwhite guards, 180n7; about Hispanic guards, 78; pleasures of reading and creating, 80, 81; racial and colonial hierarchies, 77–78; racial identifications of guards, 79; recreational offerings for detainees, 79; relationships with female guard, 80–81, 83
Ben Jelloun, Tahar, 112, 113
Bennett, Alexander, 132
Beyond Gitmo series (Cornwall), 148
Biden, Joseph, 20, 22
"bioregion," 31
The Black Arrow (Sánchez), 32; consolation in poetry, 58–59; "The Channel from the Base" poem, 59; "Impossible" poem, 59; "Secret//Noforn//20330602" poem, 61–62, 63–64; "Small Change" poem, 60; "Spotlight" poem, 59; "A Trojan Horse in the Caribbean" poem, 60–61
Black Spring (2003), 12, 176n6
Bon Appetit magazine, 113
The Book of Five Rings (Musashi), 132

INDEX

Border Brigade, 14, 69, 87–88, 100, 135–36; female soldiers in, 90; role in war on imperialism, 88–90
Borderlands/La Frontera: The New Mestiza (Anzaldúa), 31
Bosch, Carles, 152
Boti y Barreiro, Regino, 32; *Arabescos mentales*, 62; *El mar y la montaña*, 32, 62–63
Boumediène, Lakhdar, 35, 109
Brigada de la Frontera. *See* Border Brigade
Buehn, Robert, 115
Buil, Ana Mata, 58
Burch, Valmar, 127
Bush, George W., 20–22, 24, 72
Bustamante, Michael J., 143
Butler, Judith, 11, 24, 43, 167, 176n4
Buzzanco, Robert, 46

Caimanera: Una mirada diferente (García Campuzano), 129, 131–32, 136, 186n12
Calvo Ospina, Hernando, 35, 89–90, 129, 131
Camp Delta cages, 108–11
Camp Delta Standard Operating Procedures (*SOP*), 34, 72, 108, 178n2
Camp Echo, 110
Campisi, Elizabeth, 11, 152–53
Camp X-Ray, 108–10
care in Guantánamo, gestures of: gestures of compassion toward detainees, 27, 30–31; Harlow's work, 25–26, 29; lawyers, journalists and artist-activists' contribution, 28–29; writing and art by detainees, 26–30, 31. *See also* cellblock intimacies
Casal, Julián del, 56
Castro, Américo, 132
Castro, Fidel, 114, 123, 142, 152; 1961 literacy campaign, 16; 1961 speech in Havana, 176n8; apologizing for persecution of gay men, 184n28; "The Empire and the Independent Island" essay, 47; on Guantánamo Bay issue, 17–18, 47; "Reflections," 177n11; relationship with Middle East, 46; Revolutionary Offensive by, 177n10; war on imperialism, 14–15, 89, 182n13
Castro, Raúl: 1959 visit to Gaza, 46; 2016 meet with Obama, 90; on Guantánamo Bay issue, 17–18; statement on war on imperialism, 17
Cavarero, Adriana, 21
Committees for the Defense of the Revolution, 187n4
cellblock intimacies: Begg's experiences, 75–84; Errachidi's experiences, 75, 76, 84–86; experiences of detainees and of guards, 72–75; Slahi's experiences, 72–74, 76–83; transnational population of detainees, 71–72. *See also* care in Guantánamo, gestures of; guards

217

INDEX

"The Channel from the Base" poem (Sánchez), 59

"Che" Guevara, Ernesto, 88; 1959 visit to Gaza, 46; address to Tricontinental Conference, 15, 89; provocations, 181–82n11

Chekkouri, Younous, 148

Cisneros, José Felipe, 90

Clark, Edmund, 28–29, 105–6

Combinado de Guantánamo, 42, 65, 67, 86, 158, 160

"Comparative Global Humanities," 175n2

Con el alma cautiva (With a Captive Soul) (Rodríguez Lobaina), 32, 64; "Conversaciones con la luna" poem, 66; "La indignidad del hombre" poem, 66; mapping of "black sites," 66–67

confiscations, 108

Convention on the Prevention and Punishment of the Crime of Genocide, 177n12

"Conversaciones con la luna" (Conversations with the Moon) poem (Rodríguez Lobaina), 66

convivencia, 132–33, 137

Cornwall, Debi, 29, 35, 81, 85–86, 104, 148, 184n1; *Anonymous, Chinese Uighur*, 149; *Anonymous, Uzbek*, 149; free-floating images, 151; *Terry, American (United States)*, 86; *Welcome to Camp America*, 86, 163

"counterrevolutionaries," 34, 87, 91–93

Crabapple, Molly, 29

Crewe, Ben, 107

Cruz, Oscar, 58, 60

Cuba/Cubans, 105; acts of repudiation, 182n15; Adjustment Act (1966), 152, 183n17; Black Spring, 12, 176n6; Cuban Community Center, Guantánamo Bay, 125; Cuban commuters, Guantánamo Bay, 114; Cuban fortifications of land border, 91; ICAIC, 129; Law No.151 of Penal Code, 183n16; Rafter Crisis, 151–54, 156–57, 183n18; relationships in Middle East, 45–47; "Special Category Residents," 34; support to detainees, 48–50; US relationship, 14–15, 90–91

Cuban Border Brigade. *See* Border Brigade

Cuban Missile Crisis, 114

Cuban National Reconciliation, 162

Cuban Rafter Crisis, 151–54, 156–57, 183n18

Cuban Revolution, 14–15, 35, 60, 87–90, 95, 99, 136, 139, 143; teleology of, 151; vision and public rhetoric of, 47, 142

Cuban Special Category Residents, Guantánamo Naval Base, 123

Cumberbatch, Benedict, 30

INDEX

Defense Media Activity operations, 116
De Ferrari, Guillermina, 156
de Jesús Quiñónes, Roberto, 30, 96, 97–98, 100, 184n26
de la Nuez, Iván, 177n13
de la Rosa, Luis, 126
del Río, Jorge, 187n5
del Risco, Enrique, 178n4
Denbeaux, Mark P., 28, 151
Derrida, Jacques, 105, 112
"Detainee Assessment Brief" memorandum, 61–64, 179n6
Detention and Interrogation Program, 81, 181n9
Díaz-Canel, Miguel, 17
Díaz Castañón, María del Pilar, 142
Dilla, Haroldo, 177n10
documentary films about Guantánamo, 106; *Balseros*, 152, 162; *Guantánamo*, 7, 35, 129–32; *Guantánamo Diary Revisited*, 30; *Life after Guantánamo: Exiled in Kazakhstan*, 29, 147; *My Brother's Keeper*, 30, 83, 102; *Todo Guantánamo es nuestro*, 35
Domènech, Josep Maria, 152, 162
Don't Forget Us Here: Lost and Found at Guantánamo (Adayfi), 32, 41–42, 50–51
Dorticós, Osvaldo, 18
Dost, Shaikh Abdurraheem Muslim, 44
Duffy, Helen, 162
Duncan, Theresa, 26
Durán Rodríguez, Ernesto, 160

Eckstein, Susan, 152, 182n14, 183n17
Eight O'Clock Ferry to the Windward Side (Stafford Smith), 28
el-Gharani, Mohammed, 29, 41, 56, 68, 146, 182n12; "First Poem of My Life," 32, 44–45; *Poems from Guantánamo: The Detainees Speak*, 40, 42–48
El camino de la estrategia (The Way of Strategy) (Beatón and Gutiérrez), 132–33, 137
El futuro journal 35–36, 151, *155*, 156, 158, 187n5; graphic art of, 156–57
El mar y la montaña (The Sea and the Mountain) (Boti y Barreiro), 32, 62–63
"The Empire and the Independent Island" essay (Castro), 47
Enemy Combatant: A British Muslim's Journey to Guantánamo and Back (Begg), 75–76
Errachidi, Ahmed, 34, 75, 84, 111–13, 137, 144; connection around religious faith, 84–86; hospitality of, 138
Escape to Miami: An Oral History of the Cuban Rafter Crisis (Campisi), 152–53
Espacio Memoria y Derechos Humanos in Buenos Aires, 168
Estupiñán Zaldívar, Leandro, 31, 69

Fagen, Richard, 16
Falkoff, Marc, 26, 63. See also *Poems from Guantánamo: The Detainees Speak*
"Favorite Places" column, *Guantánamo Bay Gazette*, 117
Feinstein Report, 81, 181n9
Felman, Shoshana, 43
Fernández, Joseíto, 131
A Field Guide for Female Interrogators (Fusco), 81
Fink, Sheri, 148
The Fire Scroll (Musashi), 132, 136
"First Poem of My Life" poem (el-Gharani), 32, 44–45
Fischer, Sibylle, 78
Foster, Jodie, 30
Franc, Alexandre, 29, 41, 146
Franqui, Virgilio, 186n11
Funk, Marcus, 116
Fusco, Coco, 81

Gandhi, Leela, 6, 70
García Calzada, Ana Luz, 30, 96–98, 100
García Campuzano, Ofelia, 14, 131
García, María Cristina, 92, 182n15
Garth, Hannah, 151
The General: The Ordinary Man Who Challenged Guantánamo (Errachidi), 75, 76, 112
Ginsburg, Amber, 27–28, 36, 101, 161
GitmoBay Association, 118
"Gitmo Gab" column, *Guantánamo Bay Gazette*, 117
"Gitmo Shopper," *Guantánamo Bay Gazette*, 116
Goetz, John, 30
Golden, Tim, 176n3
Goldman, Dara E., 178n4; about Cuban public discourse on US occupation, 17; study of islands, 56
González, Ernesto, 124
Goulding, Cathlin, 166–67
Goyal, Yogita, 76–77
Granma newspaper, 17
Greenberg, Karen J., 21–23, 48, 71, 175n1
Gregory, Derek, 167
Guantanamera (Gutiérrez Alea), 7, 131
Guantánamo, 5, 130; asymmetries of, 5–13; battleground for consequential wars, 4; Cuban futures and Guantánamo Bay Naval Base, 151–58; detention and future, 143–51; future in Guantánamo's shadows, 158–61; geopolitical significance, 39–40; "home" (*see* home creation; navy life at); speculative futures for, 161–71; temporalities, 140–43. *See also* care in Guantánamo, gestures of; guards
Guantánamo (documentary film), 7, 35, 129–32
Guantánamo Bay Gazette newspaper, 34, 116–22, *119*, 124, 127, 176n5

INDEX

Guantánamo Bay Museum of Art and History (Paul), 36, 161, 164, 187n8; grammatical future, 168–69; museum's fictive temporality, 167; "Plan your Visit" section, 169; political agenda of, 168; recalibrates Guantánamo's openness, 170; "Reparations for Guantánamo's Torture Survivors" and, 166, 171; Symbolic Reparations Research Project, 168; vision of conciliation includes collaborative artistic work, 170

Guantánamo cell, 107–13. *See also* cellblock intimacies

Guantánamo Circus (film), 117, 185n6

Guantánamo Diary (Slahi), 9, 49, 72, 75, 140, 144, 178n1. *See also* Slahi, Mohamedou Ould

Guantánamo Diary Revisited (film), 30

"Guantánamo Docket," *New York Times*, 179n7, 181n8

Guantánamo: If the Light Goes Out (Clark), 28–29, 105

Guantánamo Kid: The True Story of Mohammed El-Gharani (Tubiana and Franc), 29, 41, 146–47

Guantánamo: My Journey (Hicks), 109

Guantánamo Public Memory Project, 152, 154, 163–64

guards: "Abducción," 69–70, 96, 98; assignments, 180n5; cellblock intimacies, 71–86; against Cuban migrants, 91, 93–95; experiences of detainees, 180n6; García Calzada's "Kites" story, 97, 98; gestures of apology and forgiveness, 102–3; guard-detainee friendships, 102; guards-enemies relationships, 33–34; intimate friendship of, 70–71; Mariel exodus, 92; Quiñónes' "La fuga" story, 97–98; Ross's *La espera* film, 98–99; Tea Project, 27–28, 101–2; Truth and Memory Project, 96; US imperialism, 100–101. *See also* cellblock intimacies

Guerra, José Sánchez, 14
Guerra, Lillian, 91–92, 128
Guha, Ranajit, 9
Gutiérrez, Pedro, 31, 35, 36, 131–33, *134*, *135*, 136–37

Habeas Corpus (Anderson), 29
Hafetz, Jonathan, 28, 151
Halbert-Brooks, Ann, 187n4
Hamlin, Janet, 29
Hansen, Jonathan, 10, 13, 114
Harlow, Barbara, 25–26, 29, 72
Harris, Harry B., Jr., 6, 176n3
Hartman-Mahmud, Lori, 20
Havana: A New Art of Making Ruins (film), 177n9
Hearty, Kevin, 187n7
Heavy Rock (García Calzada), 96
Henry, Harry, 126
Hernández-Reguant, Ariana, 93
Hernández, Orlando "El Duque," 59

INDEX

Hicks, David, 34, 176n5, 180n3; animal life in cell, 113; depiction of pre-detention life, 144–45; *Guantánamo: My Journey*, 109–11; about Guantánamo Bay Naval Base, 104; guard's apology, 101; relationships with guards, 74
Holdbrooks, Terry, 84–85, 101, 181n8
Hollander, Nancy, 26
Holzer, Jenny, 63
home creation, 105–13, 115
Hughes, Aaron, 27–28, 36, 161
Hulme, Peter, 10, 49–50, 129
Hussein, Aliya, 161
Husta, Madhya, 125

ICAIC (Cuban Institute for Cinematographic Art and Industries), 129
Imaginary of Loyalty, 135
"Impossible" poem (Sánchez), 4, 59
indefinite detention, 11, 23, 32, 107, 125, 140–41, 143, 144
"In Our Prison on the Sea" essay (Adayfi), 52
Inside the Wire (Saar and Novak), 82
Insular Cases (1902–1922), 23
interrogation techniques, 81–82, 153
"Invasion of Space by a Female" technique, 81

Jarrosay, Geny, 99, 184n25
Johnson, George, 122
Johnson, Lyndon B., 123
Johnson, Mark, 20
Joint Task Force Guantánamo, 8, 186n6

Kapcia, Antoni, 16, 141, 177n10
Kaplan, Amy, 22–23, 24, 39, 40, 71, 75, 88, 141, 182n12
Keenan, Thomas, 148
Kell, Dara, 30
Kenney, Padraic, 65
Khadr, Omar, 162
Khan, Mahvish Rukhsana, 27
Kirk, Amy, 117–18
"Kites" story (García Calzada), 97, 98
Klepak, Hal, 88, 181n10
Knight, Victoria, 107–8
Kosovo Liberation Army in Albania, 111
Kraska, James, 162
Kumaraswami, Par, 92
Kurnaz, Murat, 35, 49, 73, 144, 145, 180n3
Kuzmich, Jon, 167

La espera (film), 30, 96, 98–99
La fiesta vigilada (Ponte), 176n9
"La fuga" story (de Jesús Quiñónes), 97–98
Laguna, Albert Sergio, 182n4
"La indignidad del hombre" (The Indignity of Man) poem (Rodríguez Lobaina), 66
"La isla en peso" (The Weight of the Island) poem (Piñera), 57
Lakoff, George, 20
La maldita circunstancia del fuego

INDEX

por todas partes series (Jarrosay), 184n25
La noria journal, 58, 127–28
Lastre, Reynaldo, 96
Lawrence, Winston, 122
legal limbo, 23, 175n1
Leopold, Jason, 176n5
Levinas, Emmanuel, 112
Lezama Lima, José, 56, 178n4
Li, Daryl, 78–79
Life after Guantánamo: Exiled in Kazakhstan (Ostrovsky), 29, 147
"Life after Guantánamo" project, 147, 162–63, 184n27
Linhardt, Christina, 185n6
Lipman, Jana K., 10–11, 114, 123, 181n10; about Border Brigade, 87–88; about US military base in Cuba, 17, 18; writings about US-Cuban relations, 14
Lowe, Lisa, 6, 70, 78, 175n2
Lubin, Alex, 22
Lupton, Julia Reinhardt, 180n4

MacDonald, Kevin, 30
"magic marker" incident, 181n9
Maguire, Emily A., 142
Malone, Linda A., 178n15
Manjapra, Kris, 175n2
Margolis, Richard J., 146
Mariel exodus, 92
Martí, Irene, 107, 112
Martí, José, 56
Martínez, Gloria, 126
Massip, José, 7, 35, 129–32
Maura, Rafael, 124

The Mauritanian (film), 30, 146
McClintock, Anne, 71, 179n1
McManus, Carling, 167
McPherson, Claude, 124
Melise, Albert, 102
Menéndez Pidal, Ramón, 132
Metcalf, Josephine, 72, 146
Metres, Philip, 63
Meyer, Jane, 81, 82
Miami Herald, 28, 108, 114, 126, 179n2
Migrant Operations Center, 93
Military Family Appreciation Week, 117
Military Units for Assisting Production (UMAP), 67
Miller, Flagg, 32, 43, 45
Minnow, Martha, 187n7
Montezemolo, Fiamma, 167
Moore, Alexandra S., 76, 77, 140
Moore, Eldica, 124
Moore, Robin, 128
Morán, Francisco, 56
Morsi, Eman, 45–47
Movement of Cuban Youth for Democracy. *See* Movimiento Cubano de Jóvenes por la Democracia
Movimiento Cubano de Jóvenes por la Democracia, 64–65
Moya, Ramón, 99–100
Mubanga, Martin, 178n3
Musashi, Miyamoto, 132, 136
My Brother's Keeper (film), 30, 83, 102
My Guantanamo Diary: The Detainees and the Stories They Told Me (Khan), 27

Nadiminti, Kalyan, 52, 166
Nasser, Gamal Abdel, 46
Nasser, Latif, 30, 144, 186n2
National Defense Authorization Act (2006), 124
National Defense Authorization Act (2020–2021), 185n9
navy life at Guantánamo, 113–22
Nazaryan, Alexander, 185n7
Neely, Brandon, 48, 101, 102
Nettleton, John R., 185n7
New York Times, 28, 114
Novak, Viveca, 73, 82
Núñez, Ramón, 186n11
Nussbaum, Martha, 102

Obama, Barack: 2016 visit to Cuba, 90; order to close Cuban detention camps, 168–69; role in war on terror, 22, 24
"Oda al Mar" poem (al-Rubaish), 56–57
Odell, Jenny, 167
"Ode to the Sea" poem (al-Rubaish), 31, 44, 45, 53, 57, 62
"Odio al Mar" (Martí), 56
Oppmann, Patrick, 186n12
Organization for Security and Co-operation in Europe, 121
Ostrovsky, Simon, 147
The Other Latif (miniseries), 30, 144

Paglen, Trevor, 63
Paik, Naomi, 10
Palestinian Liberation Organization, 46
"Patria o Muerte" (Fatherland or Death) slogan, 48, 128
Paul, Ian Alan, 36, 161, 166
Pedriali, Federica, 31
Pérez Firmat, Gustavo, 186n10
Petty, Audrey, 161
photographic work about Guantánamo: Beatón's *Susurros*, 36–38, *37*, 136–37; Cornwall's *Welcome to Camp America*, 29, 35, 81, 86, 148, 150, 163, 184n1; Gutiérrez and Beatón's *Wounded by History*, 135–36
Piñera, Virgilio, 57, 178n4
Pinter, Harold, 31
Platt Amendment, 13, 19, 23, 114, 141
Poems from Guantánamo: The Detainees Speak (Falkoff), 9, 26, 31–32, 41, 52, 69, 178n3, 182n12; "Ode to the Sea" poem, 31, 44, 45, 53, 57, 62; "First Poem of my Life" poem, 32, 44–45; "Terrorist 2003" poem, 178n3; translations of, 42, 45–48, 57–58; "Two Fragments" poem, 44
Ponte, Antonio José, 9–10, 130, 143, 176n9
Porvenir: La voz independiente de Guantánamo journal, 31, 36, 87, 95, 151, 158, 162
Postprint Magazine, 52
Pratt, Mary Louise, 16
Price, Rachel, 176n7
prison cell, 107
Puchner, Martin, 168

INDEX

Qasim, Khalid, 53–54
Queair, Edward, 115
Queeley, Andrea, 123
Quesada, Pilar, 14, 88, 91
Quintero Herencia, Juan Carlos, 178n4
Quiroga, José, 178n4

Rahim, Tahar, 30
Rainsford, Sarah, 186n14
Rao, Veena, 30
Rasul, Shafiq, 102
Rath, Arun, 144
Redfield, Marc, 21, 140, 177n14
Remaking the Exceptional: Tea, Torture and Reparations | Chicago to Guantánamo, 36, 101, 161, 165
Reparations for Guantánamo's Torture Survivors (Hughes and Ginsburg), 36, 161, 164–65
Risen, James, 148, 176n3
Rochelle, Safiyah, 82
Rodríguez Lobaina, Néstor, 32, 40, 42, 68; *Con el alma cautiva*, 64, 66–67; experience as political prisoner, 65; Movimiento Cubano de Jóvenes por la Democracia, 64–65
Roman, Joe, 36
Romero, Ramón, 127
Rose, Michael L., 185n6
Rosenberg, Carol, 28, 74, 114, 186n11
Rossdale, Polly, 147
Ross, Daniel, 30, 96, 184n25

Rubio, Marco, 126, 186n11
Rumsfeld, Donald, 5, 39

Saar, Eric, 27, 72, 73, 74, 82
Sabariego, Rubén López, 129
Saito, Natsu Taylor, 141
Salcedo, Doris, 99, 184n24
Sánchez Altarriba, Claro, 95, 183n21
Sánchez, José Ramón, 4, 32, 40–42, 68, 178n5; "Animal Planet" poem, 13; *The Black Arrow*, 57–63; experience of detainees in poetry, 30; "Impossible" poem, 4, 59; publishing in *La noria*, 58; *Talibán*, 58
San Isidro Movement, 128
Santner, Eric, 180n4
Scarry, Elaine, 34, 108–9
Schmidt-Furlow Report (2005), 81, 181n9
Schwalbach, Brian, 180n5
Science magazine, 169
SCRs. *See* Special Category Residents
"Secret//NoForn//20330602" poem (Sánchez), 32, 61–62, 63–64
Ševčenko, Liz, 163
Sharpe, Harry, 127
Sharrock, Justine, 48
A Ship from Guantánamo (film), 30
Siems, Larry, 26
Sierra Madero, Abel, 67, 179n10
Single Parents Support Group, Guantánamo, 116

INDEX

Sketching Guantánamo: Court Sketches of the Military Tribunals, 2006–2013 (Hamlin), 29

Slahi, Mohamedou Ould, 9, 26, 33, 109, 140, 178n1, 181n8; connection around religious faith, 83; experiences with detainees and guards, 72–74; pleasures of reading and creating, 80, 81; post-release friendship, 102; racial identifications and misidentifications, 78–79; racial, postcolonial, and neocolonial hierarchies, 76–77; sexually abusive enhanced interrogation techniques, 82–83

Slaughter, Joseph R., 9, 63, 75

"Small Change" poem (Sánchez), 60

Smith, Steven D., 6

Solis Ybarra, Priscilla, 31

Sommer, Doris, 178n5

SOP. *See Camp Delta Standard Operating Procedures*

Special Category Residents (SCRs), 122–27

"Spotlight" poem (Sánchez), 59

Stafford Smith, Clive, 28

Suárez, Felipa, 14, 88, 91

Suñol, Jorge, 184n25

Susman, Jen, 167

Susurros (Whispers) (photography exhibit by Beatón), 36–38, *37*, 136–37

Swanson, Elizabeth, 77, 140

Sylvester, Christine, 6

Symbolic Reparation Research Project, 163

Talibán (Sánchez), 58

Taub, Ben, 29–30, 83

Taylor, Katie, 147, 184n27

Tea Project (Ginsburg and Hughes), 27–28, 101–2

"Terrorist 2003" poem (Mubanga), 178n3

Thompson, Erin, 26, 53

Todo Guantánamo es nuestro (All Guantánamo Is Ours) film, 35, 89–90, 129, 131, 134

Tomksy, Terri, 180n4

Topham, Laurence, 30, 83, 102

Traitor? (Holdbrooks), 84–85

Trapp, Erin, 43

"A Trojan Horse in the Caribbean" poem (Sánchez), 60–61

Trouillot, Michel-Rolph, 78

Trump, Donald, 22, 183n19

Truth and Memory Project, 96

Tuan, Yi-Fu, 105, 127

Tubiana, Jérôme, 29, 41, 146

Tudela Iríbar, Rolando, 162

Turner, Jennifer, 107–8

"Two Fragments" poem (Dost), 44

UMAP. *See Military Units for Assisting Production*

Untitled: Oasis (Ansi), 54

Untitled: Sunset With Bridge (Abud), 54

Untitled (Black Shore) (Ansi), 54

Untitled (Blue Mosque) (Al-Bihani), 54

INDEX

Untitled (Fins in the Ocean) (Qasim), 53–54
Untitled (Statue of Liberty) (Ansi), 54
Untitled (Two Palms) (Al-Bihani), 54–56, 55

Valladares, Armando, 12
Valls, Jorge, 12
Vamphear Circus, 117
van Nieuwkerk, Karin, 84–85
venceremos, 142, 143, 161
Vine, David, 115
Vitier, Cintier, 178n4
Voyce, Stephen, 63

Walia, Harsha, 167
Waller, Nicole, 88, 182n12; global mapping, 68; translating al-Rubaish's and el-Gharani's poems, 45
war on imperialism, 4, 13, 25, 33; 1961 literacy campaign, 16–17; disputes on US-Cuban relations, 14–15; importance to genesis and perpetuation of Cuban Revolution, 20; social initiatives in Cuba, 17

war on terror, 4, 20, 25, 33, 72; Biden's role, 22; Bush's role, 20–22, 24, 72; Guantánamo Bay Naval Base issue, 22–24; Obama's role, 22, 24; Trump's role, 22
war treatment techniques, 153
Weber, Elizabeth, 43–44
Weizman, Eyal, 148
Welcome to Camp America (Cornwall), 29, 35, 81, 86, 148, 150, 163, 184n1
Werlau, Maria C., 95
"Wet Foot, Dry Foot" migration policy, 183n17
WikiLeaks, 8, 9, 61, 63
Wild, Tim, 113
Witness to Guantánamo, 8, 146
Wohlrab-Sahr, Monika, 85
Wood, Steve, 29, 83
Worthington, Andy, 8

Yee, James, 27, 73

Zequeira y Arango, Manuel de, 56
Zevnik, Andreja, 180n4

www.ingramcontent.com/pod-product-compliance
Lightning Source LLC
Chambersburg PA
CBHW030529010526
44110CB00048B/788